THE GREEN NATIONAL PRODUCT

A Proposed Index of Sustainable Economic Welfare

Clifford W. Cobb
John B. Cobb, Jr.

with contributions by
Carol S. Carson
Hans Diefenbacher
Robert Eisner
Robert R. Gottfried
Richard D. Lamm
E.J. Mishan
Thomas Michael Power
Jan Tinbergen
Alan H. Young

UNIVERSITY
PRESS OF
AMERICA

HUMAN
ECONOMY
CENTER

Lanham • New York • London

University Press of America® Inc.
4720 Boston Way
Lanham, Maryland 20706

3 Henrietta Street
London WC2E 8LU England

Co-published by arrangement with the
Human Economy Center

Library of Congress Cataloging-in-Publication Data

Cobb, Clifford W.
The green national product : a proposed index of sustainable
economic welfare / Clifford W. Cobb, John B. Cobb, Jr. ; with
contributions by Carol S. Carson ... [et al.].
p.   cm.
Includes bibliographical references and index.
1. Sustainable development.   2. Economic development—
Environmental aspects.   3. Quality of life.   I. Cobb, John B.
II. Human Economy Center.   III. Title.
HD75.6.C59   1993   338.9—dc20   93–23426 CIP

ISBN 0–8191–9321–6 (cloth : alk. paper)
ISBN 0–8191–9322–4 (pbk. : alk. paper)

ACKNOWLEDGEMENTS

This book is the result of a series of phases of research and writing on the measurement of economic welfare.

The first phase of work was the development of a preliminary conceptual basis to analyze the well-being of a society. Because earlier work on social indicators had not challenged the ideological dominance of GNP and other national income accounts, we made a conscious choice from the beginning to focus on *economic* well-being or welfare rather than social welfare. At the instigation of John Cobb, a study group was formed to examine previous work on this question. He was joined by Sandy Dawson, Dean Freudenberger, Chris Ives, Carol Johnston, and Tokiyuki Nobuhara at the Claremont Graduate School, with Sandy Dawson conducting much of the initial research.

In the second phase, the Miller Social Ethics Fund provided financial support for more in-depth research. John Cobb and Clifford Cobb collaborated on refining the conceptual structure of the project, and the latter conducted the bulk of the data collection, computation, and writing at this stage, with revisions suggested by the members of the original discussion group. Economists Gordon Douglass and Dan Finn also offered helpful advice at this stage.

The product of that second phase, with minor modifications, is contained in part A of this book. A significant portion of that material appeared in chapter three and the Appendix of *For the Common Good* by Herman Daly and John B. Cobb, Jr. (Beacon Press, 1989). Herman Daly made significant contributions to the project from its inception. He has provided a continuing stream of information and insights. His advice on how to account for depletion of natural resources has been especially helpful.

iii

This book is the culmination of the third phase of the project. We solicited comments about our Index from leading thinkers on the costs of economic growth and the measurement of economic welfare. Each was sent material that was substantially the same as that which comprises part A of this book. We include their critiques of our Index in part B. Based on their comments and on our own continuing research, we have revised the ISEW and updated it, as presented in part C. (Since the time the respondents reviewed the Index, we have added some material at the beginning of part A and moved some material around in the first few pages. Thus, some of the material to which Carson and Young refer in their essay is slightly different than the text in its present form. We did not, however, try to correct any substantive errors in part A. Those modifications are found in part C.)

Clifford W. Cobb
Sacramento, California
and
John B. Cobb, Jr.
Claremont, California

The completion of phase three does not signify an end to the effort to improve and update the measurement of economic welfare. As the sponsoring institution for the publication of this book, the Human Economy Center has taken over the responsibility for maintaining the Index and revising it.

The Human Economy Center was started in 1979 by John Applegath to promote an economic system in which people and their home the earth came first. Instead of beginning with abstract, narrow definitions of the human person which resulted in rigid measurements and predetermined, narrowly defined goals such as "factors of production," "consumers," "GNP" and "maximization of utility" and other such constructs into which conventional economics tries to fit human beings and the planet earth, Human Economy begins by attempting to understand the needs and motivations of individual human beings and the limits of the earth and then making the models and measurements adjust. Instead of concentrating on how to produce and consume an ever larger Gross National Product (GNP), Human Economy suggests designs for new social/economic arrangements

iv

which will maximize such concerns as meaningful work and decision-making, creativity, humane communities, subsidiarity, and a sustainable healthy planet.

We at the Human Economy Center have agreed to take over the responsibility for maintaining and revising the Index of Sustainable Economic Welfare because we believe that the ISEW moves in the direction that John Applegath and others have suggested. At the same time, we did this somewhat reluctantly, given the gravity and importance of the task. We believe that the GNP is a faulty economic measuring rod that has political significance. Adding secondary subsidiary accounts, to account for environmental degradation is no real solution. Academically it may help but politically it will be ignored. In these current times with new and hopefully more sensitive leadership, action to mitigate our environmental and human crises, will be more forthcoming. In the past 12 years we had turned increasingly away from preoccupation with humane enhancement and a sustainable economy to an ever-increasing concern for individual and national economic growth at whatever cost. These are times of economic uncertainty as the global political and economic environments change at an accelerated pace requiring adoption of new values and institutions. Yet in the 1990's we believe that there exists an openness to the positive possibilities inherent in such change; possibilities for reordering individual lifestyles, for restructuring and for replacing existing institutions, for changing national goals, and for developing new economic paradigms and measurements such as the ISEW.

It is our sincere hope that those of you who share this commitment to the earth and who share the belief that the quality of human life supersedes the quantity of material things as the measure of economic success will help us in this task as we constantly strive to adjust and revise the ISEW to make our society ever more sustainable and humane.

Donald Renner
Human Economy Center
Mankato State University, Box 14
Mankato, MN 56002

Contents

Page

Part A

THE INDEX OF SUSTAINABLE
ECONOMIC WELFARE

INTRODUCTION

In *Alice's Adventures in Wonderland*, you may recall the conversation (in chapter six) that Alice has with the Cheshire Cat:

> "Would you tell me, please, which way I ought to go from here?"
> "That depends a good deal on where you want to get to," said the Cat.
> "I don't much care where--" said Alice.
> "Then it doesn't matter which way you go," said the Cat.
> "--so long as I get somewhere," Alice added as an explanation.
> "Oh, you're sure to do that," said the Cat, "if you only walk long enough."

We can see in Alice's predicament a reflection of the state of confusion surrounding economic goals in our society. Like Alice, we rely on an external authority to decide which way we ought to go, as long as we get anywhere at all. We allow ourselves to be reassured by the thought that we must be going in the right direction as long as the gross national product (GNP) keeps growing. Yet since GNP adds both beneficial and harmful activities, its growth should not comfort us any more than the Cat's crafty comments.

Alice provides another parallel to the perverse world of economic accounting in the second chapter of *Through the Looking Glass*. Alice and the Red Queen begin to run. The Queen keeps telling Alice to run faster, but no matter how fast they run, they never go anywhere at all. When they stop, and Alice comments that "Everything's just as it was," the Red Queen says that "it takes all the running you can do to keep in the same place."

Red Queen Economics

Modern economies are also partially engaged in running faster and faster just to stay in place. Although the GNP measures all economic activity as progress much of that activity is intended just to stay even, to prevent a decline in well-being. When GNP is used to measure the health of an economy, that is like measuring the speed of a car suspended on blocks by the revolutions per minute of the engine: the noise may be the same as for a car on the road, but the distance covered is not.

Critics of mainstream economics have been pointing out these anomalies for years. In particular, they have complained that the GNP lumps together spending that makes us worse off, spending that allows us to stay in the same place, and spending that makes us better off all in a single measure. In other words, national income accounts, by their very nature, give us almost no clue as to whether a nation is making progress or not.

As Manfred Max-Neef, a Chilean economist (and winner in 1983 of the Right Livelihood Award), explains:

> The GNP . . . is based on an arithmetic that would be unacceptable on page one of the simplest arithmetic book in elementary school: the only sign that exists is plus; you can only add, never subtract. So any process that generates a monetary flux or a market transaction is acceptable. It is totally irrelevant whether it is productive, unproductive, or destructive--it all adds to the GNP. In other words, if I want my GNP to grow in order to impress the International Monetary Fund, I can for instance, quickly and "efficiently" depredate a fundamental natural resource and have a beautiful GNP.[1]

This poignantly describes in a concrete way how a misguided measure can be put to ill effect, particularly in the nations of the South. Under the austerity measures imposed by the IMF, nations are forced to sell off their assets in order to raise GNP temporarily while their hungry people are forced to "tighten their belts" another notch.

In a detailed treatment of the false accounting that encourages developing countries to sell their natural resources to raise national income, Robert Repetto and the staff of the World Resources Institute have considered Indonesia's economy.[2] Although the official Gross Domestic Product of Indonesia grew by 7.1 percent annually from 1971 to 1984, when the value of the petroleum, forestry, and soil resources was subtracted from the national assets, the growth rate was reduced to 4.0 percent per year. Growth rates appeared extraordinarily high during those years because current output was based on borrowing wealth from future generations. That process of robbing the future is inherent in the way the national income accounts are currently structured.

Of course this problem is not unique to the Third World. The perverse character of the GNP is also obvious to critics in developed nations. A number of people and groups have called for a new compass to guide national economic policies because the existing compass is broken. Among the hundreds of critics are economists such as Herman Daly, Kenneth Boulding, and E.F. Schumacher, social analysts such as Hazel Henderson, Ivan Illich, Gary Snyder, and Mark Satin, feminists such as Marilyn Waring and Mary Clark, and environmentalists such as Howard Odum, Paul Ehrlich, Lester Brown, and David Brower. Green Party platforms have proposed the need for new economic accounts. The concept of alternative national accounts has also been endorsed at meetings of The Other Economic Summit in recent years. Robert Costanza, as the editor of the journal *Ecological Economics* and of a book by the same title, has been instrumental in moving the theoretical discussion forward on the many questions that need to be answered in order to develop more ecologically adequate methods of economic accounting.[3]

Needed: A "Green National Product"

In essence, what is needed is a "green national product" that would tell us whether economic activity was making us better off or worse off. In principle, it would be created by adding up the "goods" and subtracting the "bads," giving us a picture of our net condition. It would encompass the social and economic issues on which the "green" movement has focused: care for the earth and for all of the people who are sustained by it. In particular, this new GNP (green national product) would differ from the old GNP (gross national product) by addressing the long-term health of the planet and its inhabitants. In other words, sustainability would be a central issue in the new measure, rather than an afterthought.

The Index of Sustainable Economic Welfare, described in this book, is a proposal of a green national product. We hope other "green" approaches will be developed that stress different factors or that use different methods of analysis. The gross national product was not intended by its originators as a monolithic instrument for defining economic well-being. There is no reason any green national product should claim for itself that role. Thus, there are many possible ways of conceptualizing a green national product.

Since gross national product is usually referred to by its initials (GNP), it would be confusing to adopt a phrase with the same initials (green national product) as a proposed alternative to it. Thus, when we refer to GNP in this book, we are following the convention and referring to gross national product. Nevertheless, we believe that a "green national product" is descriptive of the intent of the index we have devised.

On another matter of language usage, we want to make clear that our use of the term "welfare" in this book refers only to the restricted meaning of "well-being." We use the terms "welfare" and "well-being" interchangeably. Although we recognize that "welfare" often refers in common usage to public assistance programs, we have not used the term that way in this book.

Existing Critiques: Too Theoretical

It would indeed be hard to find a countervailing idea that is as widely shared among social critics as the importance of finding an alternative to GNP. Yet for all of the desire for a new way to measure genuine progress, the official indicators still retain their power. Despite the agreement that the GNP is a terribly inappropriate measure of well-being, it remains the only indicator taken seriously in discussions of economic health.

Critics have been restricted to complaining about the GNP without offering constructive alternatives because moving from general concepts to construction of indicators is a formidable task. Consider, for example, the work of Herman Daly, who has been the leading thinker in ecological economics for over twenty years. Daly has long been aware of the shortcomings of national income accounts, and his concept of a steady-state economy is implicitly based on an alternative mode of accounting for income and assets. He argues that sustainable well-being is based on maintaining a constant level of social assets (buildings, transportation systems, food supply systems, energy systems, etc.) with as little "throughput" as possible. (Throughput means the transformation of high quality natural resources, especially energy, into low quality or high entropy wastes.) Since GNP is essentially a measure of throughputs, it values the accumulation of waste instead of the satisfaction of needs. The steady-state economy (SSE) is a measure of the amount of satisfaction that can be squeezed out of the fixed amount of resources available to us.[4]

Whereas GNP rises when a car is used up and has to be replaced, Daly's SSE would rise only if the amount of long-term transportation services derived from a car increased because of efficiency improvements. Thus, SSE can rise, but not by simply increasing the flow of throughput.

Unfortunately, while Daly's model of a steady-state economy is a valuable heuristic tool, it is not easily made operational. There is no obvious way to measure the total value of the assets created by nature and by human artifice from which we derive satisfaction. Even the measurement of the monetary value of throughputs poses grave difficulties. We might be able to evaluate throughputs in terms of energy flows, but translating them into money depends on a number of assumptions that are likely to vary with particular cases.

For example, consider a point that Daly makes about the energy captured by living plants from the sun. Photosynthesis is economically valuable work for which we do not pay. Captured solar energy is part of the stock of natural capital from which humans derive satisfaction (in the form of food and fibers). If acid rain or climatic change were to reduce the primary productivity of the soils of New England by 10 percent, this would amount to a loss of 15,000 megawatts of energy capacity.[5] How should this capacity loss be evaluated in a steady-state economy? Should it be calculated according to the cost of replacing an equivalent amount of capacity with solar collectors or only by the value of the lost income in farming and forestry? In other words, the mere knowledge of changes in energy balances does not tell us how to value them.

Daly's contribution to thinking about the proper way to evaluate economic change has been crucial. Yet like other recommendations to develop a new mode of national accounting, his approach has remained suspended at the level of a general concept, without generating a method for devising an actual measure of environmentally-adjusted economic welfare.

The same is even more true of most of the other suggested reforms of national income accounts. Suggesting changes to the GNP is
much easier than actually developing an alternative methodology and
computing it, particularly if the components of the alternative measure
are not directly countable.

Descending From the Mountain: The Need to Operationalize

When one travels down from the rarified atmosphere of the
mountain top where ideas are purely theoretical and neatly defined,
one quickly encounters a jungle of disorienting details. The search for
truth lies as much in the quest for detailed knowledge as in the formulation of general concepts. There is an element of self-deception in
speaking of abstract ideas that are not grounded in the complexities of
experience. Thus, the trip down the mountain is instructive because it
forces a more careful and concrete examination of what we value.

We learn what we most care about by paying attention to trade-
offs between conflicting values. For example, in our legal system, in
order to safeguard everyone against the potential abuse of the police
power of the state, we have established procedural rules that allow
some guilty people to avoid punishment. The idea that one could design a system that would convict only the guilty and let all of the inno-
cent free is a pipe-dream. Our Bill of Rights is a statement of our willingness to trade some of our security against crime for a guarantee
against infringement by the state in our private lives. We have opera-
tionalized the value of liberty by reducing the probability that the guilty
will be caught and convicted. We all value safety from bandits, but our
Constitution says we value safety from unchecked police power even
more. (This may be less true now than two hundred years ago.
Perhaps the apocryphal stories are true that when Americans are presented with a copy of the Bill of Rights, without being told they are
reading part of the Constitution, many regard it as "Communist" or
"subversive.")

In this book we have sought to operationalize some of the implicit trade-offs in economic activity, particularly those involving sustainability. Economists value the information provided by the price
system because it operationalizes judgments of value by revealing how
much of one item people will give up to have another. Market prices
provide information about a restricted arena, however. In our efforts
to operationalize hidden (nonmarket) relations, we have become
aware of the difficulty of doing so and of the disarray that surrounds

many of the key concepts favored by those proposing a new economic paradigm. For example, unless the term "sustainable" can be defined operationally, we will not know if we are moving toward or away from that goal as a society. Developing a functional definition of sustainability will entail acceptance of a high degree of ambiguity and approximation. Whereas standard accounting procedures ignore activities that are important but not easily measurable, we prefer to be generally accurate rather than precisely wrong.

If those who challenge the prevailing order are serious about developing a new economic paradigm, it will only come about by grappling with questions of how to measure what now remains hidden. Even in a world divided into bioregions, there would still need to be some standardized way for one jurisdiction to compensate another for damages. Should the costs of pollution be measured by the costs of pollution control equipment (theoretically wrong but relatively easy to do in practice) or by trying to estimate actual damage to health and the environment? If we choose the latter, what methodologies should be used? Should we place a value on changes in the expected death rate, and if so should it be based on the implicit risk premiums that people can be observed requiring such as higher pay for more dangerous jobs? If we do not place a value on changes in expected loss of life, how should we evaluate risks relative to benefits? These are just a few of the mundane but important questions that must be answered if we are to adopt a measure of economic welfare that can gain wide acceptance.

In other words, the time has come to move beyond the generalized critiques of GNP and to analyze the dozens of controversial elements that make up a measure of welfare. Which elements should be included and which ones left out? If an element is included, how should it be measured? For example, by what method should dollar values be assigned to unpaid household work? It is not enough to suggest that the subsistence work of child-care and home cooking should be included in total income accounts. The important issues come into focus only at the stage when one asks how that work should be valued. Similarly, with regard to the environment, the question is not whether we value clean air and water, but how much we are willing to give up elsewhere in the economy to shift from 10 parts per billion of a substance to 2 parts per billion.

The Political Relevance of Economic Indicators

Undoubtedly, this sort of debate over the fine points will seem to some people like much ado about nothing: a dispute over the number of angels that can dance on the head of a pin. But just as the distribution of benefits and costs of a policy depends on the exact wording of legislation, so also does the exact formulation of a index of economic health determine what it will reveal.

The framework of the national accounts has been determined by a handful of economists and handed down from the mountain on stone tablets. Inadvertently GNP has come to be regarded as the one general measure of economic health. Although there may be legitimate technical reasons for using GNP for a limited set of fiscal planning purposes, the failure to develop a variant economic accounting system that includes distributional, environmental, and household economic issues is a political decision. Economists who attack efforts to devise an alternative measure of welfare wear a fig-leaf of technical objectivity to mask the fact they are defending the status quo. They admit that the GNP is a grossly inadequate tool for estimating well-being, but they turn a blind eye when it is misused for that purpose.

Promoting what can be proven is much easier politically than insisting on including what is important but not tangible. Like someone who searches for lost keys under a streetlight rather than in the bushes where they were lost, economists insist that the precise verifiability of measurements is more important than their general relevance. As a result, many of the primary elements of life (such as climate and soil and nonmarket social relations) that make possible the enjoyment of secondary factors (human artifacts) are ignored in conventional accounting. The value of the primary elements is much harder to reckon because they are more ultimate and therefore less fungible (substitutable). Since there can never be incontrovertible estimates of the value of these primary elements, those who seek to include those factors will remain at a political disadvantage against the mocking voices of those who insist on the use of "hard" data.

The important political issue may not be whether a new measure of welfare is adopted either officially or unofficially. For example, if the index developed in this book were to be magically substituted for GNP as the official measure of economic welfare, we would consider that a minor victory, for the larger value of this exercise would have been lost. The enduring issue is not whether some research team can "get it right" by devising a superior index of welfare, but whether there will be an avenue by which the type of values implicit in such an index can be expressed through the political process.

Reclaiming democracy requires that citizens collectively guide decision-making. Choosing "representatives" every few years on election day is not sufficient. A key element in policy-making these days involves balancing economic values (of wetlands, biological species, and forests, for example) that have values not measured by market transactions. Deciding what price to place on those environmental factors and on the preservation of nonrenewable resources for the future is not a mere technical exercise. It lies at the heart of the self-definition of a society.

If we are to determine how to deem a society better off or worse off over time, it should be done by raising the issue in concrete ways for public discussion. The consensus a society reaches (or fails to reach) on that question will have a great impact on the way it conducts itself. The accounting system by which a nation measures its well-being is a reflection of its basic values.

The process of discussing the detailed issues of valuation is also an element in building support for policies to enhance the general welfare. For example, in order for environmental groups to gain a consensus on the need to impose some economic sacrifices in order to protect wetlands or the atmosphere, it would be helpful to be able to know that the public has expressed a willingness to raise prices of food or transportation by specific amounts to prevent particular levels of damage. Similarly, the explicit valuation of social goals, such as income distribution, could also lead to the development of some consensus on social goals (though not necessarily the methods of achieving those goals). The information that would need to be gathered to estimate national welfare would also be directly relevant to a number of environmental and social policies.

How to Measure Welfare: Some Options

So what should a measure of welfare look like? What elements should be included? One might devise an index of well-being based upon surveys of subjective factors such as perceived health, security, and comfort. Or one might construct an index based on more objective factors such as the literacy rate, infant mortality rate, and life expectancy. The latter has in fact been done in the form of the Physical Quality of Life Index. Although these social measures of welfare are useful, they have serious drawbacks. They restrict the definition of well-being to far fewer categories than most of us would consider appropriate. They also generally lack a common denominator which would allow valued results to be combined meaningfully into a single index number.

Economic measures, by contrast, have the advantage of counting all activities in the same unit of value: money. This allows the valuations by millions of individuals to be combined into a single number without having to survey them or assign arbitrary weights to their choices. Recorded market transactions unobtrusively measure the values of billions of choices made every day. (In addition, it is often possible to estimate or impute the value of an activity as if there were a market for it.) Thus, as a first approximation, the sum of purchases made in a year represents a reasonable measure of welfare. On that basis, gross national product or total output of a nation has come to be widely regarded as the primary measure of the well-being of a society. (In recent years, the United States has switched to gross domestic product, which excludes production by domestic companies in foreign countries. However, in this book, we refer entirely to GNP, for which there were historical data.)

Yet using output statistics as an indicator of economic welfare, without consideration for non-market costs and benefits as well as income distribution, is misleading. The calculation of national product combines all of the final market values of goods and services but leaves out the social and environmental costs of producing them. This leads to policies biased in favor of measured output and unfavorable to unmeasured elements--what Ivan Illich has called the "shadow economy."[6] As a result of inappropriate accounting, our leaders tell us that the economy and the environment are in conflict. An accounting system that encompassed the full range of costs and benefits of human activities would reveal that the economy/environment conflict is a mirage and that environmental protection makes economic sense.

Economists have long recognized the limitations of national income accounts for determining how well off a society is. Ordinarily, they merely pay lip service to these limitations and then proceed as if per capita national output and economic welfare were identical. However, a few economists have made an effort to face the limitations squarely and to devise alternative measures of well-being. By far the most important work in this field was done by William Nordhaus and James Tobin in an extended essay entitled, "Is Growth Obsolete?" There they developed a Measure of Economic Welfare and included the important point that genuine well-being must be sustainable: a society that lives well by devouring its stock of capital is not as well off as annual income statistics would suggest. Nevertheless, they failed to extend that insight to account for the depletion of what might be called "natural capital," the environmental capital that we use up when we erode the soil, deplete aquifers, or alter the climate. We have made some modest proposals about how to factor those elements into an accounting framework, conscious that the discussion of how these matters should be measured is still in its infancy. We hope that scholars in various fields will improve on them.

Our Proposed Index

In the absence of an accepted measure of economic welfare, per capita GNP has continued to dominate thinking on the subject, both among economists and in the general public. To rectify that situation, we believe that discussion must go beyond the mere criticism of GNP. Thus, in Part A we present our initial proposal for an Index of Sustainable Economic Welfare (ISEW). Chapter 1 describes some theoretical problems with GNP, summarizes previous efforts to create a welfare measure, and discusses the types of adjustments that are necessary to create a measure of welfare. Chapter 2 involves the actual calculation of such an index. The ISEW includes adjustments for income distribution, environmental damage, the value of housework, resource depletion, and several other categories. The results from these adjustments indicate a leveling off of sustainable economic well-being after 1970, despite the growth of national income.

Our interest in developing the ISEW was not only to show how our nation has fared since 1950 in terms of economic welfare but to establish an index that can be kept current in the years ahead. We have thus limited ourselves as much as possible to statistics that are regularly available, generally those from federal agencies. This will permit the regular measurement of future changes in economic welfare as an indication of the effectiveness of public policies.

Our aim in developing the ISEW was to further the dialogue on measurement of sustainable welfare by raising new questions and by formulating a specific index that could then be altered and amended. We therefore solicited comments and criticisms from a variety of sources. The responses we received constitute Part B of this book. Part C is our response to the critical suggestions of Part B, culminating in a revised Index of Sustainable Economic Welfare that takes into account those criticisms with which we agree and which can be given statistical expression. We are sure that further improvements are possible, but we believe that our revised ISEW is a better measure of economic well-being than the GNP and that its wide use would be a great gain.

Critical Analysis of Our Index

Part B begins with an essay by Robert Eisner, professor of economics at Northwestern University and author of *The Total Incomes System of Accounts*.[7] He comments first on the general framework by which adjustments to GNP ought to be made to create a more suitable welfare measure. He then proceeds to criticize particular elements of the ISEW: the exclusion of human capital (which plays a large role in his own work), the inadequate treatment of government capital, the methodology of analyzing income distribution, the treatment of services from capital, the correction for advertising, the calculation of commuting costs, the estimate of urbanization and pollution costs, the value of agricultural land lost, the ISEW's rejection of discounting future costs and benefits, the procedure for estimating long term environmental damage, and the method of calculating net international position. The fact that Eisner has himself carried out a statistical study of the appropriate adjustments to national income accounts gives his comments special weight. In several cases, we have followed his recommendations in making revisions to the ISEW in Part C. In other cases, we have disagreed with him and held to our original procedures, particularly on matters related to the sustainability of economic welfare.

Similarly the comments and criticisms of Allan H. Young and Carol Carson of the U.S. Bureau of Economic Analysis are of unusual significance because their office is responsible for compiling national income accounts. Carson and Young are generally critical of the effort to develop a "single-dimension aggregate measure of sustainable welfare." They favor instead the United Nations System of National Accounts whereby nonmarket values are included in "satellite" accounts rather than the main body of national accounts. This allows for the comparison of accounts among different nations, and they point out that the inability to make international comparisons is a weakness of the ISEW. Finally, they are also critical of specific columns in the ISEW: income distribution, services of consumer durables, private pollution abatement, and international investment flows. We have made several adjustments in the ISEW based on their comments.

Robert Gottfried, an economist at the University of the South who applies insights of ecological thought to economics, has also written a detailed critique of the ISEW. He raises questions both of theory (what is appropriate to include in a measure of sustainable welfare) and of methodology (how to measure the appropriate components). On the level of theory, he proposes that welfare is a function both of income flows and of capital stock or wealth, though he implies that only the services of capital and/or changes in the stock of capital should be included. He also deals extensively with the problem of how to treat depletion of non-renewable natural resources and implicitly recognizes the dilemma about how to include discounting in the development of accounts for depletion of natural capital. In addition, Gottfried comments on the methodology used to arrive at individual columns. He raises particularly important questions about the treatment of income distribution, changes in capital stock, the costs of urbanization, and net international position.

Taking a rather different approach than all of the previous authors, Thomas Michael Power, professor of economics at the University of Montana and author of *The Economic Pursuit of Quality*,[8] analyzes the problems associated with trying to measure variations in economic welfare in different locations within one nation. In particular, he criticizes the use of per capita income as a primary basis of measuring economic welfare. The New York City inhabitant with an income of $60,000 is not four times as well off as the Oregonian with an income of $15,000 because part of the difference is due to the higher cost of living in New York and the need to pay higher salaries to attract people away from the amenities of Oregon. This implies that any welfare measure (including the ISEW) that begins with composite data on national income or expenditures is beset with the problem of ignoring regional differences in the value of a given level of per capita income.

E.J. Mishan is a renowned British economist who has written numerous works on the social costs of growth.[9] In his essay in this volume, he raises the important question, "Is a welfare index possible?" Initially, Mishan discusses more specific difficulties with the ISEW: the introduction of distributional issues, the use of the concept of sustainability (and intergenerational equity), the exclusion of the value of human capital and leisure in the ISEW, the use of rising land costs as a proxy for the cost of urbanization, a methodology that leads to underestimation of environmental damage, and the incompleteness of the estimate of commuting costs and crime prevention. In his concluding remarks, however, Mishan suggests that welfare cannot be properly understood within the bounds of the principles of economics, unless one is to severely distort the most important of human values

to fit within a framework that assigns monetary value to every experience. Furthermore, he asserts that the pace of technical change has altered our lives so dramatically that the categories included in an index
of economic welfare are "incidental" to changes in welfare more broad-
ly conceived.

Two of the respondents, Jan Tinbergen and Richard Lamm, addressed issues implicitly related to changes in sustainable economic
welfare, but not made explicit in our ISEW. Both were more concerned
with the policy implications of declining economic welfare than with
the details of the techniques of how that decline might be measured.

Jan Tinbergen, a Nobel laureate in economics with a prolonged
interest in issues related to global environment, criticizes the ISEW for
failing to go far enough in several directions. First, as he correctly
points out, the ISEW deals only with economic welfare. A more complete welfare measure might try to include other elements of well-
being such as family life, ethnic relations, national security, or job satisfaction, though Tinbergen does not here propose how these elements
could be measured, much less placed in a composite index.

Second, he proposes that measures or "checks" other than the
ISEW (or GNP) are needed to evaluate fully our current situation.
These include measurement of stocks of resources, of population
growth rates, and of income distribution. In these cases, Tinbergen has
in mind measuring these quantities on an international basis.
Implicitly he is suggesting that the world, rather than each individual
nation, is the appropriate arena in which to determine how well off we
are.

Finally, Tinbergen argues that action, not just measurement, is
needed. He proposes action in four categories: disarmament, development cooperation, sustainability (maintaining welfare for future generations), and the choice of social order, focusing specifically on the role
of government in the economy. Unfortunately, Tinbergen is vague
about how desirable actions or policies are to be chosen. He does not
discuss the controversies surrounding each of the four categories with
which he deals. Nevertheless, it is important to be reminded that measures such as the ISEW are useful only if they lead to actions that will
actually correct social and environmental ills.

Richard Lamm, former governor of Colorado and author of several books, has begun where the ISEW leaves off. He examines the political meaning of living in a world of limits, a "zero sum society" of

declining resources and increasing environmental degradation in which growth of output can no longer mask social tensions.

Lamm's pessimistic conclusion is that democracy probably cannot adapt to the new limits imposed by nature in large part because of the difficulty of developing a widespread consensus on the need for making serious sacrifices. Economic stagnation and declining welfare will increase factionalization and undermine the basis of democracy. Lamm suggests the need for tools (such as the ISEW) to chart the course of society in the face of the threats now facing the world, though he is not sanguine that information about upcoming crises will be taken seriously until too late. Yet the development of information that will allow preventive responses to crises seems the only way to avoid the collapse of democracy.

Lamm's comments raise the intriguing question of how political and economic welfare are related to each other. In addition, these observations raise issues similar to those Gottfried considers in his paper regarding the difference between sustainability and "resilience" or "resistance." Yet we have no idea how to measure the resilience of an economy in maintaining democratic institutions. Thus, even though this may be a very important concept, we do not know how to include it in an ISEW.

The final paper in Part B is by Hans Diefenbacher of the Protestant Interdisciplinary Research Institute of Heidelberg, Germany. It is not a critique of the ISEW, but rather the preparation of an ISEW for Germany. This does not exactly follow the one we have prepared for the United States, because certain types of data--for example, a time series on income distribution--are simply not available in that country. Despite the unavoidable differences, the results of the German ISEW are remarkably similar to those of the U.S. Both show a leveling off of sustainable welfare after about 1970, although in Germany there is one anomalous year, 1980, that lies well outside that trend.

In Part C, we respond to the comments of our critics, and explain how we have changed many of the elements of the ISEW. In addition to recalculating a number of columns, we have also eliminated two columns and added two others. Finally, we have updated the ISEW to 1990.

Chapter 1

THE MEASUREMENT OF ECONOMIC WELL-BEING: A CONTINUING CONTROVERSY

The most commonly used measure of the economic health of a nation is the gross national product or GNP. This is defined as the value of the total output of final products (goods and services) that pass through the market in a year. This flow of goods and services can be measured either by calculating total expenditures for consumption, investment, and government, plus net exports, or by adding the aggregate income received as wages, salaries, corporate profits, proprietary income, and rent in the process of producing the nation's output. By accounting convention, expenditures for the total output must equal gross income received (plus excise taxes minus government subsidies) because every dollar spent on production must be received by someone as income.

The national income accounts yield estimates not only of gross production and income, but also of net production (derived by subtracting depreciation from GNP). Net national product (NNP) is in fact a better measure of economic health than GNP. The latter is increased by the mere replacement of worn-out capital, whereas NNP counts only the addition of new capital. Nevertheless, we will refer to GNP because that is generally the figure used in making comparisons across time and between countries.

In order to measure changes in output from year to year, the GNP is adjusted for inflation by a price index or deflator so that changes in the value of money do not distort the real growth or decline of output. Consequently, we will refer to GNP and measures of economic welfare almost exclusively in "real" or "inflation-adjusted" terms.

When economists make comparisons between countries, they generally use GNP per capita rather than aggregate GNP. Measuring output per person is certainly preferable to using a national total if one is seeking to make welfare comparisons. Unfortunately this practice also lends legitimacy to the use of national income as a measure of economic welfare. As a result, many of the economic policies in developing nations are aimed at increasing per capita GNP--despite all of the caveats made by economists that GNP is not really a measure of economic welfare.

Although GNP is often used as a measure of economic welfare by policy-makers, economists are well aware that it was not originally designed as an indicator of economic well-being. By counting those goods and services that are priced in the market, GNP ignores almost all transactions that are not measured in that way. In addition, GNP includes many market transactions that do not contribute directly to economic welfare because they are merely defensive expenditures that are undertaken to prevent conditions from worsening. On the other hand, GNP fails to subtract the amount of damage caused by pollution and other side-effects ("externalities") of production. A more satisfactory indicator of a nation's economic well-being would include nonmarket activities but deduct defensive expenditures as well as the social costs of market activities.

The valuation of nonmarket activities requires some compromise between what is conceptually desirable to measure and the availability of relevant statistics. In addition, the choice of which activities to include in a measure of welfare is inevitably a subjective process. Nevertheless, the fact that the data are somewhat messy and controversial should not deter efforts to determine true economic well-being.

The task we have set for ourselves, therefore, is not merely to criticize GNP as a measure of economic welfare but to devise a better one. Above all, we have been interested in developing an indicator that would be sensitive not only to current economic well-being but also to the sustainability of the processes that create that well-being.

GNP and Related Measures

Any effort to devise a way of measuring economic welfare is likely to begin with the GNP and its components as measured in the

National Income and Product Accounts (NIPA). Thus an understanding of the origins and composition of GNP is important as background.

Like most of what happens in the world, the explanation of why the GNP measures what it does is historical rather than systematic. The Commerce Department began reporting statistics on the net product of the national economy in 1934. However, according to Richard Ruggles,

> It was the mobilization for World War II and the consequent demand for data relating to the economy as a whole that was primarily responsible for shaping the accounts. The central questions posed by the war were how much defense output could be produced and what impact defense production would have upon the economy as a whole.[1]

Thus, the desire to measure the economic capcity of a nation to wage war was a major element that shaped the final outcome of the existing national accounts.

Marilyn Waring, in her account of the origins of national income accounts, emphasizes the way in which masculine values have determined what was included and what was left out of the final reckoning.[2] The original and continuing emphasis on war-capacity is the most obvious feature that fits her analysis. The exclusion of work performed in the household, primarily by women, is another example of the patriarchal orientation of the national accounts.

That orientation was not inevitable. Waring notes that Simon Kuznets, one of the originators of the national income accounts, expressed disappointment as early as 1947 about the way in which those accounts were becoming locked into a rigid pattern. Kuznets believed that the accounts should have been weighted more heavily toward social welfare instead of simply measuring output. For example, to make comparisons between industrial and non-industrial nations more realistic, he argued that national accounts should be flexible enough to include nutritional differences in the food consumed in each nation.[3] According to Waring, those sorts of details would have made national accounts much more relevant to measuring the aspects of well-being that women care about. She also notes that British economist J. Viner observed in 1953 that the GNP failed to differentiate between growth that was widely shared and growth that helped the rich and hurt the poor.[4] Unlike other economists, he believed that the accounts should consider income distribution.

The flexibility envisioned by Kuznets and Viner did not occur. Those who wanted to measure production won out over those who believed that the national accounts should measure welfare. The Cold War and the rise of the national security state justified the continued emphasis on military-industrial capacity. The United States had begun comparing its approach with British and Canadian accounts in 1944. The next year the League of Nations convened a meeting on national income accounting. So by 1947 the United States was ready to publish its newly developed national accounting system. Although this was supplemented in various ways in later years and revised in 1958 and 1965, it has remained basically unchanged.

Despite the emphasis on production rather than welfare, there has always been an underlying tension in the consideration of what GNP ought to measure. The national income accounts have focused on the market, but they have made modest adjustments for particular nonmarket activities. From the beginning, two major additions to market activity have been 1) the imputed value of food and fuel produced and consumed by farm families and 2) the rental value of owner-occupied dwellings. (Other imputations have also been made for the value of food and clothing provided by the military and for banking services rendered without payment to depositors.)

These particular imputations are included because they are close correlates of existing market activity. Consider a scenario. Suppose the Smiths and the Joneses each own houses but do not live in them. Instead, they rent from each other. Both rentals constitute market activity. If they now move into their own homes, market activity is reduced by two rentals. If GNP measured only market transactions, it would be reduced by the amount of the lost rental payments. Yet clearly, the output of housing services has not actually been diminished by this move; it has merely been reallocated.

The same logic that explains the inclusion of a few nonmarket categories could justify the inclusion of many others. Proposals have been advanced to impute additional values in computing GNP. However, because of the competing aims of the National Income and Product Accounts, none have been adopted. As Otto Eckstein comments:

NIPA has many purposes: to gauge economic performance, compare economic welfare over time and across
countries, measure the mix of resource use between private and public sectors and between consumption and investment, and to identify the functional distribution of
income and of the tax burden. Inevitably, these purposes
clash and the accounts must be a compromise.[5]

But why is a compromise necessary? Different accounts can be
kept for different purposes. There would be no tendency to use GNP as
a surrogate measure of economic welfare if an alternative were developed that performed that function more adequately than GNP. If a
welfare index were developed, GNP could be calculated purely in
terms of market activity, without making any adjustments to improve
its value as a measure of welfare. Then the correlation, either positive
or negative, between changes in market activity and changes in welfare
could be determined clearly and neutrally. The elimination of nonmarket imputations from GNP would be a simple matter. The creation of an economic welfare indicator is, by contrast, fraught with difficulties.

Measurement of Economic Welfare - Background

Economists have long recognized the need for a measure of economic welfare other than GNP. The 1971 Conference on Income and
Wealth raised critical questions relevant to that concern. At the conference, it became clear that many of those in attendance believed that
the focus on market transactions in the existing national income accounts gave a misleading picture of the true health of the economy. "It
was cogently argued that additional information was required on nonmarket activity, on the services of consumer and government durables
and intangible investment, and on environmental costs and benefits."[6]
There was some discussion of the evaluation of leisure. But including
that would have required estimating large values with little available
data. In addition, there was concern that including an imputation
such as leisure would have rendered the accounts less useful to
economists and business analysts who use the national accounts to
forecast changes in output, employment, and inflation.[7] (Again, this
ignores the possibility of publishing a variety of national accounts with
different purposes.)

In any case, the concerns of those interested in measuring long-term economic sustainability and social welfare have not been dealt with in the accounts. On the other hand, partly as a result of the 1971 conference and partly for reasons internal to the Department of Commerce, the Bureau of Economic Analysis (BEA) began developing estimates of nonmarket activity that could be used in modifying the GNP. Those estimates included the costs of pollution control and environmental damage, the value of time spent in household work and at leisure, and the value of the services of consumer durables and government capital.[8] Although those imputations were being developed with an eye toward inclusion in the national income accounts, none were ever formally integrated into GNP or an alternative economic indicator. In 1981, when President Reagan took office, there was a rapid change in the orientation of the federal government and an implicit faith that market prices fully reflected economic values. As a result, work on nonmarket imputations ceased.

If the BEA had completed the work on these imputations, we would have been a lot closer to an officially recognized measure of economic welfare as an alternative to GNP. However, the imputed estimates would have remained a source of controversy. As Richard Ruggles observes:

> There is no well-defined universe of nonmarket activities and imputations to be covered. The set of all possible imputations is unbounded. The only criterion that can be employed is whether the imputations are considered to be useful and necessary for the particular purpose at hand ...
>
> For all these reasons, an explicit separation of market transactions from imputations in the national accounts would seem highly desirable... It should be recognized, however, that imputations alone cannot meet the information needs for measuring economic and social performance ...
>
> No amount of imputation can convert a one-dimensional summary measure such as GNP into an adequate or appropriate measure of social welfare.[9]

Therefore, according to Ruggles, the calculation of GNP should be considered a separate matter from calculation of a more encompassing measure of economic well-being that includes imputed values. Since

GNP serves purposes unrelated to the measurement of welfare, it should be maintained as a measure of total market output. Yet Ruggles seems to doubt that modification of national income accounts with imputations could be the basis for a more adequate measure of welfare.

Perhaps, as Ruggles suggests, no single measure can grasp the full complexity of the benefits and costs of life in a modern society. The social welfare of a nation is based on many factors that are not directly tied to economic activity. For example, street crime and the disintegration of family life are often viewed as symbols of declining social well-being, but those phenomena are not related directly to economic activity. An exhaustive measure of welfare would include both economic and social categories.

Ruggles is quite correct that a comprehensive indicator could not be a "one-dimensional summary measure." A measure of social welfare, as opposed to economic welfare, would necessarily have to include factors that cannot be valued in monetary terms. Even an economic welfare measure must account for features of life that are difficult to quantify. But that should not deny the value of formulating alternative measures of economic welfare that go beyond GNP and include estimates of nonmarket activities.

An imperfect measure of well-being is better than continuing to use a measure of production for that purpose.

Measure of Economic Welfare - Nordhaus and Tobin

Without attempting to devise a comprehensive measure of social welfare, it may still be possible to develop an improved measure of the positive contribution of economic activity to well-being. The failure to make the attempt simply leaves GNP as the only measure of welfare by default. As long as the GNP continues to be misused by politicians and newspapers as a comprehensive measure of well-being, there will be reason to broaden the definition of economic health to include categories that have been left out of the national accounts. The aim, then, should not be replacement of GNP but the development of a complementary measure. Thus even if construction of a perfect welfare index is not possible, there remains a need for a less imperfect one than GNP.

Economists William Nordhaus and James Tobin sought to develop just such a measure in their pioneering 1972 essay, "Is Growth Obsolete?"[10]   However, their primary goal was to demonstrate that GNP correlates sufficiently highly with economic welfare that their new measure would not in fact be necessary. By showing that their Measure of Economic Welfare (MEW) grew between 1929 and 1965, albeit more slowly than GNP, they believed that they had demonstrated the continuing relevance of conventional measures (such as GNP) as indicators of economic welfare. Thus, in the final analysis, they contradicted their initial observation that "maximization of GNP is not a proper objective of policy."[11] If GNP growth correlates with improved welfare, then presumably we can continue to use output as a proxy for the latter.

We will return in a moment to the question of whether the conclusions reached by Nordhaus and Tobin are actually supported by their data. For now, we will turn to a summary of the procedures they use in calculating their Measure of Economic Welfare. Beginning with the national income accounts, they make three different types of adjustments: 1) They reclassify GNP into consumption, investment, and intermediate goods (which removes most government spending and redefines certain consumption as intermediate rather than final expenditures). 2) They estimate the value of leisure, housework, and the annual services of consumer durables. 3) They use wage differential between cities as a proxy for "urban disamenities."[12] With the exception of environmental costs, they covered all the questions raised in the 1971 conference mentioned above.

The task of reclassification is merely an extension of one already begun in the national income accounts. GNP is intended to measure only final production, not the production of intermediate goods. Thus the cost of a car is included in GNP, but the cost of the steel and other components paid for by the auto maker do not go into GNP because they are intermediate goods. However, some expenditures have been included in GNP as final output which Nordhaus and Tobin believe should be categorized as intermediate products in a welfare measure. The most important of these are the many government expenditures that do not directly add to well-being as they grow. Like the cost of commuting to work, they are regrettable necessities that are "overhead costs of a complex industrial nation-state."[13] As a result, government expenditures are more likely to measure costs than benefits. For example, Nordhaus and Tobin raise the question, "Has the value of the nation's security risen from $0.5 billion to $50 billion over the period from 1929 to 1965?" and answer it, "Obviously not. It is patently more reasonable to assume that the rise in expenditure was due to deterioration in international relations and to changes in military technology."[14] In other words, the rise of the defense budget does not indicate that we are more secure, only that the same level of security costs more than previously. (Indeed, it might be argued that increased defense expenditures actually reduce security if other nations arm themselves to compensate for the threat they perceive.) In addition to defense, Nordhaus and Tobin argue that a measure of economic welfare should exclude "police services, sanitation services, road maintenance," and every other government expenditure that is merely an overhead expense or regrettable necessity.

Nordhaus and Tobin also reclassify certain expenditures as investment that are classified in the national income accounts as either consumption or government expenditures. For example, they count consumer durables as a form of investment because they generate services year after year rather than being used up within one accounting period. Likewise they consider expenditures on education and health as investments rather than consumption on the theory that they increase the quantity of human capital, which is a necessary component of economic growth. They realize that excluding education and health from the category of consumption is an "admittedly extreme assumption" that "may lead to understatement of the growth of welfare."[15] Nevertheless, they believe that including them as both consumption and investment would constitute double-counting and that they are more appropriately classified as the latter.

Having made those reclassifications, Nordhaus and Tobin can begin to construct a Measure of Economic Welfare. They use personal consumption from NIPA as the base from which to make adjustments because that is the closest approximation to a welfare measure in the national accounts. They then subtract durable goods purchases, expenditures on health, education, and personal business (which includes items like banking and legal fees), and an estimated cost of commuting (set at one-fifth of total transportation costs).

The second type of adjustment they make is the imputation of capital services, leisure, and nonmarket production. The first of these imputations involves adding the value of services derived from household appliances and furniture as well as from government structures (excluding military). (They also add the services from government activities that can be classified as directly furthering personal welfare--such as postal services and parks and recreation programs. These values are not imputed; they are taken directly from the national income accounts.) The second and third imputations can have an overwhelming effect on the estimation of economic welfare, and Nordhaus and Tobin recognize that there is no indisputable method for valuing free time or household labor. Thus when they add the value of those activities, they offer three alternative methods of imputation, differing primarily in their assumptions about how technological progress affects leisure and nonmarket work. The authors prefer the measure that regards the value of leisure as being unaffected by technology in contrast to nonmarket production which is assumed to become more efficient as a result of technology. They also consider the possibilities that neither or both have been affected. (However, even where they assume no change due to technology they value the time spent in leisure or household labor as being equal to the real wage rate, which itself is affected by technological change over time.)

Finally, Nordhaus and Tobin subtract an imputed value of urban disamenities. This is determined by using a regression analysis that allows them to estimate the wage differential necessary to attract people to live in more densely populated areas. To a very limited extent, this may measure the environmental costs of urbanization, such as exposure to higher concentrations of air and noise pollution. But on the whole, we assume that the correlation between wages and density represents the higher cost of living in cities, primarily because land rents are bid up. Moreover, the greater anonymity of the city brings with it more crime and less sense of community. The urban wage differential must in part compensate for those social ills.

After making all of the adjustments discussed above--reclassification of expenditures; addition of imputations for services from capital, for leisure, and for housework; and subtraction of imputed urban disamenities--Nordhaus and Tobin arrive at an estimate of total consumption, which they call the Measure of Economic Welfare (MEW). They define "actual MEW" as the amount of annual consumption. They then add an imputed value of net investment (which is in fact often negative) to arrive at an estimate of "sustainable MEW." By sustainable they mean capable of maintaining a level of growth in per capita consumption equal to the growth of labor productivity. Thus, for net investment to be positive, the increase in the capital stock in a given year must be greater than the combination of capital consumption and the growth requirement, where the latter equals the stock of net capital times the combined percentage growth of the labor force plus productivity.

Nordhaus and Tobin's Findings Considered

Nordhaus and Tobin draw two primary conclusions from their analysis. First, they note that there are substantial differences between their Measure of Economic Welfare and GNP or other conventional measures of output. In particular, estimates of the consumption of leisure and the products of housework increase the magnitude of consumption in MEW far above the level in GNP. Second, they argue that the growth of MEW paralleled the growth of NNP. Although MEW grew more slowly than NNP from 1929 to 1965 (1.0 percent for MEW, 1.7 percent for NNP), Nordhaus and Tobin emphasize the fact that the two measures grew simultaneously, which suggests to them that NNP could serve as a reasonable approximation of a measure of welfare. "The progress indicated by conventional national accounts is not just a myth that evaporates when a welfare-oriented measure is substituted."[16]

Their calculations thus seem to prove their contention that growth as measured by GNP or NNP is indeed associated with growth of welfare. If that is true, then there would seem to be little value in developing more refined measures of welfare. The national income accounts presumably give us a rough approximation of economic welfare.

Yet when the findings in their study are examined for time-frames other than the full period from 1929 to 1965, the relatively close association between growth of per capita GNP and MEW disappears.[17] For example, between 1945 and 1947 per capita GNP fell about 15% (from $2,528 to $2,142) while per capita sustainable MEW rose by over 16% (from $5,098 to $5,934). Of course, this is the period of demobilization after World War II, so no conclusions should be drawn from this short-term negative relationship. Yet the presumption that the growth of GNP could be used as a reasonable proxy for MEW growth does not find confirmation in other periods either. From 1935 to 1945, while per capita GNP rose almost 90% (from $1,332 to $2,528), per capita sustainable MEW rose only about 13% (from $4,504 to $5,098). More significantly, during the postwar period, 1947-1965, when neither depression nor war nor recovery had a major impact on growth rates, per capita GNP rose about 6 times as fast as per capita sustainable MEW.[18] (Per capita GNP grew by 48% or about 2.2% per year, while per capita sustainable MEW grew by 7.5% or about 0.4% per year.) Moreover, if we assume, as Nordhaus and Tobin did in one of their options, that the productivity of housework has not increased at the same rate as the productivity of market activities, then per capita sustainable MEW actually registers a decline of 2% during the period 1947-1965. Alternatively, we might consider the growth of per capita sustainable MEW in the absence of any imputation for leisure or household production because, as Nordhaus and Tobin admit,

> [i]mputation of the consumption value of leisure and nonmarket work presents severe conceptual and statistical problems. Since the magnitudes are large, differences in resolution of these problems make big differences in overall MEW estimates.[19]

If that imputation is omitted, per capita sustainable MEW grew by 2% from 1947 to 1965. In any case, whether the appropriate figure for the change during that period in per capita sustainable MEW is 7.5%, 2%, or -2%, each of these results suggests that in fact "[t]he progress indicated by conventional national accounts is.just a myth that evaporates when a welfare-oriented measure is substituted." With their own figures, Nordhaus and Tobin have shed doubt on the thesis that national income accounts serve as a good proxy measure of economic welfare.

Nordhaus reflected again on the significance of his work with Tobin five years later. His interpretation of the results was unchanged.

> Although GNP and other national income aggregates are imperfect measures of the economic standard of living, the broad picture of secular progress that they convey remains after correction for their most obvious deficiencies.[20]

He had still failed to remark upon the lack of similarity between the growth of MEW and GNP during the last 18 years of the period that he and Tobin had reviewed.

Net National Welfare - Japan

Although Nordhaus and Tobin decided that the similarity between MEW and GNP was sufficient enough to drop pursuit of the former as an independent measure, others have taken up where they left off. Their work attracted interest in Japan, and a team of leading economists developed a measure of Net National Welfare (NNW). Although based on the work of Nordhaus and Tobin, it differs in several respects. The Japanese study does not dismiss considerations of environmental damage, and it includes an item for the cost of highway accidents. On the other hand, it makes no imputations for housework or leisure.

The Japanese team presented figures for the period 1955-1970. This was a period of extremely rapid growth in the Japanese economy, and, by any measure, the economic welfare of the Japanese people rose. Indeed, the correspondence between the growth rates of per capita NNW and per capita Net Domestic Product (NDP) was high from the beginning and increased over time. Per capita NNW grew at 6.3% per year from 1955 to 1960, while per capita NDP grew at 8.9% per year during the same period. During the last five years of their study period, 1965-1970, the gap closed. Per capita NNW grew at 13.5% per year, and per capita NDP grew at 14.9%. The contrast between this close association between NNW and NDP in Japan and the lack of one between MEW and GNP in the U.S. may be due either to real differences in national experience or in the differing methodologies used in the studies. Since we have only summary figures for the Japanese study, we were unable to determine the relative importance of those two possibilities.

Economic Aspects of Welfare - Zolotas

The most recent proposal for a measure of economic welfare is the Index of the Economic Aspects of Welfare (EAW-index) proposed by Xenophon Zolotas in his book, *Economic Growth and Declining Social Welfare*.[21] Zolotas differs from Nordhaus and Tobin by more sharply focusing on the current flow of goods and services and by largely ignoring capital accumulation and the issue of sustainability. Also, he considers only changes in aggregate national welfare rather than in per capita welfare.

Despite these major conceptual differences, the largest items in his EAW are much like those in MEW: personal consumption and imputations for leisure and household services. EAW resembles MEW in a number of other ways as well. Like the MEW, EAW subtracts the cost of commuting to work as a regrettable necessity. It deducts expenditures on consumer durables and public buildings and adds the imputed annual services derived from them. EAW treats most educational expenditures as investment rather than consumption, but unlike MEW, it does not reintroduce investments under the category of sustainability. Zolotas merely omits consideration of investment as a factor in welfare altogether. Another difference, minor by comparison, is the deduction in EAW of half the cost of advertising, on the assumption that only half of it provides a valuable information service to consumers.

Environmental damages enter only very obliquely into MEW as an imputation for urban disamenities. Zolotas, by contrast, directly addresses the issue by deducting half the pollution control costs for air and water pollution and all of them for solid waste. (His aim is to subtract only those anti-pollution expenditures that are paid for by private parties rather than by the government.) He also subtracts the estimated damage cost of air pollution. Finally, because he believes that much of the increase in medical expenses has been necessitated as a response to greater environmental stresses, he subtracts half of the per capita growth in real health care costs both public and private.

EAW is the first index to include a figure for resource depletion. Zolotas recognizes that this is particularly controversial; so he regularly gives his summary conclusions with and without this figure. Nevertheless, his procedure is based on the standard economic view that nonrenewable resources should rise in price at a rate equal to the "the long-term interest rate plus a premium for risk and user cost." Since resource prices have not in fact risen at that rate, Zolotas reasons that the market does not function properly at setting prices for the optimal depletion of resources. Thus, as part of EAW he deducts the difference between actual resource prices and imputed prices derived from the long-term interest rate and an estimated risk premium.

In order to compare EAW with MEW, we have calculated the former on a per capita basis. Given the significant difference in the elements included and excluded in the respective calculations, the results are surprisingly close. From 1950 to 1965, per capita growth of EAW was around 9% for the full period, or 0.57% per year. During the closest comparable period for MEW, 1947-1965, per capita sustainable MEW grew by approximately 7.5%. That amounted to 0.4% per year. In other words, both increased less than one-third as rapidly as the 2.2% per year growth of per capita GNP from 1947 to 1965. Furthermore, Zolotas carried his statistics down to 1977. From 1965 to 1977, the approximately one-to-three ratio of the growth of per capita EAW and GNP remained the same as during the earlier period. Per capita EAW grew at 0.71% per year while per capita GNP continued to increase by 2.2% per year. Thus the gap in the growth rates of EAW and GNP continued, although it remained less than the gap between the growth rates of MEW and GNP in the post-war period.

Constructing a New Index of Economic Welfare - Modifications of and Additions to Existing Indices

The task of developing an appropriate welfare index is worth pursuing. All of the foregoing studies have shown that there is much in GNP that does not express economic welfare and that there are welfare concerns not expressed in GNP. National income and welfare measures overlap, chiefly in personal consumption, but elsewhere they are quite different. Furthermore, the correlation between the two is not sufficiently high to justify continuing use of GNP as a welfare indicator.

None of the measures we have examined is entirely satisfactory. Each has some appropriate elements, but each ignores other features that are of value. There are some aspects of economic welfare that none of the measures include. Hence, a new measure is needed. In our own Index of Sustainable Economic Welfare (ISEW), we have included many of the components of MEW, NNW, and EAW; in addition, we have made adjustments not previously considered.

Income Distribution

We have factored in changes in income distribution on the assumption that an additional thousand dollars in income adds more to the welfare of a poor family than it does to a rich family. Though economists generally consider the question of distributional equity to be important, they regard it as a separate issue from the magnitude of economic welfare. Thus one might ask: "If the aggregate quantity of benefits (units of welfare) decreases by X per cent while the measure of income distribution improves by Y per cent, are we better off or worse off?" From the perspective of neo-classical economics, there is no way to answer this question. We are aware of the conceptual problems involved in including a distributional component in our Index of Sustainable Economic Welfare. Nevertheless, we believe that continuing to treat distribution as a separate issue has the effect of devaluing its importance in the analysis of economic welfare. Thus we have chosen to make it an integral part of our index.

Net Capital Growth

We have considerably altered what Nordhaus and Tobin did in the calculation of changes in net capital stock. Specifically, we have included only changes in the stock of fixed reproducible capital and excluded land and human capital in this calculation.

First, we have not treated changes in the value of land as increases in capital in the same way as Nordhaus and Tobin did. Rather than adding the value of land as part of the capital stock, we have assumed that since the stock of land is fixed, its increased value represents merely the effect of growing demand for a fixed resource. In other words, rising land costs contribute to growth of GNP but not to welfare gains.

Second, we have excluded "human capital" from our calculations of changes in the stock of capital even though we recognize its theoretical importance in sustainable economic welfare. Human capital--the characteristics of the workforce, such as health and skillfulness, that make it productive--certainly contributes to economic well-being. Yet having granted that general principle, we question the validity of measuring inputs such as expenditures on medical care or on schooling to derive meaningful estimates of the stock of human capital. We regard the actual sources of human capital formation as yet undefined and thus unmeasurable. To the extent that we include health and education expenditures in our calculations, we treat portions of them as consumption.

The relation between increased medical expenditures and improved health in a well-nourished society is tenuous, and we have not seen evidence that demonstrates any clear contribution of health expenditures to productivity. Intuitively, we might assume that more money spent on medical care will lead to a healthier population, which will in turn lead to lower absenteeism at work and higher productivity. Yet the record on this relationship is ambiguous. According to the U.S. National Center for Health Statistics (as reported in *Statistical Abstract*), the number of "restricted-activity days" per person increased from 16.4 in 1965 to 19.1 in 1980, a period during which real per capita expenditures on health care increased by over 70%. This does not mean that we were less healthy in 1980 than in 1965. Other statistics might indicate some degree of health improvement. We cite the "restricted-activity days" statistic merely to demonstrate the ambiguity of any presumed connection between health expenditures and enhancement of productivity.

The effect of increased schooling on productivity is also far from definitive. In the work of economists Edward Denison and Theodore Schultz (the latter being a source for Nordhaus and Tobin's human capital calculations), the contribution of education to productivity is *assumed* to be correlated with inputs such as years of schooling and expenditures per pupil.[22] On its face, that assumption may seem plausible. However, both theoretical and empirical issues raise serious doubts about the validity of using these inputs to estimate "educational capital."

On a theoretical level, the correlation between levels of formal education and earned income differentials may not indicate a causal relation between them, or at least the cause may not fit the human capital model. Lester Thurow suggests that the correlation between education and income may be explained by a model of what he calls "job competition."[23] In contrast to the usual concept of wage competition, in which workers receive wages according to the skills that they have when they seek employment, the jobs competition model proposes that workers are hired on the basis of their "relative position in the labor queue," which is determined more by their academic degrees than by their actual job-related skills. According to this model, job skills are learned primarily at work rather than through formal education. The higher earnings of college graduates compared to high school graduates is thus based not on their greater stock of knowledge or skills (human capital) but on the fact that employers use academic degrees as a device to screen out those they expect will require higher training costs. Thurow argues that insofar as this model is valid,

> The function of education is not to confer skill and therefore increased productivity and higher wages on the worker; it is rather to certify his [or her] "trainability" and to confer upon him [or her] a certain status by virtue of this certification. Jobs and higher incomes are then distributed on the basis of this certified status.[24]

The model helps to explain why equalization of the distribution of education since 1950 has not led to a comparable equalization of income distribution and why overall levels of productivity growth have not kept pace with growth in educational expenditures. It also explains why investment in education continues to provide a relatively high rate of return for an individual even though it provides only a small return to society. The value of formal education lies not in gaining skills but in placing the individual higher in the labor queue than others. *"In effect, education becomes a defensive expenditure necessary to protect one's 'market share'.* The larger the class of educated labor and the more rapidly it grows, the more such defensive expenditures become imperative."[25] In other words, an individual is forced to obtain a college degree to gain access to certain jobs simply because others have the degree. If much of what is spent on education is designed to preserve the relative positions of individuals, the massive increases in educational expenditures since 1950 cannot be counted as a significant factor in productivity gains or as a source of human capital.

Even if Thurow's model of "jobs competition" is completely invalid, other empirical evidence also casts doubt upon the importance of formal education in the creation of human capital. In particular, the correlation between earned income and education appears to be very weak. Jacob Mincer, one of the leading analysts of investments in human capital, has shown that among white, male, nonfarm workers only 7% of the variation in earned income is accounted for by differences in their levels of education.[26] (If the whole workforce were included, education would account for an even smaller portion of the variation because of discrimination based on race and gender.) In other words, 93% of the variation is due to other factors, ranging from luck and personal connections to ambition, native ability, and skills learned on the job.

As a consequence of these considerations, we have omitted any estimates of human capital from our calculations of changes in the stock of capital. In principle we agree that human capital should be included, but we believe that medical and educational expenditures vastly overstate actual changes in the stock of human capacities that enhance productivity.

In addition to removing the land and human capital components from the procedure used by Nordhaus and Tobin, we have also redefined the growth requirement as the growth of capital necessary to compensate for depreciation and population growth, without including any consideration of changes in labor productivity. It was not evident, even to Nordhaus and Tobin, why sustainability should mean growth rather than a steady-state, i.e., why net capital should grow at the combined rate of population and productivity growth.

> [T]he capital stock must be growing at the same rate as population and the labor force. This capital-widening requirement is as truly a cost of staying in the same position as outright capital consumption. This principle is clear enough when growth is simply increase in population and the labor force. Its application to an economy with technological progress is by no means clear. Indeed the concept of national income becomes fuzzy.[27]

When they proposed to include productivity growth as part of the growth requirement, Nordhaus and Tobin may not have foreseen the possibility that productivity would decline, which it has during many of the years since they published their paper. Using their procedure the growth of sustainable MEW is enhanced by a fall in productivity, which is an absurd result.[28] Instead, declining productivity should expand the growth requirement, because capital must be used to compensate for reduced productivity if the same level of consumption is to be maintained. As a result, one reasonable way of calculating a growth requirement would be to subtract (rather than add) the percentage growth of productivity from the growth of population and the labor force. For our ISEW, we have chosen the more conservative method of leaving productivity changes out of calculations of sustainability altogether.

Foreign vs. Domestic Capital

Besides calculating whether net capital formation is sufficient to keep up with a growing population, we have included a category that takes into account whether the source of capital can be sustained. In the early stages of a nation's economic development, growth may depend on borrowing capital from other countries. However, when an advanced capitalist nation finances its capital accumulation by borrowing from foreign sources, we assume that that reflects a fundamental weakness in the long-term viability of that economy. We therefore add the change in the net U.S. investment position (or subtract it when negative) on the assumption that sustainability requires long-term national self-reliance.

Natural Resource Depletion

We have also extended the concern for sustainable production to include the availability of natural resources or "natural capital" rather than merely humanly created capital. Under the category of natural capital we include not only fuels and minerals but wetlands and farmland as well. Zolotas took this issue into account to some extent by correcting for what he regarded as the slight underpricing of fuels and minerals by the market. MEW omits the cost of depleting natural resources altogether. However, this is not an oversight. Instead Nordhaus and Tobin believe that exhaustion of resources does not involve any threat to sustainability because they assume that "reproducible capital is a near-perfect substitute for land and other exhaustible resources."[29] They further believe that technological innovation will overcome any problems that arise if substitution fails or if any given resource is exhausted. In other words, they explicitly reject the pessimistic assumptions of absolute resource scarcity and the limits of technology that have provoked environmental concern for resource depletion. They admit that if their optimistic assumptions are invalid the growth of output would necessarily cease. If resources are scarce in the strong sense of lacking substitutes, growth would indeed be "obsolete."

Thus the question of whether an adjustment for resource depletion needs to be made under the category of sustainability hinges upon this issue of substitution and technological advance. In support of their optimistic view, Nordhaus and Tobin cite a study by Edward Denison that shows a declining proportion of national income being contributed by natural resources from 1909 to 1958.[30] They also refer to a 1963 study by Barnett and Morse which concluded that, with the exception of forest products, the price of resource-intensive goods had not risen more rapidly than the price of goods in general.[31] Thus substitution and technological change had "come to the rescue of scarcity."

The faith in the infinite substitutability of non-renewable resources is founded on the experience of a peculiar period in history, during which energy was extremely cheap. But now that that era is over, the cost of all resources will increase because of the increasing energy costs of extraction and processing. The falling price of natural resources during the first seventy years of this century was a one-time phenomenon upon which a faulty view of the future has been built.

The path-breaking book, *Beyond Oil: The Threat to Food and Fuel in the Coming Decades*, explains why economists have underestimated the consequences of resource depletion. The problem is that energy is now expensive, not merely in the financial sense of costing more money but also in terms of requiring increasing amounts of energy to obtain useful energy. The energy output/input ratio--the amount of energy made available as output from a given input of energy for exploration, extraction, and processing--declined for oil from about 100 in the 1940s to 23 in the 1970s.[32] A similar decline occurred for coal. Yet even when the energy cost of energy was rising (because the energy output/input ratio was falling), the cost of energy in dollars could continue to decline. This paradox was possible as long as the dollar price of fossil fuels was low relative to labor costs. Energy-intensive technologies for extraction and refining of energy reduced dollar costs as long as they cut labor requirements. Since the price of fossil fuels was falling, the unit price of other resources could be cut as well by the same process of substituting cheap energy inputs for expensive labor. Now that the energy output/input ratio for newly discovered oil has fallen to about 8 and for most other energy sources to less than 5, the days of declining resource costs are permanently at an end.[33]

Thus the money cost of energy rose in the 1970s and will continue to rise in the long-run, not simply because of producers' cartels but because of the increasing energy inputs required for discovery and extraction and processing of new sources of energy. According to the authors of *Beyond Oil*, "by 2005 it will be pointless to continue exploring for oil and gas as energy sources in the United States: after that more energy would be used to look for these fuels than the oil and gas we found would contain."[34] Moreover, even when expected new discoveries are included, their analysis shows that "domestic oil and gas stores will be effectively empty by 2020 [while] . . . world oil and gas supplies will last perhaps three decades longer, or more if Third World economies fail to develop."[35]

The point is not that resources are finite. Economists have long recognized that fact, but they have assumed that resources are *effectively* infinite if one is willing to pay a sufficiently high price to get them. Yet energy analysis allows us to see that a resource may be exhausted even when there are vast stocks in the ground, if the energy cost of extraction and processing exceeds the energy content of the unmined resource. Nor is the development of non-petroleum based energy sources likely to change the general outlook. Unless unproven technologies such as fusion provide cheap, unlimited energy (which seems doubtful given the track-record of fission compared to its initial promise), no technical changes will substantially alter the basic trend of declining energy resources and higher costs.[36] Even if technological breakthroughs cannot dramatically expand production, economists argue that rising prices will encourage technological improvements in energy efficiency as well as reduced energy consumption. The idea is that we will be able to maintain our standard of living and even continue to grow by using the dwindling supply of energy more efficiently. The authors of *Beyond Oil* explain why technology offers little hope of achieving this goal. First, they note that advances in the material standard of living have been dependent on two factors working in combination: knowledge and resources. Growth depended on the embodiment of new ideas in the form of capital, which required the use of energy. As long as energy was declining in cost, the limiting factor in material growth was knowledge. Under those circumstances, a certain degree of optimism that growth could be sustained indefinitely seemed justified.   There was no obvious limit to increases in knowledge. However, in recent years, resources have become the limiting factor in growth. By having to spend a larger and larger amount of our resources just to make more resources available, less is left over for improvements in welfare. Thus, Cleveland, et al., have calculated that "in the last ten years alone [1974-1984], the fraction of GNP accounted for by natural resource extraction has grown from 4 percent to 10 percent."[37] We can now see that technological advances have traditionally involved a combination of inventiveness and cheap energy. New technology can marginally improve energy efficiency, but, for the most part, material growth is a thing of the past.

Second, the authors of *Beyond Oil* point out that previous estimates of the nation's capacity to conserve energy were overly optimistic because much of what appeared to be conservation actually involved shifts of the kinds of fuels used for particular purposes (fuel efficiency rather than energy efficiency per se). In addition, optimistic estimates of possible improvements in energy efficiency have been based on extrapolations from individual sectors to the entire economy. Yet when the *indirect* energy costs of the technology used to increase energy efficiency are included, the gains in efficiency appear minimal.

If · *all* companies substituted labor and capital for fuel, more fuel would be needed somewhere in the economy to increase the amount of labor and capital, and the nation's net savings in energy are reduced. In agriculture, for example, the amount of fuel used *directly* on a cornfield to grow a kilogram of corn fell 14.6 percent between 1959 and 1970. However, when the calculation includes the fuel used elsewhere in the economy to build the tractors, make the fertilizers and pesticides, and so on, it turns out that the total energy cost of a kilogram of corn actually rose by 3 percent during that period.[38]

Thus, technologically achieved energy conservation does not offer a comprehensive remedy for the declining stock of energy resources. The precise extent to which energy efficiency gains will be offset by in-direct energy costs is not clear. In some sectors of the energy economy, such as household heating and automobile fuel consumption, Amory Lovins has calculated that tremendous energy savings can be achieved by shifting to technologies that are more energy efficient but require lit-tle more capital than current technologies. In the economy as a whole, however, the declining energy output/input ratio suggests that gains from energy efficiency improvements will be limited.

Nevertheless, some economists have argued that resource de-pletion leaves future generations better off than our own if a suffi-ciently large proportion of those resources are transformed into capital rather than being consumed in the present.[39] According to this view, true inter-generational equity is not served by depriving ourselves of present enjoyment so that the future will have even more than we now have. The implicit assumption behind this view is that capital constitutes a perfect substitute for (or even an improvement upon) the natural resource base of a society. At one level this seems plausible. A machine made of steel might reasonably seem like a better gift to the next generation than the deposits of minerals that were used to make it. Yet as E.J. Mishan notes:

> A common belief among economists, that the consump-tion of finite resources . . . is offset in value by the forma-tion of other capital, is erroneous. Under familiar be-haviour assumptions, no more than a fraction of the value of the finite resource is replaced, and this fraction could be negligible.[40]

Even if the entire value of the finite resource were replaced with capital, this often would not benefit future generations as much as leaving the resources untapped. First, the production of the capital would consume resources that future generations might wish to use for other purposes. Second, capital goods would deteriorate over time, imposing maintenance costs on future generations that would not occur if the resources were left in their natural state. (An example of this can be seen in the massive cost of restoring highways in the U.S., a cost which would have been imposed by weathering even if they had never been used to carry traffic.) Third, capital cannot ultimately substitute for resources because capital itself is composed of resources. In other words, labor and capital complement rather than substitute for the material resources that are transformed into a product. Capital provided for future generations must be accompanied by natural resources to be of any value.

We have already begun to pay the price of profligate use of resources that made possible rapid economic growth in the past. The decline in real wages after 1972 and the stagnation of productivity for about a decade were signs of the effect of rising real resource costs, particularly energy resources.

The implications of this prospect of diminishing resources and rising costs for Nordhaus and Tobin's study are clear. The issue of resource exhaustion needed to be included in their measurement of sustainable welfare. Current welfare should have been reduced to the extent that present enjoyment deprives the future of the potential for the same level of economic welfare. Having introduced the idea of sustainability with respect to net capital accumulation, they should have carried over the same logic to the depletion of "natural capital."

Yet even if Nordhaus and Tobin had entertained the notion that depletion of resources in the present would impoverish future generations, they would likely have minimized the significance of this inter-generational conflict by suggesting that the effects on the future be discounted at the real interest rate. From the perspective of neo-classical economic theory, the damage caused by exhaustion of resources (either renewable or non-renewable) should be counted in the present only after it has been discounted (reduced) in proportion to the long-term interest rate. In effect, this theory says that a resource should be exhausted as long as the rate of increase in its price *in situ* is less than the interest rate. We regard this process of discounting the effects of our present policies on future generations as socially inappropriate, even though the practice is reasonable on an individual level. In other words, the rational procedure for an individual, given the existing set of incentives, is not necessarily a rational policy for a society as a whole. Thus we reject in principle the idea of discounting the effects of resource depletion (and environmental damage) on the future.

Instead we propose the view that any reduction in economic welfare in the future below the level currently enjoyed should be counted as if the cost occurred in the present.

The attitude of benign neglect toward the future implicit in the concept of discounting has troubled some leading members of the economics profession. As A.C. Pigou noted in 1924,

> There is wide agreement that the state should protect the interests of the future in some degree against the effects of our irrational discounting, and of our preference for ourselves over our descendants. The whole movement for "conservation" in the United States is based upon this conviction. It is the clear duty of government which is the trustee for unborn generations as well as for its present citizens, to watch over and if need be, by legislative enactment, to defend exhaustible natural resources of the country from rash and reckless spoliation.[41]

Yet in effect, Pigou merely recognized the problem without suggesting an appropriate basis for addressing it. By implying that consideration of the distant future lies outside the bounds of economic theory, he washed his hands of any professional responsibility for thinking about the issue of sustainability.

In our ISEW, we have thus deducted an estimate of the amount that would need to be set aside in a perpetual income stream to compensate future generations for the loss of services from non-renewable energy resources (as well as other exhaustible mineral resources). In addition, we have deducted for the loss of biological resources such as wetlands and croplands (due to shifts in land use and to erosion and compaction). This may be thought of as an accounting device for depreciation of "natural capital" similar to the depreciation of capital subtracted from GNP to arrive at NNP.

Environmental Damage

In the studies by Nordhaus and Tobin and by Zolotas, there is some recognition of the fact that pollution and other environmental damage should be deducted in the calculation of economic welfare. In the area of air and water pollution, we have updated Zolotas's estimates using more recent data and different methodologies for constructing time series. We have also included an estimate for noise pollution. The most important change, however, is the addition of a rather speculative estimate of long-term environmental damage, particularly from climate modification. We have assumed that that damage is cumulative and directly correlated with energy consumption. Also, as in the case of resource depletion, we have not discounted future costs.

Value of Leisure

We have omitted any imputation of the value of leisure from our Index of Sustainable Economic Welfare for two theoretical reasons: 1) the imputation for leisure would outweigh all other elements of the ISEW and 2) the rather arbitrary assumptions upon which such a calculation are based strike us as being particularly problematic. In addition, the data on leisure seem to indicate that it has changed little in the past forty years.

First, the imputation for leisure tends to be so large that variations in the assumptions about how to calculate it have an enormous impact on any welfare index that includes it. The rate of growth of the MEW, for example, varies by approximately a factor of 2 according to which assumption one makes about the relation of technological progress to the value of leisure and nonmarket labor. Nevertheless, in each variant, the value of leisure is by far the largest item in the index, constituting from half to three-fifths of total MEW. Excluding leisure raises the growth of per capita sustainable MEW to 0.86% per year during the period 1947-1965 compared to 0.40% per year when it is included. Thus the omission of leisure significantly reduces the gap between the growth of MEW and GNP (the latter of which grew annually by 2.2% during this period).[42] In the absence of a solid framework, the massive contribution of leisure to the outcome of welfare measurements is not justified.

Second, the meaning of leisure is not entirely clear. Does it simply mean all time spent on activities for which there is no remuneration? In that case, it would include the time of all those who are unemployed, underemployed, or involuntarily retired and who would like to be working. Does it include time spent in such activities as child-care and cooking, which may fall into the categories of either work or pleasure within the same household under various circumstances? Marilyn Waring also points out that the division of leisure within households between women and men is extremely skewed. She cites the work of Lisa Leghorn and Katherine Parker, who suggest that throughout the world, women's household work is designed specifically to increase the leisure of men.[43] If one person's leisure is based directly on another person's drudgery, how can that leisure be counted as a net gain?

Finally, how should the value of leisure time be calculated in dollar terms? As Nordhaus and Tobin explain, "In general, time is to be valued at its opportunity cost, the wage rate."[44] Yet is it appropriate to value the leisure of women and minorities as less than that of white males because the hourly earnings of the former are smaller due to discrimination? These are just a few of the imponderables that make any measurement of the value of leisure conceptually doubtful.

Finally, turning to the empirical evidence on leisure, we find that the growth in the value of leisure, at least since the 1954 survey used by Nordhaus and Tobin, has been due almost exclusively to an increase in the real wage rate, not to any decrease in the number of hours of work being performed. As Zolotas explains:

> [F]or the period prior to 1965, leisure data from a sample survey by Robinson and Converse suggest that there has been no change in the amount of free time available to the four major population segments, namely male workers, male non-workers, female workers and female non-workers. This conclusion coincides with the findings of a 1954 survey, which have been used by Tobin and Nordhaus.[45]

He later adds that the findings of a 1975 survey show that the number of weekly hours devoted to paid employment had "remained virtually unchanged over the period 1965-1975." He concludes that the reason for the rise in total hours of leisure during that decade (from 34.8 hours per week to 38.5) "is mainly attributable to a decrease in hours devoted to family care from 25.4 a week in 1965 to 20.5 a week in 1975."[46] The extent to which the rise of leisure time is a function of declining fertility rather than a change in child-care patterns is not clear. Nevertheless, since the trade-off here is not between work and leisure, to count this change as a welfare gain is dubious.

Rather than allowing us to work less and enjoy more leisure, increased market activity has merely intensified status competition. As

Zolotas so aptly observes:

> It was originally believed that economic growth would
> eventually shorten working time. This belief has not
> been confirmed in today's advanced economies. The im-
> plication is that mankind is constantly being driven far-
> ther away from the point of long term equilibrium,
> where it could sit back and enjoy the fruits of civilization
> in peace and quiet. The reason is that the growth of the
> physical product, in the way it takes place in modern
> economies, is a source of constant stress and compels peo-
> ple to work harder in order to be able to afford the unend-
> ing stream of "new" goods being supplied by the system.[47]

If this image of perpetual striving is in fact correct, then the absence of
significant growth in leisure should come as no surprise.

Given the disproportionate size of most calculations of leisure,
the difficulties of knowing precisely what is meant by leisure, and the
problem of being able to measure changes in it over time, we regard
the inclusion of leisure time in a welfare measure as inappropriate. If,
in the future, the average work week were to decline significantly (as it
apparently did between 1929 and 1954), some imputation for leisure
might be called for. Even then conceptual problems of valuing the
leisure time of the underemployed and unemployed and of men and
women at their various real wage rates would continue to plague the
effort. For now, at least, we omit the imputation for leisure because of
the dubious calculations involved in it and because it would outweigh
all other components in a measure of welfare.

Value of Unpaid Household Labor

The imputation for the value of household services has many
of the same problems as the imputation for leisure, yet the warrant is
so strong for including nonmarket labor that we could not omit it.
The idea that the production of services by members of the household
should be included alongside services produced in and for the market
is intuitively compelling. In addition, because the figure is much
smaller than the imputation for leisure, it does not overwhelm the
index. Nevertheless, it, too, has serious problems, and it is a large
enough factor that questionable judgments about it have a major effect
on the total outcome. After the removal of leisure, the imputation for

household services constitutes between a third and a half of the total MEW for Nordhaus and Tobin.

Though we agree in principle that the value of housework should be included in an indicator of economic welfare, the conceptual and empirical difficulties of measuring it are formidable. Conceptually, the main difficulty is in the definition of housework or household production. Which of the activities within the household should be classified as work as opposed to leisure or an intrinsically satisfying activity? Those who have studied this issue in some detail, particularly the Berks, have discussed some of the rather subtle issues that interfere with any simple calculation of the value of time spent on housework because of these definitional quandaries. For example, when survey respondents are asked to specify whether household activities are work or leisure, some activities (notably cooking and child-care) are frequently classified as both.[48] Moreover, how should those who are assigned the ultimate responsibility for managing the household (generally women, by virtue of gender expectations) be regarded differently than those who merely carry out specific tasks under supervision?[49] If the distinction between management and labor is important in the market, it should also be considered as significant in the home. The time of women, who bear the brunt of this burden, should then be valued not at their wage rate but on the basis of a managerial salary from which the market generally precludes them.

The foregoing comments should clarify why empirical measurement of either "household production functions" or even time spent in housework presents enormous difficulties. Yet even though researchers have not known exactly what they were measuring, the few studies that have taken place of household time allocation have shown surprisingly similar results in terms of time spent in housework. Despite all of the "labor-saving" devices introduced into the household in the past eighty years, the effect on the number of hours spent in housework has been trivial or perhaps non-existent. Whereas housewives spent an average of 56 hours per week doing housework in the 1910s, they still spent about 53 hours per week in 1965-66. Similar findings were discovered by studies in 1924-25 and 1930-31.[50] For the 1980s, Berk's study showed that the average number of *weekday* hours devoted to housework was 8.5 for housewives and 7 for women who were employed.[51] Since this study required respondents to keep diaries only of weekday activities, it is not precisely comparable to previous studies. Nevertheless, it suggests that average weekly hours devoted by women to housework are probably still in the neighborhood of fifty. Berk also notes that the widely touted increase in men's level of housework is largely a mirage, not confirmed by any large-scale studies.[52]

Despite the enormous difficulties in defining the exact boundaries of nonmarket household labor and in measuring its contribution to economic welfare, we could not ignore it. We have chosen to use the rather conservative estimates derived by Robert Eisner who computes the value of time spent on unpaid household work on the basis of the average wage rate of household domestic workers.[53] Though this undervalues the managerial element of household production, it avoids the problem of using differential market wage rates for men and women.

Caveats and Limitations

Nothing is better calculated to make one realize the difficulty of estimating economic welfare over time than the effort to devise an index. Consider the limitations of this one.

First, it relies for its base on personal consumption, which is certainly a more appropriate measure of welfare than production, though it is still questionable. There are many questions one could raise about the extent to which human beings become better off as a result of increased consumption. Above all, it seems likely that there are diminishing returns with respect to the satisfaction gained by marginal increases in consumption. In fact, by using distribution of income to weight consumption, we have implicitly assumed that marginal increases in consumption by the poor are of greater value than marginal increases by the rich.

On the other hand, our calculus of economic well-being has failed to take into account the fact that happiness is apparently correlated with relative rather than absolute levels of wealth or consumption. Having more is less important than having more than the "Joneses."[54] Yet in the absence of any way to quantify this sense of relative well-being, we have ignored this important finding in our index just as others have.

Second, there are many possible categories of additions and deductions that we have omitted. To the extent that unreported income from the "underground economy" (excluding illegal activities) is not already imputed in NIPA, we would like to include it in a measure of welfare. Changes in working conditions should also be included, if there were some reasonable way to calculate such a change.[55] On the deletion side, one might be tempted to subtract expenditures for junk food, tobacco, pornography, and innumerable other items that make questionable contributions to genuine economic welfare. We recognize that this would lead to highly subjective judgments, though we suspect that a consensus might be formed around certain items.

Third, we have been forced to make some heroic assumptions in the process of compiling the ISEW. In some cases, we have included estimates of quantities that are inherently unmeasurable, as in the imputation of the cost imposed upon future generations by the depletion of natural resources. In the case of long term environmental damages, the estimation of costs is clouded by a high degree of uncertainty about the precise physical effects of human actions. (How high will temperatures rise as a result of the greenhouse effect and what will the ecological ramifications be? Are there any geological structures that can *permanently* hold high level radioactive wastes and prevent them from contaminating the environment?) We certainly do not presume to have any definitive answers to these and other questions. We have merely made what we regard as moderate conjectures, ones that do not overwhelm the index, but which play a substantial role in its final outcome.

Chapter 2

THE INDEX OF SUSTAINABLE ECONOMIC WELFARE: DETAILED CALCULATIONS

This chapter contains a detailed explanation of the components of the measure we have devised: the Index of Sustainable Economic Welfare. Per capita ISEW is compared graphically to per capita GNP in figure 1 on page 79. The calculation of the ISEW is presented in table A.1, on pages 80 to 83, and in the supporting tables (A.2 through A.11) which follow it.

Because the methodologies for estimating the costs of natural resources and long-term enviromental damage (columns T and U in table A.1) are more speculative than the procedures used for other estimates, we have also calculated the Index of Sustainable Welfare excluding those columns. (In other words, we *added* the amount in columns T and U to the amount in column X in table A.1 because they were originally subtracted in the calculation of column X.) Although we have not shown this calculation in table A.1, we have included a revised estimate of per capita ISEW, which we label ISEW*, in figure 1 (following table A.1) and in table A.12. In the latter, we have calculated annual growth rates of three alternative measures of economic welfare: per capita GNP, ISEW, and ISEW*.

We have tried to provide enough information in each case to make possible the duplication of our calculations from the original data. However, it is possible that in some cases the process by which we adjusted for minor differences in the reported data from year to year and for inflation may cause our figures to diverge slightly from calculations made by others. Since we regard our calculations as rough approximations anyway, we make no claims for their precision.

Explanation of Columns in Table A.1

Column A - Year

Column B - The value of personal consumption expenditures comes from table 1.2 of the *National Income and Product Accounts* (*NIPA*) and July issues of *Survey of Current Business*, both published by the Bureau of Economic Analysis, U.S. Department of Commerce. Up to 1984, this was available in 1972 dollars. Since the inflation adjustment for 1985 and 1986 is in 1982 dollars, we estimated GNP for 1985 and 1986 in 1972 dollars by calculating the percentage increase in 1982 dollars from 1984 to 1985 and to 1986, then added those proportional increases to the 1984 figure in 1972 dollars.

Column C - The "index of distributional inequality" was derived from the Census Bureau, U.S. Department of Commerce, *Current Population Reports: Consumer Income*, Series P-60, No. 159, table 12, page 39, "Income at Selected Positions and Percentage Share of Aggregate Income in 1947 to 1986 Received by Each Fifth and Top 5 Percent of Families and Unrelated Individuals by Race of Householder." We created an index of inequality that is similar to the Gini Coefficient except that our index assigns weights according to the degree of difference between each of the four lowest quintiles (fifths) of income and the highest (richest) quintile. In 1975, for example, the top quintile received about 7.6 times as much income as the lowest quintile, 3.5 times as much as the second quintile, 2.3 times as much as the third quintile, and 1.7 times as much as the fourth quintile. We then added those four numbers (plus 1 to represent the highest quintile's relation to itself) and divided by 5 (that being the number that would be obtained by perfectly uniform distribution of income). The lowest possible number for a given year is 1 (5 divided by 5), but there is no upper maximum (unlike the Gini coefficient which varies between 0 and 1). We then used the numbers we derived from this procedure (numbers which ranged from 3.1 to 3.75) to make an index, setting the 1951 value at 100. (See table A.2.)

The income figures we used may not accurately reflect actual income differences for two reasons. First, they may overestimate inequalities to the extent that they do not include transfer payments made to the poor in the form of AFDC, Food Stamps, public housing, and other welfare programs. On the other hand, the disproportionate benefits received by the middle and upper classes from government services offsets the modest transfer payments to the poor. Second, the before-tax income reported in the surveys we used does not take into account the graduated scale of income taxes, thereby overestimating inequalities. At the same time, however, tax benefits to the middle and upper income brackets (such as the write-off of mortgage interest payments) tilt the distributional balance the other way. We encourage a thorough study of this very complex issue of income inequality, net of all taxes, transfer payments, and hidden benefits. In the meantime, we must use the data available to us.

Column D - Weighted personal consumption is column B (personal consumption) divided by column C (index of distributional inequality). (The reason for division rather than multiplication is that in column C larger numbers indicate greater *i*nequality.)

Column D is the base number from which other modifications are either added or subtracted. We first add four columns (E, F, G, and H) that represent streams of services that are not counted as part of personal consumption in the national income accounts. Next, we subtract nine columns (I through Q) that represent items intended to compensate for implicit overestimates of welfare in the measure of personal consumption. We then subtract four columns (R, S, T, and U) that represent our estimate of how present activities undermine the sustainability of our natural resource base. Finally, we add two columns (V and W) that represent the degree to which the level of capital accumulation and shifts in control of capital between domestic sources and foreign sources affect the sustainability of the U.S. economy. Thus columns R through W represent items that reflect the capacity of the economy to continue to provide the same level of welfare over a prolonged period.

Column E - Household services such as cooking, cleaning, and childcare contribute to economic welfare even though they are not sold in the market at an observable price. In chapter 1 we pointed to several theoretical and empirical problems involved in imputing the value of household, non-market labor. We have nevertheless included it because of its tremendous significance as a factor in overall economic welfare. We have derived this column from figures presented by Robert Eisner in "The Total Incomes System of Accounts," *Survey of Current Business*, January 1985. He provides estimates in 1972 dollars for 1946, 1956, 1966, 1971, 1976, and 1981. We have used a regression on the logarithm of those estimates to interpolate and extrapolate for other years. Eisner explains the methodology he used:

The value of unpaid household work is taken conservatively to be the product of annual hours in relevant household activities and the average hourly compensation of household domestic workers. The time estimates were derived from the Michigan Survey Research Center time use studies of 1965, 1975, and 1981, with the 1975 survey used as the benchmark.[1]

Column F - In order to count only the value received each year from capital equipment rather than its initial purchase price, we add the value of the services that flow from consumer durables here and subtract the actual expenditures on consumer durables elsewhere (column I). To the extent that household equipment wears out more quickly than it might, it inflates the personal consumption account without contributing to welfare. If washing machines, on average, lasted 100 years rather than 15, fewer would be bought, and personal consumption would not rise as rapidly as it would otherwise, but welfare would not be diminished. By using the estimated value of the service from such equipment rather than its purchase price, we have attempted to overcome this distortion in current measures.

To calculate this column, we used the table entitled "Constant Dollar Net Stock of Consumer Durables" in the *Survey of Current Business*, March 1979, April 1981, October 1982, and August of 1983, 1984, and 1987. For each year we multiplied the total net stock by ten per cent to approximate the ratio of housing services to net housing stock given in the *National Income and Product Accounts*. (Actual proportions for a sample of years are: 1950, 8.5%; 1955, 9.6%; 1960, 10.7%; 1965, 11.7%; 1971, 11.2%; 1974, 10.0%; 1977, 9.7%; 1980, 9.5%; and 1983, 11.3%)

Column G - With the exception of this column and column H (certain expenditures for health and education), we have not included government expenditures as adding to welfare because they are largely defensive in nature. That is, the growth of government programs does not so much add to net welfare as prevent deterioration of well-being by maintaining security, environmental health, and the capacity to continue commerce. In addition, some government enterprises, such as transit systems and sewer or water districts, provide services for a fee in a manner similar to private businesses. These payments already show up as personal consumption in the national income accounts. However, some services are provided by the government that could theoretically be offered through the market but which are difficult to meter. The main item in that category is the provision of streets and highways. Since the annual value of services from roads is not calculated, we have imputed it from estimates of the value of the stock of streets and highways.

To calculate this column, (see table A.3) we used the table entitled "Constant Dollar Gross Stock of Government-Owned Structures, Excluding Military, By Type of Structures" in the *Survey of Current Business*, March 1980, February 1981, October 1982, August 1983, and August 1984. (Because later estimates of the stock of government-owned structures--for 1984-1986--were not disaggregated by type of structure, we had to make estimates for those years based on aggregated figures.) We added together the "Highways and streets" columns for Federal and State and local governments. We estimated the net stock as being two-thirds of the gross stock, based on the approximate ratio of net to gross for all government-owned non-military structures. We then estimated that approximately three-fourths of all vehicle-miles (for both passenger and freight travel) are for non-commuting travel and therefore contribute to welfare. The net stock of roadways that contributes to welfare is thus two-thirds times three-fourths--i.e., one-half--of the value of the gross stock in each year. To find the annual value of services from this stock, we multiplied by ten per cent, which is the approximate ratio of housing services to net housing stock that appears in the *NIPA*. (See note to column F).

Column H - We have excluded most government expenditures from our estimate (except see column G) because they measure inputs or costs rather than outputs or benefits. The correlation between increases in government spending and real increases in welfare is tenuous because of the difficulty of measuring the demand for the kinds of services that government offers. Nevertheless, we have assumed that a portion of the money spent on education and health contributes to welfare and should be added to personal consumption.

With the exception of one-half of public spending on higher education, we regarded most expenditures on education as being neither consumption nor investment. In chapter 1, we explained why we have not counted education as investment: the evidence suggests that it contributes little to productivity. On the other hand, it would be inappropriate to count education as consumption because most schooling appears to be defensive. In other words, people attend school because others are in school and the failure to attend would mean falling behind in the competition for diplomas or degrees that confer higher incomes on their recipients. (We assume that compulsory attendance laws are not the primary motivation for going to school.) We assume, nevertheless, as Zolotas did in his study, that one-half of post-secondary education is pure consumption, in the sense that it is sought for its own sake rather than to serve another purpose. Thus, we have added one-half of public expenditures (federal and state and local) for higher education from tables 3.15 and 3.16 of the *National Income and Product Accounts*. (See table A. 4, column c of this Appendix.)

In the case of expenditures on health by the public sector, we have assumed that they are valued as highly as private expenditures for the same purpose. We have added only that portion of public health expenditures that are assumed to add to social welfare. (See table A.4, column e.) From the inflation-adjusted expenditure in each year, we subtracted the amount spent in 1950 (also in 1972 dollars) to determine the *increase* over the base year. We divided that difference by two to take into account the "defensive" expenditures necessary to compensate for the growth of environmental stresses on health (as we do for private health expenditures in column J). All figures are derived from the *Statistical Abstract of the United States*, 1988, table 129, p. 86. Expenditures are adjusted for inflation using the "medical care" component of the Consumer Price Index, in the *Statistical Abstract*, 1988, table 738, p. 450. (Please note that for this and all later references to the *Statistical Abstract*, we have cited only the 1988 edition. In fact, we often referred to previous editions to fill in gaps in the data.)

Column I - The value of private expenditure on durable goods in constant (1972) dollars comes from the *National Income and Product Accounts*, table 1.2. The estimates for 1985 and 1986 were derived in the same manner as the estimates of personal consumption. The reason for subtracting expenditures on consumer durables is explained in the note on column F.

Column J - This is the inverse of column H. Here we *subtracted* private education and health expenditures that do not contribute to welfare. We subtracted them because they are included in column B, personal consumption, and not subtracting them here would involve double counting.

We subtracted all expenditures on private education except one-half of private expenditures on higher education, based on the same rationale given in the explanation of column H. (See table A.5, column d.) The cost of private education, for both total and higher education, was taken from the *NIPA*, the table entitled "Personal Consumption Expenditures by Type of Expenditure" (table 2.4), and adjusted to 1972 dollars by the implicit price deflator for private education in table 7.12.

Similarly, we subtracted defensive private health expenditures from total welfare. As in the case of public expenditures on health, we assumed that half of the real growth in private health expenditures is purely defensive in nature, i.e. compensating for growing health risks due to urbanization and industrialization. We subtracted the inflation adjusted expenditure level in 1950 from the expenditure in each subsequent year to determine the increased spending on health above a base level. We then divided the difference by two to represent the proportion of expenditures that are defensive in nature. (See table A.5, column f.) Total private health expenditures come from *Statistical Abstract*, 1988, table 129, p. 86. Costs are adjusted for 1972 prices by the "medical care" component of the Consumer Price Index, from *Statistical Abstract*, 1988, table 738, p. 450.

Column K - The value of national advertising expenditures comes from the *Statistical Abstract*, 1988, table 896, p. 529, and is adjusted for inflation using the "Services Deflator" in the *National Income and Product Accounts*, table 7.12. We subtracted national, but not local, advertising expenditures (in contrast to Zolotas, who subtracted one-half of total advertising expenditures) because we reasoned that local advertising (especially in newspapers and on the radio) tends to offer information of value to consumers about the location and price of goods. By contrast, national advertising (especially on television and in magazines) tends to be aimed at creating demand for products and brand name loyalty through the use of images that have little to do with the actual product.

Column L - The direct (out of pocket) costs of commuting were calculated as follows (see table A.6):

$$C = 0.3 (A - 0.3 A) + 0.3 B$$
$$= 0.3 (0.7 A) + 0.3 B$$
$$= 0.21 A + 0.3 B \quad \text{where:}$$

C is the direct cost of commuting.

A is the cost of user-operated transport (mainly cars) from the *National Income and Product Accounts*, table 2.4). This figure was adjusted to constant (1972) dollars with the implicit price deflator for personal consumption expenditures on motor vehicles and parts found in the *NIPA*, table 7.12.

0.3 A is the estimated cost of depreciation of private cars (which is excluded here to avoid double counting since it was already included as an element in column F) from the *Statistical Abstract*, 1987, table 1040, p. 593.

0.3 is the estimated portion of total non-commercial vehicle miles used in commuting in 1983 (see *Statistical Abstract*, 1987, table 1033, p. 591).

B is the price of purchased local transportation (see *National Income and Product Accounts*, table 2.4)

0.3 is the estimated portion of passenger miles on local public transportation used for commuting.

We did not include indirect costs of commuting (the value of the time lost in commuting) in our calculations because we lacked reliable data. In theory, we regard this as a significant cost of the presumably increased congestion that accompanies urban growth, but we could not find a time series showing changes in the amount of time spent commuting to work. Zolotas used an estimate made in 1965-66 of 52 minutes for men and 42 minutes for women. He then assumed an increase of 2 minutes per year after that period. That would indicate that commuting time in 1980 should have been 80 minutes for men and 70 minutes for women. In fact, according to the 1980 Census, average commuting time in 1980 was 43 minutes, less than the combined average for men and women in 1965-66.[2] Did commuting time actually decrease over time? Were the methodologies or populations of the two surveys sufficiently different to account for this difference? We simply do not know. Therefore, we have not subtracted the indirect costs of commuting, though doing so would certainly reduce economic welfare each year by tens of billions of dollars.

Column M - A partial measure of the cost of urbanization is the higher cost of living associated with increasing density. In other words, as population grows in urban areas, the cost of land increases without any compensating increase in welfare. In order to measure this aspect of the cost of urbanization, we computed the proportion of rental (and imputed rental) payments that reflect the price of land rather than structures built on land.

To arrive at the figures in column M (see table A.7), we multiplied (a) the value of residential land as a percent of the total value of residential property (land value divided by the combined value of land and improvements) times (b) aggregate annual expenditures on housing (including the imputed rental value of owner occupied dwellings). The first part of the equation (value of land divided by total value of property) is derived from Federal Reserve Board, *Balance Sheets For the U.S. Economy 1947-86*, pages 11 to 15, lines 4 and 9. The second part of the equation (aggregate housing expenditures--including imputed expenditures) comes from the *National Income and Product Accounts*, table 2.4, adjusted for 1972 prices by the implicit price deflator for housing, table 7.12.

Column N - Damage due to accidents represents a real cost of industrialization and higher traffic densities. Figures are available only for the damages due to motor vehicle accidents. They are derived from *Statistical Abstract*, 1987, table 997, p. 579 and adjusted for inflation using the Consumer Price Index.

Column O - The figures in this column are a composite of two estimates: 1) damage to water quality, primarily from point source discharges (sewage and industrial wastes) and 2) damage due to siltation resulting from erosion from farms, construction sites, and roadways. Although this may involve some double counting (insofar as siltation also damages water quality), we suspect that on the whole we have underestimated the first type of damage because of the lack of data on non-point sources of pollution. If they are marginally included under erosion costs, that only partially corrects for a more general underestimation of the total damage.

Damage due to point source discharges. We have estimated the cost of damage from water pollution as $12.0 billion in 1972 and derived estimates for earlier and later years based on subjective estimates and surveys. (We did not include the cost of building sewage treatment facilities because that is a public expenditure and therefore not included in our initial estimate of welfare--aggregate private consumption or column B.) The numbers in this column are of limited reliability, though we consider them reasonable and plausible.

A number of factors contribute to the difficulty of making reliable estimates of the dollar value of the damage caused by water pollution:

1) No universally acknowledged measure of "water quality" exists. A number of different elements may contribute to poor water quality, such as biological oxygen demand (or conversely, low dissolved oxygen levels), phosphorus, nitrogen, suspended solids, dissolved solids, turbidity, and temperature. With no means of developing a single composite measure of their joint effects, the term "water quality" has no precise meaning.

2) Even if we had a single composite measure of water quality, the actual measurement of water samples is not very reliable. Infrequent samples, measurement inaccuracy due to the imprecision of laboratory tests, and faulty monitoring and laboratory procedures all contribute to a low level of confidence in measured results.[3]

3) Precise numerical relations have not been established between the components of water quality (number 1 above) and the capacity of water to support fish or other wildlife or to support swimming and other recreational activities.

4) If a reliable estimate of water pollution could be devised for a particular water basin, aggregating data across regions would still elude us. Unlike the problem of air pollution, where the entire atmosphere serves as a "sink" for airborne wastes and where speaking of national air quality has some meaning, an aggregate measure of water quality is complicated by the fact that there may be improvements in one river basin or lake while another is becoming more polluted.

5) Even if a reliable baseline estimate could be derived for one year, we would still not know whether water quality were improving or deteriorating without comparable data for other years. Such data exist only in the form of highly subjective estimates.

6) Unlike the relatively direct estimation of air pollution damage (see the note on column P), many of the costs of water pollution must be calculated almost entirely from indirect evidence such as the loss of swimming, fishing, and boating opportunities. Thus, to determine recreation benefits of improving water quality, economists have had to rely on proxy measures such as changes in the amount of time and money spent on *transportation* to alternative recreation sites in re-sponse to changes in water quality. (In other words, the measure of pollution damage comes from estimating the additional money people are willing to spend to drive to a new recreational site if a closer one has been contaminated by pollution.) The outcome of these studies is heavily dependent on the assumptions about the magnitude of shifts in participation rates in water-based recreation in response to meeting the 1985 water quality objectives set by Congress.

7) Finally, estimates of the cost of water pollution generally at-tempt to measure only damage resulting from point source discharges (i.e., pollution coming out of municipal and industrial sewers). The cost of damage caused by urban and farmland runoff is not included. Since those non-point sources of pollution are often at least as serious

as point sources, neglecting the impact of the former considerably underestimates the actual costs or damage from water pollution. As of the late 1970s, after several years of efforts to control point sources but with minimal control of non-point sources, the latter contributed 57% of biological oxygen demand, 98% of suspended solids, 83% of dissolved solids, 87% of phosphorus, and 88% of nitrogen discharged into U.S. waterways.[4]

Keeping those caveats and conditions in mind, we have estimated the total damage from water pollution in 1972 as approximately $12 billion. Our source is Myrick Freeman, an economist who has done comprehensive work on the value of clean air and water.[5] Three of the studies he cites came to the conclusion that the upper limits of the range of estimated damage to recreation from point source pollution was around $18 billion in 1978 dollars. Freeman's own upper estimate of recreation benefits that would be realized by eliminating point source discharges is $8.7 billion in 1978 dollars (or about $6 billion in 1972 dollars). Adding damage to aesthetics, ecology, property values, and diversionary uses (household and industrial water supplies), his upper estimate of damage is $18.4 billion in 1978 dollars ($12 billion in 1972 dollars). Though Freeman's best estimate for damage from point source pollution is only $9.4 billion ($6 billion in 1972 dollars), we have used the less conservative figures on the assumption that the inclusion of non-point source pollution would at least double the *total* pollutant load in many river basins and increase it several-fold in others. Thus, a $12 billion estimate of water pollution damage in 1972 may even be conservative.

In the absence of any reliable time series data about water pollution, our estimates of changes in pollution damages over time are not very reliable. According to the Conservation Foundation, "the years 1974 to 1981 saw little change in water quality with respect to the conventional pollution indicators."[6] This finding is based on the U.S. Geological Survey's National Ambient Stream Quality Accounting Network. It is confirmed by a 1984 survey of the Association of State and Interstate Water Pollution Control Administrators and the 1982-83 National Fisheries Survey. We assume that this overall lack of improvement means that the improvements that did take place as a result of more stringent pollution controls were offset by the growth of population and polluting activities. By contrast with the unvarying levels of the 1970s and 1980s, we have assumed that water quality declined during the 1950s and 1960s at 3% per year before a concerted national effort was undertaken to address the issue.

Damage due to siltation. In addition to the estimates of damage to water quality, we have included data on the effects of erosion from farmland as well as streambanks, roadbanks, and construction sites. We assume here that the deterioration of water quality due to these non-point sources has already been included in a general way in the calculations of point source discharges. Our estimate here is of the costs of dredging navigable rivers and the damage posed by siltation to dams and other water impoundments, as well as costs of sediment-related flooding and other off-stream effects. The Conservation Foundation estimated that this damage was in the range of $3.2 to $13.0 billion in 1980, with a best estimate of around $6.0 billion. That would be about $3.3 billion in 1972 dollars (using the implicit GNP deflator).

Estimating changes in these costs over time is difficult. Two point estimates of the amount of total erosion exist for 1977 and 1982, derived from the National Resources Inventory, which was undertaken in both of those years by the Soil Conservation Service in conjunction with Iowa State University. In both 1977 and 1982, total erosion was estimated at 6.5 billion tons. We have assumed that that 5 year trend has remained constant until the present and that it began in 1972 when the massive growth of grain exports led to shifts in land use, particularly the plowing of marginal, erosion-prone soils, in an attempt to profit from the high levels of world demand. We have assumed that during the previous 22 years erosion increased by an average of 1% per year. We recognize that estimates for these previous years are essentially speculative and would prefer reliable data. We also realize that farmland erosion may have remained approximately constant during that period in the absence of data to the contrary. Nevertheless, we believe that the overall problem of sedimentation from erosion probably increased during this period as a function of general economic growth, particularly from urban construction and the development of the interstate highway system.

Column P - Following Myrick Freeman's analysis, we have divided estimates of the costs of air pollution into 6 categories: 1) damage to agricultural vegetation, 2) materials damage, 3) costs of cleaning soiled goods, 4) acid rain damage, 5) urban disamenities, and 6) aesthetics.[7]

1) We have estimated damage to agricultural vegetation at $4 billion. According to a study by Heintz, Herschaft, and Horak in 1976, entitled "National Damages of Air and Water Pollution," the level of damage to agricultural vegetation due to oxidants in 1973 was $2.8 billion. Freeman suggests this estimate is too low because it fails to reflect the fact that farmers have not only sustained crop damage from air pol-

lution but that they have also shifted to less profitable crops. We have assumed this added cost would raise the total cost of air pollution damage to crops to approximately $4 billion in 1970 (in 1972 dollars).

2) We have estimated materials damage due to corrosion of paint, metals, rubber, and so on at $6 billion. Zolotas uses an estimate from Liu and Yu of $38.4 billion in 1970, and since that amount is only about three per cent of the net stock of fixed reproducible wealth owned by households for that year (including all residential structures and durable equipment), that rate of deterioration due to air pollution may in fact be plausible. We have chosen $6 billion as our estimate to bring it more into line with Freeman's middle estimate of $3.2 billion.

3) We are using the same figure as Zolotas for our estimate of the cost of cleaning soiled materials as a result of air pollution--$5 billion. That figure is derived from Liu and Yu. It is confirmed by Freeman's estimate that a 20% reduction in airborne particulates would reduce cleaning costs by $0.6 to $3.8 billion. Though additional reductions in particulates would not have correspondingly dramatic results, this nevertheless suggest that an estimate of $5 billion for total damage in this category is reasonable and perhaps conservative.

4) Based on Freeman, we have conservatively estimated total damage to forests and aquatic ecosystems due to acid rain as $1.5 billion in 1972 dollars.[8]

5) We have estimated the total reduction in the quality of urban life as a result of air pollution to be approximately $9 billion. This involves two components: 1) a reduction in property values in proportion to the level of pollution in an area and 2) the necessity of paying higher wages to attract people to work in areas with high levels of pollution. Freeman estimates reduced property values to be $4 billion as a result of stationary sources and $1.5 billion as a result of mobile sources (both in 1972 dollars). For wage differentials, he cites a study by Meyer and Leone that concluded that wage differentials necessary to attract workers to pollution prone areas were $6.1 billion for particulates, $2.1 billion for sulfur dioxide, and $5.1 billion for nitrogen oxides. If all of these factors (reduction in property values and wage differentials) were simply additive, the total reduction in quality of life would be $18.8 billion. Since there is overlap among their effects and with other damage estimates (such as between cleaning costs and property values), we have included only $9 billion, or approximately one-half of the total from this category.

6) We have assumed a total of $4.5 billion in damage to aesthetic values due to loss of visibility and enjoyment in national parks and other scenic areas. This is based on a study in the region surrounding the Four Corners Power Plant where residents said that they would be willing to pay $85 per year to improve the aesthetic conditions of the area considerably. Since our estimate of $4.5 billion amounts to about $20 per person per year to pay for visibility improvements, we believe that it is a plausible figure.

Adding these figures (vegetative damage, $4 billion; corrosion and materials damage, $6 billion; cleaning and soiling, $5 billion; acid rain, $1.5 billion; reduction in urban quality of life, $9 billion; and aesthetic costs, $4.5 billion) we arrive at a total of $30.0 billion in costs associated with air pollution for 1970 (in 1972 dollars).

If this $30 billion estimate seems excessive, we would like to point out that we consider it conservative because we have attempted to exclude from our calculations all estimates of damage to health due to air pollution. That damage may be included indirectly in the estimate of wage differentials, but we have consciously avoided including health costs as a separate category. We have also excluded health costs because we have put in two other columns (H and J) that specifically eliminate "defensive" health expenditures from the estimation of health benefits. Despite this, we suspect that some portion of health damage due to air pollution *could* be included here without double counting because many respiratory ailments (such as colds, flu, bronchitis, etc.) do not require medical attention, yet they are exacerbated and prolonged by exposure to air pollution. Other chronic conditions that cause discomfort and reduce productivity but which do not require medical attention--from shortness of breath to headaches to burning eyes--would all constitute damage to health from air pollution that would not show up as "defensive" health expenditures. We suspect that these costs would amount to several billion dollars per year.

Furthermore, we have not included any estimate of the cost of increased mortality in our calculation of the costs of air pollution, in part because this might involve some double counting. We are also not entirely satisfied with the idea of setting a dollar value on human life. On the other hand, neglecting this category altogether, as we have done, implicitly places zero value on human life (or more precisely on the value of living a longer life). We are not entirely happy with that result either. Nevertheless, if we were to include some measure of the costs of increased mortality, we would base it on the value of life revealed in the willingness of people to pay to reduce the overall death rate in a large population. Since all of us make trade-offs between activities involving a higher probability of death and measurable benefits, this procedure reflects the value we implicitly place upon the probability of remaining alive. If the value per death avoided (in this probabilistic sense) is approximately $1 million in our society as some studies suggest, we can determine the dollar cost of air pollution on mortality rates at least within an order of magnitude. With that dollar value as a baseline figure, it is possible to estimate the damage of air pollution once the physical relation between air pollution and mortality is known. Freeman cites a number of studies that derive estimates of the elasticity of mortality with respect to air pollution of between 0.01 and 0.09 (meaning a 1% increase in air pollution causes an increase in mortality of between 0.01% and 0.09%). Using those figures and Freeman's calculations, we arrived at a best estimate of the cost of increased mortality due to air pollution of about $13 billion (in 1972 dollars). This is based on estimates of mortality benefits of about $10.5 and $12 billion for 20% and 60% reductions in air pollution, respectively. We assume that elimination of the remaining 40% of air pollution would add only $1 billion in benefits. In any case, we assume that the addition of the costs of higher mortality associated with air pollution would add another $10 to $15 billion in 1970 to the $30 billion estimate we are in fact using.

Our estimate of time series for air pollution damage is based on EPA's *National Air Pollutant Emission Estimates*, as summarized in the *Statistical Abstract*, 1988, table 332, p. 192. The volume of emissions in 1986 is an extrapolation from previous years since data were not available. We combined the emissions of particulates, sulfur oxides, and nitrogen oxides for each year and created an index number to show changes over time. (See table A.8.) A better model would calculate the damage from each type of pollutant each year and add the sum of those dollar figures together, but we do not have the sophistication to develop such a model.

Column Q - The damage caused by noise pollution in the U.S. in 1972 was estimated to be $4 billion by the World Health Organization.[9] We have assumed that increasing industrialization and expansion of the highway system and of the number of airports caused noise pollution to get worse during the period from 1950 to 1972 at 3% per year. We have assumed that since 1972 noise abatement regulations have slowed the rate of growth of the noise level to 1% per year.

Column R - To calculate the value of the loss of wetlands, we first estimated the value per acre of the flow of services from an acre of wetland at $600 (1972 dollars). This is approximately one-third more than the median value of $448 per acre per year estimated for flood protection, water purification, provision of wildlife habitat, and aesthetics by Gupta and Foster.[10] We estimated a higher figure than Gupta and Foster because they did not account for what economists call "consumers' surplus" in their valuations. (Consumers' surplus means the amount that purchasers or beneficiaries of an item or service would have been willing to pay above and beyond the actual price. We do not know how much this would actually be in the case of wetland services, so we have made a reasonable estimate.) In addition, $600 is a relatively conservative figure since calculations of the value of salt water wetlands have arrived at estimates three to twenty times as high.[11] The estimated loss of 600,000 acres per year through 1973 comes from the Council on Environmental Quality, *Annual Report*, July 1982, and the estimated loss of 300,000 acres per year in subsequent years comes from the testimony of Robert A. Jantzen, Director of the U.S. Interior Department's Fish and Wildlife Service before the Senate Environment and Public Works Committee on November 20, 1981.

The loss of the stream of benefits from wetlands is a cumulative process. In other words, if 600,000 acres of wetlands were filled or drained in two successive years, at the end of the second year the loss would equal the stream of benefits flowing from 1.2 million acres of wetlands. Thus we have added the loss of benefits from wetlands each year to the total from the previous year.

Our base figure of $10 billion for 1950 is largely arbitrary. We estimated that a total of approximately 100 million acres of wetlands were filled in North America to make way for farming and other activities from the colonial period to 1950. This is based on a decline from approximately 215 million original acres to about 110 million in 1950.[12] We reasoned that the value of each of the initial tens of millions of acres of lost wetlands was lower than the marginal value of the remaining acres that were filled in recent decades. (Likewise, the value of the last million acres on the continent will be greater than $600 per acre because of the greater scarcity of the resource at that time.) Thus we multiplied an average value of $100 an acre of services from wetlands by 100 million acres to arrive at $10 billion as a plausible estimate of the cumulative loss to that time.

Column S - This column reflects two logically distinct ways in which the biologically productive capacity of farmland has been reduced. On the one hand, urban expansion (including the construction of highways) permanently removes land from production by paving it over.

On the other hand, poor land management that destroys the soil through erosion, compaction, and decomposition of organic matter removes land gradually from production by lowering its productivity. Measuring either of these losses in dollar terms is both complicated and somewhat arbitrary, but because of the importance of food production in the long-run sustainability of the economy, we feel that it is imperative to make an attempt at measuring this loss.

As a result of the industrialization of agriculture, particularly since World War II, the productivity of labor and other non-energy inputs (including farmland) increased steadily over time as those inputs were replaced by increasing amounts of energy (including embodied energy such as fertilizers or machines that themselves required energy to produce). This led to the assumption that crop yields would continue to increase indefinitely as new genetic strains were developed and new techniques were applied. From that perspective, the loss of a fraction of a percent of the cropland base to non-agricultural uses each year or a slight annual decline in productivity of the underlying soil base is insignificant if technological progress grows faster than those sources of decline.

In a world of continuously declining real energy costs, that perspective would be partially valid (though with some reservations because chemical inputs cannot entirely substitute for the organic content of the soil beyond a certain point). However, as we noted in chapter 1, the real cost of energy is rising and will continue to rise in the future because of the increasing energy cost required for discovery and extraction and processing of new sources of energy. The implications of the rapid depletion of low-cost energy resources available for agriculture are staggering. For over forty years, the use of energy-intensive inputs to agriculture has masked the declining size and quality of the soil base upon which farming ultimately depends. Fertilizer has increased crop yields dramatically, but at a cost of breaking down the humus in the soil, oxidizing the soil carbon, and allowing farmers to ignore the effects of erosion. As long as fertilizer is relatively cheap, the effects of this degradation can be temporarily overcome by adding more fertilizer, though that merely exacerbates the problem in the long-run. Likewise, irrigation can boost yields considerably as long as water can be pumped from rivers or aquifers at low cost. However, as energy (including embodied energy) costs rise and as aquifers are depleted, this source of growth in agriculture will be shown to be unsustainable. Moreover, the process of irrigation can itself lead to soil degradation if it increases either erosion or the salinity of the soil.

Economists also tend to downplay the reduction in quantity and quality of cropland by pointing out that there are over one hundred million acres of land that are currently unused or are being used as rangelands or pasture that could be brought into crop production. Undoubtedly some of this land will in fact be brought into production in the future as energy inputs to agriculture become more expensive and as some of the land currently used for crops becomes exhausted from overuse. Nevertheless, this land is not already being used as cropland for economic reasons and because it has high erosion potential.

> Most of the land with high or medium potential for conversion is in soil classes IIe, IIIe, or IVe, and "e" stands for erodible. According to the 1980 RCA draft (p.3-4), even the better of those soils are dangerously erodible when in crop production. [13]

In other words, the sanguine view that the loss of valuable cropland can be compensated by conversion of other land to more intensive use is not supported by the facts.

Another pernicious idea in economics that downplays the significance of soil loss is the discounting of future costs and benefits. Thus the present value of farmland is based on the productivity of the land, but only after the value of future yields has been reduced by a compound interest formula. The damage caused by erosion or urbanization to future productivity thus appears as insignificant in conventional economic analyses. In effect, this theory says a profit-maximizing farm *should* deplete the soil as long as the discounted stream of net revenues from unsustainable farming is greater than the discounted stream of net revenues from a farm managed on a sustained-yield basis. If farming unsustainably yields a higher stream of revenues, the surplus can be invested elsewhere, making the next generation better off (in theory) than if the farmer had transferred the land in its undepleted state.

Our purpose is to calculate the *sustainable* economic welfare of our activities. We have therefore subtracted the cumulative damage to long-term productivity of land that results from urbanization and poor land management. We would like to have estimated the undiscounted costs our current practices impose on our descendants who will no longer be able make up for the loss of land area and declining soil quality with fossil fuels. However, we were forced to settle for estimates that are undoubtedly based only on the discounted value of lost productivity. Thus we believe that our estimates understate the magnitude of the cost being imposed on the future as a result of unsustainable practices.

Losses due to urbanization. The amount of farmland that has been lost to urbanization is the subject of a great deal of controversy. The 1981 National Agricultural Lands Study (NALS) created a furor by arguing that the rate of farmland loss had grown from about one million acres per year in the period 1958-1967 to about three million acres per year in the period 1967-1975. Recognizing certain methodological and definitional problems in the study, we have chosen to assume that the one million acres per year figure has probably been constant throughout the period of our study (1950-1986) and that the proportion of cropland being converted to urban uses has remained at about 30% of that. In other words, we have adopted a conservative estimate for cropland loss due to urbanization of 300,000 acres per year. (This compares to the estimate in the NALS of 600,000 acres per year of cropland or 800,000 acres per year of cropland plus potential cropland.)

We then estimated that the value of an average acre of converted cropland, based on its productivity in the absence of high applications of fertilizers and other energy-intensive inputs, would be $100 per acre per year or a capitalized value of $1,000 per acre (in 1972 dollars). We are assuming that the underlying value of farmland exceeds the market value today. Since our aim is to calculate *sustainable* economic welfare, we have chosen a figure that represents the value of land *as if* cheap energy sources had already been depleted. Without nitrogen fertilizer (derived from natural gas), for example, farm output would be lower, and food prices would be higher. The demand by farmers for high quality agricultural land would increase, raising its price. We regard that (unknown) price as the appropriate one to use when calculating the value of land lost to urbanization. We believe $1,000 per acre to be conservative, even if it seems high in terms of current market prices. It should be remembered that the best land for urban uses is generally the highest quality farmland in terms of slope, drainage, and other soil characteristics. Thus urbanization has generally caused the conversion of the most valuable croplands.

We began this calculation with an estimated accumulated loss of $1 billion to represent the value of services from farmland that had already been lost through urbanization by 1950. Since 15 million acres were in urban areas by that date and another 24 million had been transformed into highways and rights-of-way by then, our estimate of $1 billion implies that the average value of the loss to agriculture was about $25 per acre per year.[14] As in the case of wetlands, we have assumed that the marginal utility or value of the first acres removed from agriculture is lower than the value of the land most recently urbanized.

In summary, we have calculated that urbanization annually removes from the cropland base a stream of agricultural services worth $30 million (300,000 acres times $100 per acre) and that the total cost is an accumulation of these losses, beginning with a loss of $1 billion in 1950. (See table A.9, column d.)

Losses due to deteriorating soil. The visible loss of land to urbanization is probably not as serious a problem as the less evident reduction in the quality of land as a result of poor management practices. Economists tend to downplay productivity losses resulting from mismanagement because tangible productivity (in terms of yield per acre, though not in terms of yield per unit of energy input) has increased rapidly over the past forty years. In addition, productivity losses due to soil depletion are probably not linear, which means that the effects of erosion and compaction and loss of organic matter from the soil may not show up in yield reductions until the soil is irreversibly damaged. This is especially true, as noted above, when chemical fertilizers mask the effects of soil depletion temporarily, even as they contribute to it.

As a result, calculation of the loss of soil productivity is difficult. We expect that our estimates of this cost are underestimates of the true cost of current practices because the impact on the future has presumably been discounted and because loss of productivity is measured only against yields inflated by energy-intensive inputs.

In 1980 economists at the Soil Conservation Service of the U.S. Department of Agriculture estimated that agricultural productivity losses resulting from erosion were approximately $1.3 billion (or about $0.7 billion in 1972 dollars).[15] Since we do not know the methodology for arriving at that result, we checked it using an alternative method of calculation and a different data source. The National Agricultural Land Study estimated in 1977 that 1.7 million acre-equivalents of land were lost each year due to erosion. If we assume that about one-half of the serious erosion takes place on cropland, then a per acre cost of about $800 for this eroded land would yield the same result as the SCS estimate. (Thus, 1.7 million acre-equivalents divided by 2, times $800 per acre = $680 million or $0.68 billion).

We have assumed, as we did in the discussion of erosion impacts on watercourses (see note to column O), that the rate of erosion has remained fairly constant since 1972 and that it increased by one percent per year from 1950 up to that point. We have also assumed that some damage had already occurred prior to 1950. Thus we have begun our calculation with a cumulative loss of $5 billion in 1949, with further costs added to that. (See table A.9, column b.)

The damage to soil from compaction by heavy machinery was estimated at $3.0 billion in 1980 ($1.67 billion in 1972 dollars) by R. Neil Sampson.[16] We assume that that figure increased by 3% per year both before and after 1980. (See table A.9, column c.)

The amount in column S represents the total from the two types of soil loss: urbanization and deterioration, of which the latter is divided into two components. (See table A.9, column e.)

Column T - We consider the depletion of non-renewable resources as a cost borne by future generations that should be subtracted from (debited to) the capital account of the present generation.

In order to estimate the proper amount to subtract for depletion of "natural capital," we have examined a procedure developed by Salah El Sarafy of the World Bank in an article entitled, "The Proper Calculation of Income from Depletable Natural Resources." El Serafy's approach is to estimate the amount of money that would need to be set aside from the proceeds of the liquidation of an asset (such as a mineral deposit) to generate a permanent income stream that would be as great in the future as in the present.

> An owner of a wasting asset, if he is to consume no more than his income, must relend some part of his receipts in order for the interest on it to make up for the expected failure of receipts from his wasting asset in the future. This proposition, which can be found in J.R. Hicks's *Value and Capital*, led me to convert the mineral asset concerned into a perpetual income stream. The finite series of earnings from the resource, say a 10-year series of annual extraction leading to the extinction of the resource, has to be converted to an infinite series of true income such that the capitalized value of the two series be equal. From the annual earnings from sale, an income portion has to be identified, capable of being spent on consumption, the remainder, the capital element, being set aside year after year to be invest-

ed in order to create a perpetual stream of income that
would sustain the same level of "*true*" income, both during the life of the resource as well as after the resource had
been exhausted. I set out to find the two constituent portions of current receipts: the capital portion and the income portion. Under certain assumptions which are neither too restricting nor unrealistic, I arrived at the ratio of
true income to total receipts, viz:

$$X/R = 1 - \frac{1}{(1 + r)^{n + 1}}$$

where X is true income; R total receipts (net of extraction
cost); r the rate of discount; and n the number of periods
over which the resource is to be liquidated. R - X would be
the "user cost" or "depletion factor" that should be set
aside as a capital investment and totally excluded from
GDP [or in this case from ISEW].[17]

We applaud this model as the best attempt we have seen to come
to grips with the proper method of accounting for depletion of non-renewable resources or "natural capital." As a general principle, we agree
with the capitalization of current income to yield a permanent income, but we are not entirely satisfied with the details of El Serafy's
model.

First, the calculation of n, the number of years to exhaustion of a
resource, poses some conceptual problems. The longevity of a mineral
deposit at a specified rate of extraction is not a simple physical fact. The
availability of the resource is a function not only of how much is "out
there" but also of the intensity of the effort (in labor, capital, and energy) used to extract it. In other words, in El Serafy's equation, n (years to
exhaustion of resource) is dependent on an exogenous variable, extraction costs. The equation is thus unspecified or indeterminate.[18] If extraction costs are assumed to remain constant, then n will be quite
small for most mineral deposits. (In other words, for a given level of
extraction only certain easily accessible deposits will be tapped.) Then
X/R will tend towards 0, the set-aside value of R - X will approach the
value of R, and most receipts will be counted as investment.

On the other hand, if we assume in the equation that n varies directly with extraction costs, n will be indefinitely large because deposits
will be included that are not currently profitable due to their enormous

extraction costs. As a result, X/R will tend towards a value of 1, and the value of R - X will decline towards zero. (In addition, the value of R will be reduced because R is calculated net of extraction costs). This leads to the perverse conclusion that the more dispersed the mineral deposit is (and thus the higher the extraction cost), the less should be set aside for the permanent income stream. Put simply, this amounts to saying that the scarcer the resource the less should be set aside for investment.

Second, we question the assumption in El Serafy's model that the price of non-renewable resources in relation to the general price level will remain constant in the future. From before 1900 to 1972, the declining cost of energy permitted resource prices to remain stable. During that period the proportion of GNP devoted to mineral resources fluctuated between 3% and 4%. However, that trend has shifted, presumably irreversibly. As noted earlier, the proportion of GNP devoted to mineral resources jumped from 4% to 10% from 1972 to 1982. Although this drastic increase has been somewhat reversed as a result of temporary declines in demand for oil and thus of oil prices, the analysis in *Beyond Oil* suggests that the real price of oil and other energy sources can be expected to begin climbing again in the 1990s, pushing up the price of all energy-intensive mineral exploration and mining as well.

As a result of rising resource prices, the amount set aside to maintain a permanent income stream in El Serafy's model should be some portion of the future price of extracted minerals, not of the current price. Otherwise the income stream would pay for less in the future than in the present, thus violating the avowed principle of creating equal real incomes in each time period. Consequently, using R calculated on the assumption of constant prices would provide an insufficient amount to cover future claims against the income stream. However, since we cannot predict the future price of resources (other than to say that they will almost certainly be considerably higher than today), we cannot offer a specific way to replace R in the equation.

Third, on a very practical level, we are not clear how one would estimate the value of R from existing sources, at least in the U.S. The *Census of Minerals* provides data on the value of shipments, capital expenditures, cost of supplies, and value added in mining, and it defines value added as the sum of the first two values minus the third. Presumably, in El Serafy's equation, R is supposed to indicate rent, the return or "profit" to the enterprise holding the mineral rights. In principle, this could be calculated as a residual after subtracting wages, interest, and other production costs from value added, but in practice the data are not presented in a way that makes that possible.

Summarizing these criticisms of El Serafy's model, we can see that there is a great deal of arbitrariness in any effort to account for depletion of "natural capital." Our arguments suggest that the appropriate value of R might be several times as large as current market prices (to account for future price increases). The value of n cannot be specified in the equation without taking into account some estimate of extraction costs. In addition, since the real cost of a resource is a function of both its cost of extraction as well as the limitation of its total quantity, R should not be calculated net of extraction costs. We may also think of extraction costs as "regrettable necessities" so that they should not be eliminated from this column which will be subtracted to arrive at a welfare measure.

Consequently, we have chosen to subtract the *total* value of mineral production each year. We did not try to arrive at the figure of 100% of value through any precise means. Instead we offer several general considerations that lead to this result within the basic framework of El Serafy's model. First, with a zero discount rate we would always set aside 100% of receipts as capital, regardless of the life expectancy of the resource. Consequently, our earlier arguments against social (as opposed to individual) discounting may be invoked in this context. Combinations of low discount rates and low life expectancy of resources also produce a capital set-aside approaching 100%. A moderate discount rate of 4% combined with a life expectancy of 35 years, however, results in a 25% set-aside. Yet if we assume a four-fold increase in resource prices relative to prices in general over that period, which is not unreasonable, then the set-aside would again be 100%.

The source for the value of mineral production is *Historical Statistics: Colonial Times to 1970,* Series M 13-37, and updates in *Statistical Abstracts.* The original source is the *Minerals Yearbook,* and, for years after 1976, information on fuels comes from *Energy Data Reports.* For 1986, the value of fossil fuel production was unavailable, so we estimated it according to the quantity produced using 1985 prices.

The deflator we used is the Consumer Price Index (CPI) for all commodities. This may seem like an inappropriate index for this purpose, but we have chosen it deliberately. The more logical choice might seem to be the Producers Price Index (PPI) for energy (which is a fairly good proxy for price changes in all minerals). If our purpose were to determine changes over time in the physical quantity of energy produced, weighted by changes in energy sources (such as from coal to natural gas), the PPI would be the correct index. However, our purpose in selecting a deflator has to do with compensating for the effect of relative changes in price between minerals (especially energy resources) and the general price level that confronts consumers. In other words, we wish to separate out the rise in price of minerals due to general inflation from the price increases in this sector due to increased scarcity of particular resources. The use of CPI as a deflator has the effect of showing how much the price of minerals has changed in relation to prices in general.

We are far from satisfied with the arbitrary approach we have taken. Nevertheless, we regard the issue of resource depletion as too important to ignore. We hope, therefore, that others will pursue different approaches to this problem of estimating an amount that, subtracted from current welfare, would adequately compensate future generations for the resources we consume today. One way to do this might be to estimate the size of a tax on non-renewable resources that would be high enough to prevent them from increasing in price faster than prices in general. The tax would achieve what Talbot Page calls the "conservation criterion" for equitable resource depletion.[19] Nevertheless, we are not clear how to estimate the appropriate size of the hypothetical tax or how to incorporate it into the ISEW, so we have not followed this procedure.

Column U - In addition to using up mineral and fuel resources, our collective behavior also loads costs onto the future by dumping waste products into the environment that will have long-term consequences. The cost of keeping radioactive elements with long half-lives out of the environment for thousands of years is anybody's guess, since we have not yet devised a method of long-term storage. The costs to the future imposed by industrial activities that add carbon dioxide, nitrogen dioxide and methane to the atmosphere (thereby contributing to the "greenhouse effect" and global climate change) and chlorofluorocarbons (which destroy ozone in the upper atmosphere) have only recently begun to be recognized. The full extent of the physical damage that has already been irreversibly inflicted upon future generations is not yet known in each of these cases. The observable effects of flooded cities and completely eroded beaches as a result of higher sea levels as well as an exponential increase in cases of skin cancer from greater ultraviolet radiation represent only the first level of the threat. Even the disruption of established patterns of agriculture as a result of increased variations and unpredictability of weather will not be the most serious consequence of these changes. The greatest threat is ecological. The almost instantaneous change (on a geological scale) of the global climate and of ultraviolet radiation could have harmful effects on all but the most resilient species of plants and animals in those regions of the planet most drastically affected by climate change.

Almost no effort has been undertaken to estimate any of these damages in economic terms other than one EPA study which estimated that a sea-level increase of five feet would inundate 25% of Charleston, South Carolina and increase storm damages in Galveston, Texas by $82 million per year. Nevertheless, if we are to have a measure of net sustainable welfare, we cannot simply neglect the effect of these tremendous ecological catastrophes which our economic activities have begun to produce in such a short time.

We have assumed that the amount of damage to the future in terms of ecological disruption is directly proportional to the consumption of fossil fuels and nuclear energy--in effect to nonrenewable energy consumption. We have therefore begun by adding the total quantity of nonrenewable energy consumed each year in quadrillions of BTUs, starting in 1900.[20] Assuming that a barrel of crude oil contains approximately 5.8 million BTUs, we calculated the total barrel equivalents of energy consumed each year from 1900 to 1986. We then imagined that a tax or rent of $0.50 per barrel-equivalent had been levied on all nonrenewable energy consumed during that period and set aside to accumulate in a non-interest-bearing account, as in the case of resource depletion. (See table A.10.) That account might be thought of as a fund available to compensate future generations for the long-term damage caused by the use of fossil fuels and atomic energy. We are implicitly assuming that the cumulative undiscounted damages in the future caused by consuming a barrel of oil or its equivalent in the present are equal to $.50 in 1972 dollars. This is of course speculative, but considering the billions of dollars of property and recreational damage already caused by the rising of the oceans, it is not unreasonable.[21]

Column V - In order for economic welfare to be sustained over time, the supply of capital must grow to meet the demands of increased population. More specifically, we have assumed that one element of economic sustainability is constant or increasing quantities of capital available for each worker. We have followed the general procedure used by Nordhaus and Tobin. However, unlike them, we have excluded human capital from our estimates for reasons explained in chapter 1. We have thus calculated net capital growth by adding the amount of new capital stock (increases in fixed reproducible capital) minus the capital requirement, the amount necessary to maintain the same level of capital per worker. We estimated the capital requirement by multiplying the percent change in the labor force by the stock of capital from the previous year. (See table A.11, column h.) Actually, we used a five year rolling average of changes in labor force and capital to smooth out year to year fluctuations. (See table A.11, columns d and f.)

Fixed reproducible capital is derived from the *Survey of Current Business*, August 1982 to August 1987. The size of the labor force comes from the *Economic Report of the President*, table B-29, which uses the estimates of the U.S. Bureau of Labor Statistics, *Employment and Earnings*.

Column W - The U.S. net international position measures the amount that Americans invest overseas minus the amount invested by foreigners in the United States. The annual change in the net international position indicates whether the U.S. is moving in the direction of net lending (if positive) or net borrowing (if negative). If the change is positive, the U.S. has in effect increased its capital assets. If it is negative, part of U.S. capital formation is in fact based on the borrowed wealth of foreign interests that must eventually be repaid. We have thus included annual changes in the net international position as a measure of the sustainability of the welfare of our economy. Some years from 1950 to 1975 have had to be interpolated. The figures each year have been adjusted for inflation using the implicit GNP deflator in the *National Income and Product Accounts*, table 7.4. For net international position, see *Statistical Abstract*, 1988, table 1330, p. 758 or *Survey of Current Business*.

Column X - The column marked ISEW (Index of Sustainable Economic Welfare) equals columns C+D+E+F+G-H-I-J-K-L-M-N-O-P-Q-R-S-T+U+V.

Column Y - Per capita ISEW is calculated by dividing ISEW by the population (from *Statistical Abstract*, 1988, table 2, p. 7).

Column Z - The value of GNP comes from the *National Income and Product Accounts*, table 1.2. We made the same adjustment for 1985 and 1986 as we did for personal consumption. (See column B.)

Column AA - Per capita GNP is GNP divided by the population.

Conclusion

To the extent that the Index of Sustainable Economic Welfare measures the true health of our economy over the past 36 years, the results are rather discouraging. Per capita ISEW is only about 20% higher now that it was at the beginning of the period--approximately $3,403 per person in 1986 compared to $2,831 in 1951. (See the note below about the choice of 1951 as the base year.) According to table A.12, the average annual increase from 1951 to 1986 was 0.53% per year.

The overall increase in ISEW masks a more important pattern of changes decade by decade. From 1951 to 1960, per capita ISEW increased by an average of 0.84% per year. From 1960 to 1970, however, it increased by about 2.01% per year, about one-half a percentage point slower than per capita GNP (which grew at a rate of 2.64% per year that decade). The period from 1970 to 1980 marked a very slight decline of per capita ISEW by 0.14% per year. The decline during the 1980s has thus far been 1.26% per year. Thus an overall increase during the period from 1951 to 1986 masks the leveling off of per capita ISEW during the 1970s and the decline of the 1980s.

Even when we exclude resource depletion and long-term environmental damage (columns T and U from table A.1) from the calculation of per capita ISEW, the results still show a similar pattern of improvements in the 1960s, little growth in the 1970s, and decline in the 1980s. This can be seen in table A.12 in the column marked "PC-ISEW*." Thus the general pattern of changes in economic welfare is not simply a function of the assumptions we have made about these relatively controversial issues.

We emphasize the variation in the decades and especially the rise during the 1960s in order to point out that we have not simply chosen components for the ISEW that create a pessimistic outlook. Even in the face of declining resources and growing environmental threats, ISEW was able to grow faster than GNP during at least one segment of the period of our study.

A major factor in the dramatic increase in per capita ISEW during the 1960s (and decline during other periods) was the change in income distribution. For example, whereas personal consumption increased by about 37.5% from 1961 to 1968, weighting personal consumption by changes in income distribution led to an increase of more than 57%. (This weighting factor--along with the jump in net capital growth from negative to positive--is also largely responsible for the anomalous increase in ISEW from 1950 to 1951.) By contrast, in the 1980s the grow-ing gap in income inequality had a tremendous effect on the decline in economic welfare as measured by the ISEW. The almost 13% deepen-ing of inequality caused weighted personal consumption to grow by only about 10%, while measured personal consumption grew by 24%.

Changes in net capital growth also had a strong influence on the shifts in ISEW. From the mid-1950s to the early 1970s, net capital growth advanced steadily. It has risen only slowly since then, except from 1983 to 1986. However, part of the apparent improvement in in-vestments during that latter period was offset by the decline in the net international position from 1983 to 1986. The growth of net capital in-vestment in recent years seems therefore to be largely based on borrow-ing capital from abroad and therefore not sustainable.

Efforts to control air pollution and to reduce accidents have paid off by improving economic welfare during the 1970s and 1980s. The cost of air pollution peaked in 1970 and the economic damages caused by car accidents peaked in 1978. Improvements in both areas since those dates have had the effect of countering the generally downward trend in ISEW. They offer evidence that the choice of policies by the govern-ment can indeed have a positive effect on economic welfare even if they do not increase physical output.

In order to compare the ISEW with the MEW by Nordhaus and Tobin as well as the EAW by Zolotas, we have calculated the annual growth of per capita ISEW from 1951 to 1965 and from 1951 to 1977. (We used 1951 rather than 1950 because the latter was so radically differ-ent from the results for the rest of that decade.) From 1951 to 1965, per capita ISEW increased by 1.36% per year, while per capita MEW grew at a rate of 0.40% per year from 1947 to 1965. Similarly, from 1951 to 1977 per capita ISEW grew at 0.99% per year while per capita EAW showed an increase of only 0.63% from 1950 to 1977. Thus ISEW suggests more improvement than either EAW or MEW during comparable periods.

Despite the year to year variations in ISEW, it indicates a long-term trend from the late 1970s to the present that is indeed bleak. Economic welfare has been deteriorating for a decade, largely as a result of growing income inequality, the exhaustion of resources, and the fail-ure to invest adequately to sustain the economy in the future. Although these three factors might be addressed through separate poli-cy initiatives, they are in fact intertwined. The most fundamental problem in terms of sustainable economic welfare is the decline in the quality of energy resources as measured by the ratio of energy output to

energy input. As a result of this entropic process, the discovery and extraction of oil will soon take more energy than is made available, thereby bringing to a close the era of cheap energy. This also means that the
production of capital equipment will become increasingly expensive
because capital is largely embodied energy. Thus efforts to reverse the
trend towards decreasing net investment will be made more difficult.
Finally, reductions in the amount of energy and capital available per
worker will lead to a long-term decline in worker productivity, though
improved management may be able to counter that trend for short periods. As competition for the returns to labor grows along with higher
return to scarce capital, the income gap is likely to worsen if actions are
not taken to improve equality.

The purpose of an index that strives to measure economic well-
being is not simply to show us how we are presently faring or are likely
to fare. It should also reveal the kinds of policies that would enable a
nation to improve its welfare. As we have seen, reductions in car accidents and in air pollution have made small but important contributions to raising the level of economic welfare. During the 1960s, the
Great Society programs of President Johnson seem to have improved
economic welfare by reducing income inequality. Economic welfare can
thus be improved by enacting appropriate policies.

Clearly the important question then becomes whether our nation is going to continue in its efforts to increase total output or
whether we are going to redirect our focus towards the enhancement of
sustainable economic welfare. Are the policies of our government
going to be guided by GNP, by ISEW, or some other measure of sustainable welfare?

Figure A.1

Alternative Measures of Economic Welfare

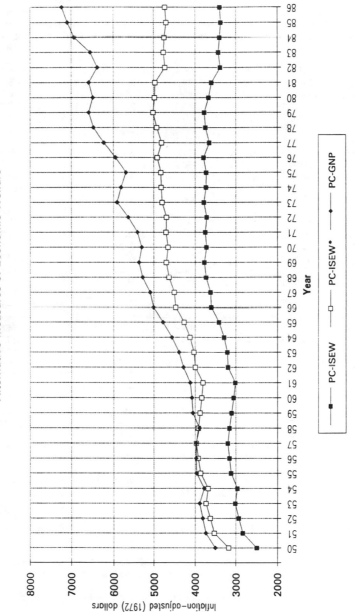

Note: ISEW is Index of Sustainable Economic Welfare (Table A.1, Col. Y); ISEW* is ISEW without Cols. T and U.

Table A.1. Index of Sustainable Economic Welfare 1950-1986

Year A	Personal consumption B	Distributional inequality C	Weighted personal consumption (B/C) D	Services of household labor E(+)	Services of consumer durables F(+)	Services of streets and highways G(+)
1950	337.3	109.0	309.5	311.4	13.4	6.4
1951	341.6	100.0	341.6	315.4	14.6	6.6
1952	350.1	102.0	343.2	319.5	15.5	6.8
1953	363.4	100.8	360.4	323.6	16.6	7.0
1954	370.0	106.2	348.5	327.8	17.5	7.3
1955	394.1	101.2	389.3	332.0	18.8	7.7
1956	405.4	98.1	413.2	336.3	19.6	8.0
1957	413.8	95.3	434.0	340.6	20.3	8.3
1958	418.0	97.1	430.6	345.0	20.6	8.8
1959	440.4	99.6	442.1	349.5	21.2	9.2
1960	452.0	101.3	446.3	354.0	21.7	9.6
1961	461.4	105.3	438.1	358.5	22.0	10.0
1962	482.0	99.6	484.2	363.2	22.7	10.5
1963	500.5	99.2	504.3	367.9	23.6	11.0
1964	528.0	98.5	536.3	372.6	25.0	11.5
1965	557.5	96.5	577.7	377.4	26.8	12.0
1966	585.7	92.0	636.5	382.3	29.0	12.5
1967	602.7	92.5	651.7	387.2	30.9	13.1
1968	634.4	92.0	689.6	392.2	33.4	13.6
1969	657.9	92.4	712.3	397.2	35.7	14.1
1970	672.1	95.0	707.8	402.4	37.3	14.6
1971	696.8	94.9	734.2	407.5	39.3	15.1
1972	737.1	96.6	763.1	412.8	42.1	15.5
1973	767.9	95.1	807.7	418.1	45.3	15.9
1974	762.8	94.7	805.6	423.5	47.2	16.3
1975	779.4	95.9	812.3	429.0	48.8	16.5
1976	823.1	95.9	857.9	434.5	51.1	16.7
1977	864.3	99.0	873.2	440.1	54.1	17.0
1978	903.2	99.0	912.1	445.8	57.3	17.1
1979	927.6	99.5	932.5	451.5	60.0	17.3
1980	931.8	100.1	930.9	457.3	61.3	17.5
1981	950.5	102.4	928.6	463.2	62.7	17.6
1982	963.3	107.9	892.4	469.2	63.8	17.8
1983	1009.2	108.1	933.5	475.3	66.1	17.9
1984	1058.6	108.9	975.9	481.4	69.6	18.1
1985	1108.2	111.9	990.3	487.6	74.3	18.3
1986	1155.5	112.8	1024.4	493.9	79.8	18.5

Notes: 1. All figures are in billions of inflation adjusted (1972) dollars except column A (year), column C (an index number 1951 = 100), and columns Y and AA (dollars, not billions of dollars).

2. The explanation of the columns in Table A.1 can be found on pages 50 through 70.

3. Calculations of columns C, G, H, J, L, M, P, S, U, and V can be found in tables A.2 through A. 11 on pages 84 through 93.

Table A. 1 continued

Year A	Public expenditures on health and education H	Expenditures on consumer durables I	Defensive private expenditures health and education J	Expenditures on national advertising K(-)	Costs of commuting L(-)	Costs of urbanization M(-)	Costs of auto accidents N(-)
1950	1.1	42.6	2.8	6.9	9.0	5.8	11.6
1951	1.2	39.1	3.3	7.4	8.5	6.2	13.2
1952	1.4	38.0	3.8	7.8	8.4	6.6	13.3
1953	1.5	42.1	4.4	8.2	9.3	7.0	13.9
1954	1.7	42.5	5.0	8.4	9.6	7.3	13.3
1955	2.1	51.1	5.8	9.3	10.9	7.7	13.9
1956	2.4	48.8	6.8	9.9	10.4	8.8	14.4
1957	2.8	48.6	7.8	10.1	10.5	9.2	14.3
1958	3.1	45.3	8.4	9.9	9.9	9.7	14.0
1959	3.5	50.7	9.2	10.4	10.7	10.2	14.3
1960	4.0	51.4	10.0	10.8	11.3	11.6	14.4
1961	4.8	49.3	11.8	10.5	10.9	12.1	14.4
1962	5.7	54.7	13.7	10.9	11.7	12.8	15.4
1963	6.7	59.7	15.5	11.4	12.4	13.3	16.2
1964	7.6	64.8	17.3	12.0	12.8	14.0	17.4
1965	8.5	72.6	19.0	12.7	14.3	14.7	18.8
1966	11.4	78.4	20.7	13.4	14.9	17.1	19.4
1967	13.8	79.5	21.4	13.0	15.2	17.8	19.5
1968	15.5	88.3	22.5	13.3	16.7	18.7	20.8
1969	17.0	91.8	23.0	13.4	17.7	19.6	23.0
1970	18.7	89.1	23.4	12.7	17.4	20.4	25.3
1971	20.1	98.2	24.7	12.3	19.5	21.3	26.3
1972	21.7	111.1	26.8	12.9	21.6	22.5	28.7
1973	23.3	121.3	28.8	13.1	23.1	24.4	28.6
1974	25.3	112.3	28.5	13.1	22.4	25.6	25.8
1975	26.0	112.7	28.4	12.5	22.4	26.5	28.1
1976	27.6	126.6	29.7	14.3	25.0	29.5	30.1
1977	28.1	138.0	31.0	15.1	27.2	32.6	32.1
1978	29.3	146.8	32.3	15.8	28.2	36.0	33.7
1979	30.5	147.2	33.7	16.5	29.2	39.3	32.5
1980	32.2	137.5	35.1	16.7	28.6	41.4	29.0
1981	33.4	140.9	37.0	17.2	29.0	45.4	27.0
1982	33.0	140.5	38.1	17.7	27.7	40.9	26.1
1983	33.2	157.5	39.7	18.8	30.2	46.4	26.3
1984	33.6	177.9	41.6	20.1	32.8	47.4	27.8
1985	34.9	195.5	42.8	20.6	35.3	48.8	29.6
1986	34.9	212.0	44.2	20.9	33.5	51.5	30.5

4. Figure A.1 on page 79 compares in graphic form, columns Y and AA plus a revised estimate (not shown) of per capita ISEW excluding columns T and U.

5. Calculations of the annual changes of per capita GNP and per capita ISEW (columns Y and AA) ca be found in table A.12 on page 94.

Table A.1 continued

Year A	Costs of water pollution O	Costs of air pollution P	Costs of noise pollution Q(-)	Loss of wetlands R(-)	Loss of farmland S(-)	Depletion of nonrenewable resources T(-)	Long term environmental damage U(-)
1950	9.0	25.2	2.0	10.0	7.2	20.6	84.0
1951	9.2	25.2	2.1	10.4	7.8	21.8	86.9
1952	9.4	25.2	2.2	10.7	8.5	21.1	89.9
1953	9.7	25.2	2.2	11.1	9.1	22.6	92.9
1954	9.9	25.2	2.3	11.4	9.7	22.1	95.8
1955	10.2	25.2	2.4	11.8	10.4	24.9	99.0
1956	10.4	25.1	2.5	12.2	11.0	26.9	102.4
1957	10.7	25.1	2.5	12.5	11.7	27.1	105.7
1958	10.9	25.1	2.6	12.9	12.4	24.1	109.1
1959	11.2	25.1	2.7	13.2	13.0	24.9	112.5
1960	11.5	25.1	2.8	13.6	13.7	25.5	116.2
1961	11.8	25.6	2.9	14.0	14.4	25.5	120.2
1962	12.1	26.1	2.9	14.3	15.1	26.1	124.0
1963	12.4	26.6	3.0	14.7	15.8	26.8	128.0
1964	12.7	27.1	3.1	15.0	16.5	27.8	132.2
1965	13.1	27.6	3.2	15.4	17.2	28.5	136.6
1966	13.4	28.0	3.3	15.8	17.9	29.6	141.2
1967	13.8	28.5	3.4	16.1	18.7	29.7	146.0
1968	14.1	29.0	3.5	16.5	19.4	30.0	151.0
1969	14.5	29.5	3.7	16.8	20.1	30.7	156.3
1970	14.9	30.0	3.8	17.2	20.9	30.9	161.8
1971	15.3	28.9	3.9	17.6	21.6	31.7	167.4
1972	15.3	28.9	4.0	17.9	22.4	32.2	173.3
1973	15.3	29.3	4.0	18.3	23.2	34.6	179.5
1974	15.3	27.4	4.1	18.5	24.0	46.8	185.4
1975	15.3	25.7	4.1	18.6	24.7	46.6	191.2
1976	15.3	26.2	4.2	18.8	25.5	48.4	197.4
1977	15.3	26.3	4.2	19.0	26.3	50.4	203.7
1978	15.3	25.5	4.2	19.2	27.1	52.6	210.2
1979	15.3	25.4	4.3	19.4	27.8	61.6	216.7
1980	15.3	24.3	4.3	19.5	28.6	74.5	223.0
1981	15.3	23.6	4.4	19.7	29.4	86.1	229.1
1982	15.3	22.4	4.4	19.9	30.2	77.6	234.9
1983	15.3	21.6	4.5	20.1	31.0	70.9	240.6
1984	15.3	22.4	4.5	20.3	31.7	72.2	246.6
1985	15.3	22.4	4.6	20.4	32.5	64.9	252.7
1986	15.3	22.4	4.6	20.6	33.3	62.4	258.7

Table A.1 continued

Year A	Net capital growth V(+)	Change in net interna- tional position W(+)	Index of Sustainable Economic Welfare ISEW X(sum)	Per capita ISEW Y	Gross National Product Z	Per capita GNP AA
1950	-26.3	0.0	378.8	2488.0	534.8	3512.2
1951	0.1	0.2	438.5	2831.2	579.4	3741.0
1952	19.8	0.2	461.4	2928.7	600.8	3813.3
1953	31.2	0.2	482.9	3014.9	623.6	3893.0
1954	42.1	0.2	482.6	2960.0	616.1	3779.2
1955	50.3	0.2	517.9	3121.2	657.5	3962.5
1956	40.8	2.4	533.2	3156.9	671.6	3976.2
1957	37.5	2.3	550.1	3198.7	683.8	3976.0
1958	36.3	2.3	552.3	3158.3	680.9	3893.5
1959	32.6	2.2	551.9	3103.5	721.7	4058.4
1960	31.4	2.2	551.4	3051.9	737.2	4080.3
1961	38.8	4.8	553.8	3014.7	756.6	4118.9
1962	43.8	4.8	595.0	3189.7	800.3	4290.3
1963	45.5	4.7	607.7	3211.5	832.5	4399.1
1964	47.1	4.7	631.9	3293.1	876.4	4567.2
1965	50.8	4.6	664.3	3419.0	929.3	4782.7
1966	51.9	-0.9	709.5	3609.4	984.8	5010.2
1967	47.3	-0.8	720.7	3626.9	1011.4	5089.8
1968	49.8	-0.7	749.5	3734.4	1058.1	5271.9
1969	50.1	-0.7	765.6	3777.4	1087.6	5366.2
1970	51.1	-0.7	763.4	3723.1	1085.6	5294.3
1971	48.0	3.2	778.8	3750.4	1122.4	5405.0
1972	40.2	3.1	780.7	3719.6	1185.9	5649.9
1973	32.6	3.0	802.5	3786.8	1254.3	5919.1
1974	27.6	2.8	799.1	3736.9	1246.3	5827.8
1975	27.4	2.5	805.6	3730.1	1231.6	5702.6
1976	22.3	7.1	826.2	3789.5	1298.2	5954.1
1977	21.7	-7.8	805.2	3656.0	1369.7	6219.2
1978	16.4	2.3	833.5	3744.6	1438.6	6463.1
1979	15.5	11.3	849.9	3776.4	1479.4	6573.5
1980	8.4	6.4	836.3	3672.0	1475.0	6476.7
1981	8.7	17.9	828.0	3599.3	1512.2	6573.6
1982	8.3	-2.0	786.8	3386.3	1480.0	6369.8
1983	24.6	-22.0	806.0	3436.5	1534.7	6543.5
1984	27.3	-38.2	807.0	3405.2	1642.5	6930.4
1985	37.4	-49.6	807.9	3376.1	1697.5	7094.3
1986	44.0	-63.4	822.1	3402.8	1745.9	7226.4

Table A.2
Index of Income Inequality

Year a	% income received 1st quintile b	% income received 2nd quintile c	% income received 3rd quintile d	% income received 4th quintile e	% income received top quintile f	Sum ((f/b) +(f/c)+.+ (f/f))/5 g	Index income inequal-ity h
50	4.5	12.0	17.4	23.4	42.7	3.67	109.0
51	5.0	12.4	17.6	23.4	41.6	3.36	100.0
52	4.9	12.3	17.4	23.4	41.9	3.43	102.0
53	4.7	12.5	18.0	23.9	40.9	3.39	100.8
54	4.5	12.1	17.7	23.9	41.8	3.57	106.2
55	4.8	12.3	17.8	23.7	41.3	3.40	101.2
56	5.0	12.5	17.9	23.7	41.0	3.30	98.1
57	5.1	12.7	18.1	23.8	40.4	3.21	95.3
58	5.0	12.5	18.0	23.9	40.6	3.26	97.1
59	4.9	12.3	17.9	23.8	41.1	3.35	99.6
60	4.8	12.2	17.8	24.0	41.3	3.41	101.3
61	4.7	11.9	17.5	23.8	42.2	3.54	105.3
62	5.0	12.1	17.6	24.0	41.3	3.35	99.6
63	5.0	12.1	17.7	24.0	41.2	3.34	99.2
64	5.1	12.0	17.7	24.0	41.2	3.31	98.5
65	5.2	12.2	17.8	23.9	40.9	3.25	96.5
66	5.6	12.4	17.8	23.8	40.5	3.10	92.0
67	5.5	12.4	17.9	23.9	40.4	3.11	92.5
68	5.6	12.4	17.9	23.7	40.5	3.09	92.0
69	5.6	12.4	17.7	23.7	40.6	3.11	92.4
70	5.4	12.2	17.6	23.8	40.9	3.19	95.0
71	5.5	12.0	17.6	23.8	41.1	3.19	94.9
72	5.4	11.9	17.5	23.9	41.4	3.25	96.6
73	5.5	11.9	17.5	24.0	41.1	3.20	95.1
74	5.5	12.0	17.5	24.0	41.0	3.18	94.7
75	5.4	11.8	17.6	24.1	41.1	3.23	95.9
76	5.4	11.8	17.6	24.1	41.1	3.23	95.9
77	5.2	11.6	17.5	24.2	41.5	3.33	99.0
78	5.2	11.6	17.5	24.1	41.5	3.33	99.0
79	5.2	11.6	17.5	24.1	41.7	3.35	99.5
80	5.1	11.6	17.5	24.3	41.6	3.37	100.1
81	5.0	11.3	17.4	24.4	41.9	3.44	102.4
82	4.7	11.2	17.1	24.3	42.7	3.63	107.9
83	4.7	11.1	17.1	24.4	42.7	3.64	108.1
84	4.7	11.0	17.0	24.4	42.9	3.66	108.9
85	4.6	10.9	16.9	24.2	43.5	3.76	111.9
86	4.6	10.8	16.8	24.0	43.7	3.79	112.8

Table A.3
Value of the Services of Highways and Streets

Year a	Gross stock of federal highways b	Gross stock of state & local highways c	Imputed services of highways 5%(b+c) d
50	2.3	126.6	6.4
51	2.4	130.0	6.6
52	2.4	133.7	6.8
53	2.5	138.2	7.0
54	2.7	144.2	7.3
55	2.8	150.5	7.7
56	2.9	157.0	8.0
57	3.1	163.8	8.3
58	3.3	171.7	8.8
59	3.4	180.0	9.2
60	3.6	188.0	9.6
61	3.8	196.6	10.0
62	4.1	205.7	10.5
63	4.4	215.4	11.0
64	4.6	225.1	11.5
65	4.9	235.1	12.0
66	5.2	245.5	12.5
67	5.6	255.7	13.1
68	5.9	266.3	13.6
69	6.1	275.9	14.1
70	6.4	285.2	14.6
71	6.7	294.4	15.1
72	6.9	302.7	15.5
73	7.2	310.9	15.9
74	7.4	317.7	16.3
75	7.6	322.7	16.5
76	7.8	327.1	16.7
77	8.1	331.0	17.0
78	8.3	334.4	17.1
79	8.5	337.3	17.3
80	8.6	340.4	17.5
81	8.9	343.1	17.6
82	9.1	346.1	17.8
83	9.3	349.6	17.9
84	9.5	352.6	18.1
85	9.7	356.0	18.3
86	9.9	360.0	18.5

Table A.4
Public Expenditures on Health and Education
Counted as Personal Consumption

Year a	Public expenditures on higher education b	Public expenditures on higher education for consumption (b/2) c	Public expenditures on health d	Public expenditures on improving health (d-7.6)/2 e	Public expenditures on health & education for consumption (c+e) f
50	2.2	1.1	7.6	0.0	1.1
51	2.0	1.0	7.9	0.1	1.2
52	2.2	1.1	8.1	0.2	1.4
53	2.2	1.1	8.4	0.4	1.5
54	2.4	1.2	8.7	0.6	1.7
55	2.6	1.3	9.0	0.7	2.1
56	2.9	1.4	9.5	1.0	2.4
57	3.2	1.6	9.9	1.2	2.8
58	3.6	1.8	10.1	1.3	3.1
59	4.1	2.1	10.4	1.4	3.5
60	4.8	2.4	10.7	1.6	4.0
61	5.4	2.7	11.8	2.1	4.8
62	6.0	3.0	12.9	2.7	5.7
63	7.0	3.5	13.9	3.2	6.7
64	7.8	3.9	14.9	3.7	7.6
65	8.8	4.4	15.9	4.1	8.5
66	10.3	5.1	20.0	6.2	11.4
67	12.0	6.0	23.2	7.8	13.8
68	12.4	6.2	26.2	9.3	15.5
69	13.0	6.5	28.5	10.5	17.0
70	14.5	7.3	30.5	11.5	18.7
71	15.3	7.7	32.4	12.4	20.1
72	16.1	8.0	35.0	13.7	21.7
73	16.9	8.4	37.3	14.9	23.3
74	16.7	8.3	41.5	17.0	25.3
75	17.6	8.8	41.9	17.2	26.0
76	17.6	8.8	45.1	18.8	27.6
77	17.9	8.9	45.9	19.2	28.1
78	18.1	9.0	48.1	20.2	29.3
79	18.6	9.3	50.0	21.2	30.5
80	19.6	9.8	52.4	22.4	32.2
81	19.8	9.9	54.5	23.5	33.4
82	19.0	9.5	54.5	23.5	33.0
83	19.3	9.6	54.7	23.6	33.2
84	19.1	9.6	55.7	24.1	33.6
85	19.5	9.7	57.8	25.1	34.9
86	19.4	9.7	58.0	25.2	34.9

Table A.5
Defensive Private Expenditures on Health and Education

Year a	Private expenditures on education b	Private expenditures on higher education c	Defensive expenditures on private education (b-(c/2)) d	Private expenditures on health e	Defensive expenditures on private health (e-22.1)/2 f	Defensive expenditures on private health & education (d+f) g
50	3.6	1.7	2.8	22.1	0.0	2.8
51	3.7	1.6	2.9	22.9	0.4	3.3
52	3.9	1.6	3.1	23.6	0.7	3.8
53	4.1	1.8	3.2	24.5	1.2	4.4
54	4.3	1.7	3.4	25.3	1.6	5.0
55	4.6	1.9	3.6	26.4	2.1	5.8
56	4.8	2.0	3.8	28.0	3.0	6.8
57	5.1	2.1	4.1	29.4	3.7	7.8
58	5.4	2.4	4.3	30.5	4.2	8.4
59	5.6	2.3	4.5	31.5	4.7	9.2
60	6.0	2.4	4.8	32.6	5.2	10.0
61	6.3	2.7	4.9	35.9	6.9	11.8
62	6.6	2.8	5.2	39.0	8.5	13.7
63	7.0	2.8	5.5	42.0	10.0	15.5
64	7.4	3.2	5.8	45.1	11.5	17.3
65	8.1	3.9	6.1	47.8	12.8	19.0
66	8.8	4.1	6.7	50.1	14.0	20.7
67	9.3	4.2	7.1	50.7	14.3	21.4
68	10.0	4.4	7.8	51.5	14.7	22.5
69	10.6	4.7	8.2	51.7	14.8	23.0
70	10.9	4.8	8.5	51.9	14.9	23.4
71	11.2	5.0	8.7	54.1	16.0	24.7
72	11.7	5.2	9.1	57.7	17.8	26.8
73	11.9	5.2	9.3	61.2	19.5	28.8
74	11.7	5.2	9.1	61.0	19.4	28.5
75	12.1	5.2	9.5	60.0	18.9	28.4
76	12.2	5.2	9.6	62.2	20.0	29.7
77	12.2	5.3	9.6	64.9	21.4	31.0
78	12.7	5.3	10.1	66.5	22.2	32.3
79	13.1	5.5	10.4	68.6	23.3	33.7
80	13.3	5.6	10.5	71.2	24.6	35.1
81	13.7	5.8	10.7	74.6	26.2	37.0
82	14.1	5.7	11.2	75.9	26.9	38.1
83	14.8	5.8	11.9	77.7	27.8	39.7
84	15.4	6.0	12.4	80.5	29.2	41.6
85	16.4	6.2	13.4	81.1	29.5	42.8
86	17.4	6.3	14.2	82.1	30.0	44.2

Table A.6
Cost of Commuting

Year a	User operated transportation b	Purchased local transportation c	Cost of commuting (.21b+.3c) d
50	34.2	6.1	9.0
51	32.4	5.6	8.5
52	32.3	5.4	8.4
53	37.1	5.1	9.3
54	39.2	4.7	9.6
55	45.7	4.4	10.9
56	43.3	4.3	10.4
57	43.8	4.2	10.5
58	41.8	3.9	9.9
59	45.6	3.9	10.7
60	48.4	3.9	11.3
61	46.6	3.6	10.9
62	50.5	3.6	11.7
63	53.9	3.5	12.4
64	56.2	3.4	12.8
65	63.2	3.3	14.3
66	66.5	3.3	14.9
67	64.5	3.2	15.2
68	74.7	3.3	16.7
69	79.2	3.5	17.7
70	78.3	3.4	17.4
71	87.8	3.4	19.5
72	97.8	3.4	21.6
73	105.3	3.4	23.1
74	101.5	3.5	22.4
75	101.8	3.5	22.4
76	113.8	3.6	25.0
77	124.4	3.6	27.2
78	129.0	3.7	28.2
79	133.4	3.8	29.2
80	131.2	3.5	28.6
81	133.6	3.2	29.0
82	127.8	3.0	27.7
83	139.4	3.0	30.2
84	152.1	3.0	32.8
85	163.6	3.0	35.3
86	155.2	3.1	33.5

Table A.7
Cost of Urbanization

Year a	Value of residential land b	Value of residential structures c	Land as % of total b/(b+c) d	Housing expend- itures e	Urbanization cost (d x e) f
50	26.2	145.3	15.3%	38.1	5.8
51	29.5	163.8	15.3%	40.9	6.2
52	32.8	182.3	15.3%	43.4	6.6
53	34.9	194.1	15.3%	45.8	7.0
54	37.7	209.6	15.3%	47.9	7.3
55	41.6	231.0	15.3%	50.3	7.7
56	49.7	248.3	16.7%	52.8	8.8
57	52.3	261.3	16.7%	55.4	9.2
58	55.1	275.4	16.7%	57.9	9.7
59	58.3	291.5	16.7%	61.0	10.2
60	67.2	305.7	18.0%	64.1	11.6
61	70.0	318.0	18.0%	67.1	12.1
62	72.8	331.0	18.0%	70.7	12.8
63	74.8	339.9	18.0%	73.9	13.3
64	79.6	361.6	18.0%	77.4	14.0
65	83.3	378.8	18.0%	81.5	14.7
66	102.1	408.4	20.0%	85.3	17.1
67	107.4	429.6	20.0%	89.1	17.8
68	120.1	480.3	20.0%	93.6	18.7
69	131.1	524.4	20.0%	98.2	19.6
70	138.0	551.9	20.0%	102.0	20.4
71	153.6	614.3	20.0%	106.4	21.3
72	171.9	687.4	20.0%	112.5	22.5
73	205.8	791.7	20.6%	118.1	24.4
74	234.8	902.9	20.6%	124.2	25.6
75	254.4	978.6	20.6%	128.2	26.5
76	309.7	1106.1	21.9%	134.9	29.5
77	388.8	1296.1	23.1%	141.2	32.6
78	488.7	1527.1	24.2%	148.5	36.0
79	589.6	1734.0	25.4%	154.8	39.3
80	666.0	1902.9	25.9%	159.9	41.4
81	783.6	2062.1	27.5%	164.8	45.4
82	685.9	2017.5	25.4%	161.1	40.9
83	875.0	2187.5	28.6%	162.2	46.4
84	923.0	2307.5	28.6%	166.0	47.4
85	952.2	2380.5	28.6%	170.6	48.8
86	1087.6	2589.6	29.6%	174.0	51.5

Table A.8
Cost of Air Pollution

Year a	Sum of NOx + SOx + particulate b	Index of air pollution c	Cost of air pollution c x 30 d
50	54.1	84.0	25.2
51	54.1	84.0	25.2
52	54.1	83.9	25.2
53	54.0	83.9	25.2
54	54.0	83.9	25.2
55	54.0	83.9	25.2
56	54.0	83.8	25.1
57	54.0	83.8	25.1
58	53.9	83.8	25.1
59	53.9	83.7	25.1
60	53.9	83.7	25.1
61	55.0	85.3	25.6
62	56.0	87.0	26.1
63	57.1	88.6	26.6
64	58.1	90.2	27.1
65	59.2	91.8	27.6
66	60.2	93.5	28.0
67	61.2	95.1	28.5
68	62.3	96.7	29.0
69	63.3	98.4	29.5
70	64.4	100.0	30.0
71	62.0	96.3	28.9
72	62.1	96.4	28.9
73	62.8	97.5	29.3
74	58.8	91.3	27.4
75	55.2	85.7	25.7
76	56.2	87.3	26.2
77	56.4	87.6	26.3
78	54.7	84.9	25.5
79	54.6	84.8	25.4
80	52.1	80.9	24.3
81	50.7	78.7	23.6
82	48.0	74.5	22.4
83	46.4	72.0	21.6
84	48.1	74.7	22.4
85	48.0	74.5	22.4
86	48.0	74.5	22.4

Table A.9
Loss of Agricultural Land
(Erosion, Compaction, Urbanization)

Year a	Erosion productivity loss b	Compaction productivity loss c	Agricultural land lost by urbanization d	Total loss of agricultural land (b+c+d) e
50	5.6	0.7	1.0	7.2
51	6.1	0.7	1.0	7.8
52	6.7	0.7	1.1	8.5
53	7.3	0.7	1.1	9.1
54	7.9	0.8	1.1	9.7
55	8.5	0.8	1.2	10.4
56	9.0	0.8	1.2	11.0
57	9.7	0.8	1.2	11.7
58	10.3	0.9	1.2	12.4
59	10.9	0.9	1.3	13.0
60	11.5	0.9	1.3	13.7
61	12.1	0.9	1.3	14.4
62	12.8	1.0	1.4	15.1
63	13.4	1.0	1.4	15.8
64	14.0	1.0	1.4	16.5
65	14.7	1.1	1.5	17.2
66	15.4	1.1	1.5	17.9
67	16.0	1.1	1.5	18.7
68	16.7	1.2	1.5	19.4
69	17.4	1.2	1.6	20.1
70	18.1	1.2	1.6	20.9
71	18.7	1.3	1.6	21.6
72	19.4	1.3	1.7	22.4
73	20.1	1.3	1.7	23.2
74	20.8	1.4	1.7	24.0
75	21.5	1.4	1.8	24.7
76	22.2	1.5	1.8	25.5
77	22.9	1.5	1.8	26.3
78	23.6	1.6	1.8	27.1
79	24.3	1.6	1.9	27.8
80	25.0	1.7	1.9	28.6
81	25.7	1.7	1.9	29.4
82	26.4	1.8	2.0	30.2
83	27.1	1.8	2.0	31.0
84	27.8	1.9	2.0	31.7
85	28.5	1.9	2.1	32.5
86	29.2	2.0	2.1	33.3

Table A.10
Energy Consumption as a Measure of Long Term Environmental Damage

Year a	Total energy consumption, quadrillions of BTUs b	Barrel equivalents of energy consumed (billions of barrels) c	Cumulative $.50 tax per barrel (billions of $) d	Year e	Total energy consumption, quadrillions of BTUs f	Barrel equivalents of energy consumed (billions of barrels) g	Cumulative $.50 tax per barrel (billions of $) h
1900	7.3	1.3	0.6	1944	30.4	5.2	68.1
1901	8.0	1.4	1.3	1945	30.1	5.2	70.7
1902	8.4	1.5	2.0	1946	29.0	5.0	73.2
1903	9.9	1.7	2.9	1947	31.4	5.4	75.9
1904	9.8	1.7	3.7	1948	32.5	5.6	78.7
1905	11.0	1.9	4.7	1949	30.0	5.2	81.3
1906	11.5	2.0	5.7	1950	31.7	5.5	84.0
1907	13.4	2.3	6.8	1951	34.1	5.9	86.9
1908	11.8	2.0	7.9	1952	33.8	5.8	89.9
1909	13.0	2.2	9.0	1953	34.9	6.0	92.9
1910	14.3	2.5	10.2	1954	33.9	5.8	95.8
1911	14.0	2.4	11.4	1955	37.4	6.4	99.0
1912	15.1	2.6	12.7	1956	38.9	6.7	102.4
1913	16.1	2.8	14.1	1957	38.9	6.7	105.7
1914	14.9	2.6	15.4	1958	38.8	6.7	109.1
1915	15.4	2.7	16.7	1959	40.5	7.0	112.5
1916	17.1	2.9	18.2	1960	42.1	7.3	116.2
1917	18.8	3.2	19.8	1961	46.2	8.0	120.2
1918	19.7	3.4	21.5	1962	44.7	7.7	124.0
1919	16.8	2.9	22.9	1963	46.5	8.0	128.0
1920	19.0	3.3	24.6	1964	48.6	8.4	132.2
1921	15.8	2.7	25.9	1965	50.6	8.7	136.6
1922	16.5	2.9	27.4	1966	53.6	9.2	141.2
1923	21.0	3.6	29.2	1967	55.3	9.5	146.0
1924	19.8	3.4	30.9	1968	58.7	10.1	151.0
1925	20.2	3.5	32.6	1969	61.5	10.6	156.3
1926	21.7	3.7	34.5	1970	63.7	11.0	161.8
1927	21.0	3.6	36.3	1971	65.0	11.2	167.4
1928	21.5	3.7	38.2	1972	68.4	11.8	173.3
1929	22.9	4.0	40.1	1973	71.3	12.3	179.5
1930	21.5	3.7	42.0	1974	69.1	11.9	185.4
1931	18.1	3.1	43.6	1975	67.2	11.6	191.2
1932	15.7	2.7	44.9	1976	71.2	12.3	197.4
1933	16.2	2.8	46.3	1977	73.7	12.7	203.7
1934	17.2	3.0	47.8	1978	74.9	12.9	210.2
1935	18.3	3.2	49.4	1979	75.7	13.1	216.7
1936	20.6	3.6	51.1	1980	72.8	12.6	223.0
1937	21.9	3.8	53.0	1981	70.8	12.2	229.1
1938	19.0	3.3	54.7	1982	67.1	11.6	234.9
1939	20.8	3.6	56.4	1983	66.5	11.5	240.6
1940	23.0	4.0	58.4	1984	70.1	12.1	246.6
1941	25.7	4.4	60.6	1985	70.4	12.1	252.7
1942	26.7	4.6	62.9	1986	70.2	12.1	258.7
1943	29.1	5.0	65.5				

Table A.11
Net Capital Growth

Year	Labor force (000's)	% change in labor force	Rolling average % change in labor force	Net stock fixed capital	Rolling average of net stock of fixed capital	Change in rolling average of capital stock $f-f_{(t-1)}$	Capital require-ment for labor $dxf_{(t-1)}$	Net capital growth (g-h)
a	b	c	d	e	f	g	h	i
45	53060			1170				
46	56720	6.90%		1183				
47	59350	4.64%		1196				
48	60621	2.14%		1203				
49	61286	1.10%	3.69%	1220	1194.4			
50	62208	1.50%	3.26%	1233	1207.0	12.6	38.9	-26.3
51	62017	-0.31%	1.81%	1291	1228.6	21.6	21.9	-0.3
52	62138	0.20%	0.93%	1350	1259.4	30.8	11.4	19.4
53	63015	1.41%	0.78%	1412	1301.2	41.8	9.8	32.0
54	63643	1.00%	0.76%	1480	1353.2	52.0	9.9	42.1
55	65023	2.17%	0.89%	1545	1415.6	62.4	12.1	50.3
56	66552	2.35%	1.42%	1596	1476.6	61.0	20.2	40.8
57	66929	0.57%	1.50%	1648	1536.2	59.6	22.1	37.5
58	67639	1.06%	1.43%	1703	1594.4	58.2	21.9	36.3
59	68369	1.08%	1.45%	1758	1650.0	55.6	23.0	32.6
60	69628	1.84%	1.38%	1816	1704.2	54.2	22.8	31.4
61	70459	1.19%	1.15%	1888	1762.6	58.4	19.6	38.8
62	70614	0.22%	1.08%	1962	1825.4	62.8	19.0	43.8
63	71833	1.73%	1.21%	2041	1893.0	67.6	22.1	45.5
64	73091	1.75%	1.35%	2121	1965.6	72.6	25.5	47.1
65	74455	1.87%	1.35%	2203	2043.0	77.4	26.6	50.8
66	75770	1.77%	1.47%	2297	2124.8	81.8	29.9	51.9
67	77347	2.08%	1.84%	2394	2211.2	86.4	39.1	47.3
68	78737	1.80%	1.85%	2495	2302.0	90.8	41.0	49.8
69	80734	2.54%	2.01%	2603	2398.4	96.4	46.3	50.1
70	82771	2.52%	2.14%	2715	2500.8	102.4	51.3	51.1
71	84382	1.95%	2.18%	2809	2603.2	102.4	54.4	48.0
72	87034	3.14%	2.39%	2906	2705.6	102.4	62.2	40.2
73	89429	2.75%	2.58%	3007	2808.0	102.4	69.8	32.6
74	91949	2.82%	2.64%	3111	2909.6	101.6	74.0	27.6
75	93775	1.99%	2.53%	3220	3010.6	101.0	73.6	27.4
76	96158	2.54%	2.65%	3319	3112.6	102.0	79.7	22.3
77	99009	2.96%	2.61%	3421	3215.6	103.0	81.3	21.7
78	102251	3.27%	2.72%	3526	3319.4	103.8	87.4	16.4
79	104962	2.65%	2.68%	3634	3424.0	104.6	89.1	15.5
80	106940	1.88%	2.66%	3718	3523.6	99.6	91.2	8.4
81	108670	1.62%	2.48%	3799	3619.6	96.0	87.3	8.7
82	110204	1.41%	2.17%	3855	3706.4	86.8	78.5	8.3
83	110550	0.31%	1.58%	3941	3789.4	83.0	58.4	24.6
84	113544	2.71%	1.59%	4071	3876.8	87.4	60.1	27.3
85	115461	1.69%	1.55%	4205	3974.2	97.4	60.0	37.4
86	117834	2.06%	1.64%	4344	4083.2	109.0	65.0	44.0

Table A.12
Annual Per Capita Growth of ISEW and GNP

	PC-GNP	PC-ISEW	PC-ISEW*		PC-GNP	PC-ISEW	PC-ISEW*
50-60	1.51%	2.06%	1.91%	51-60	0.97%	0.84%	0.92%
51-60	0.97%	0.84%	0.92%	60-70	2.64%	2.01%	1.97%
50-65	2.08%	2.14%	1.99%	70-80	2.04%	-0.14%	0.66%
51-65	1.77%	1.36%	1.36%	80-86	1.84%	-1.26%	-0.84%
50-77	2.14%	1.44%	1.55%	PC-ISEW* means PC-ISEW excluding			
51-77	1.97%	0.99%	1.19%	Column T (resource depletion) and			
50-86	2.02%	0.87%	1.11%	Column U (long-term environmental			
51-86	1.90%	0.53%	0.84%	damage)			

(Note:　We have given 1950 and 1951 as alternative base years for calculations of annual changes because the change in per capita ISEW between those years was greater than at any other time during the period from 1950 to 1986. (See table A.1, Column Y.) Due to this anomaly, we consider 1951 to be the appropriate year from which to make comparisons.)

Part B

CRITICAL RESPONSES

Chapter 3

THE INDEX OF SUSTAINABLE ECONOMIC WELFARE: COMMENT

Robert Eisner
William R. Kenan Professor of Economics
Northwestern University

Reviewing the Index of Sustainable Economic Welfare, I cannot help but be reminded of the reported comment of the Queen upon being informed of the sexual habits of her subjects. "Isn't that too good for the common people," she asked.

It is not that the creators of this well-intentioned effort are prudes. They do at one point consider the possibility of including pornography among the negatives in their index, but reject it. In general, though, they appear a bit too ready to claim to know better what is good for people or their economic welfare than the people themselves.

Economists generally set a more modest task. We are inclined to accept revealed preferences of economic agents. If they buy something at a particular price we assume that the good or service was worth at least that much to them. Otherwise they would not have bought it.

Why, then, do we not all accept the market value of what people buy in a certain period as a good measure of their economic welfare? The first very large problem is that a great deal of economic activity-- the production of goods and particularly services--is done outside of the market, without purchases or sales. This nonmarket activity frequently is similar or identical in character to market activity, that is, similar goods and services are produced for the market and outside of the market. What is more, the proportions of this output that are non-market vary over time and across countries. To ignore nonmarket output, whether the housing services provided by owner-occupied residences, which conventional accounts do "impute," or the unpaid housework of cooking, cleaning and care of home and children, is to leave out major and varying amounts of the outputs that constitute economic contributions to human welfare.

Recognition of nonmarket output also suggests major adjustments in government accounts since government, at least in a non-socialist economy, essentially provides services that are not sold through the market. These include major amounts in the way of education, roads and other transportation facilities, and police and national defense.

Critical complications arise in both conventional and extended accounts in the necessity of avoiding double counting--the rubber and metal going into a car and the final automobile. In general, the process of production requires the output of many intermediate goods and services which enter into the "final product" with which we are concerned. Most important are the vast amounts of capital that are used, and used up in delivering the goods and services of final output.

Since it is this final product presumably that contributes to welfare, we wish to exclude from any measure related to welfare both the intermediate goods and services already counted and absorbed completely in that product and the portion of capital used up in the process of production. We would then, to the extent we are concerned only with the contribution of economic activity to *current* welfare, also want to exclude the net acquisition of capital to be used in the production of future output.

If the size of the population and the labor force are constant, however, and capital is defined comprehensively as the total stock, tangible and intangible, contributing to production, the rate of output can be kept constant without any additional capital, that is, with zero net investment. It follows that an appropriate measure of sustainable economic welfare is the consumption that could be undertaken if all of the resources devoted to net investment were instead directed to consumption. It is this concept that underlies ISEW, the index of sustainable economic welfare and, essentially, MEW, Nordhaus and Tobin's measure of economic welfare (1972), Zolotas's less well-known EAW, the economic aspects of welfare (1981), my own TISA, the total incomes system of accounts (1985, 1988, and 1989), and other extended measures of national income and product.[1]

With this clearly understood, the corrections, adjustments and extensions to conventional income and product accounts to make them serve better as a measure of the contribution of economic activity to some aggregate of human welfare become, at least conceptually, straight-forward. I refer advisedly to the contribution of *economic* activity, to acknowledge that human happiness or "welfare" may depend as well on the work of psychiatrists and sex counselors, on political propaganda and religion. Perhaps people in sack cloths and ashes can be persuaded to be happier and enjoy more welfare than the cursed rich. But economists generally, as I, would leave to others the analysis and measure of the factors contributing to these aspects of welfare.

The indicated corrections regarding economic welfare then relate to including properly the flow of final product of goods and services and the calculation of net investment. The net investment, though, must be comprehensive. It must include the changes in all kinds of capital: in government, nonprofit institutions and households, as well as in business; human and nonhuman; the intangible capital represented by the contribution of research to knowledge and technology as well as physical plant and equipment; the investment in our natural resources and land, water and air, as well as its exhaustion or despoiling; and our holdings of foreign assets net of foreign holdings of ours.

Many of the ISEW's additions to and subtractions from the official measure of personal consumption expenditures fit the conceptual framework I have outlined. But some of the potentially most important are lacking, others are inadequate, and some of those included would appear to be arbitrary and questionable.

The greatest lack involves the almost complete exclusion of human capital. I am quite unconvinced, in particular, by the arguments that our vast expenditures on education serve little more than to provide a screening device so that employers will know who will make the more trainable and better workers and hence who will get better pay. My own view, shared by many others, is that human capital is the most critical factor of production. It certainly constitutes, when measured at the cost of its creation, the largest single share of the total capital of the nation--$10.7 trillion out of a total of $23.7 trillion by my TISA measures for 1981. Changes in the amounts of human capital available promise to make more difference to sustainable consumption and welfare than business tangible investment, which usually gets so much more attention. Preventing much of another generation from growing up with large numbers of functionally illiterate school dropouts would appear likely to be a vital factor in determining sustainable welfare. Declines in the value of our investment in human capital, as indicated by declining scores on scholastic aptitude examinations and results such as those in the news recently showing American thirteen-year olds last among youngsters of a number of nations on tests of math and science skills, cry out for incorporation in our measures. And so do investment in basic and applied research and development. Without measures of investment and depreciation of all of this intangible capital, it is hard to make much of ISEW's critical measure of "net capital growth."

Aggravating the problem here is the grossly inadequate treatment of government tangible capital and investment. Sustainable economic welfare must certainly depend importantly on the nation's infrastructure of roads, bridges, harbors, airports, sewers and water supply, schools, hospitals, government research laboratories and public as well as private buildings. A measure of sustainable economic welfare should include both the net investment in government capital and the value of its final product services.

A major innovation of ISEW is the adjustment for income inequality. The rationale, I would presume, is that the welfare-income coefficient is lower for higher incomes. In the familiar terms of economic theory, marginal utility for each individual or household is a declining function of income. Even if utility functions are not identical across individuals, if there are no systematic differences among utility functions on the basis of income, we can infer that aggregate utility or welfare will be higher the more equal is the income distribution. Since the marginal income of the rich adds little to their utility or welfare while the marginal income of the poor adds much, redistributing income from the rich to poor must add to aggregate utility.

That said, there are serious questions as to the methods pursued by ISEW in this adjustment. First, it should properly be applied to the end product of aggregate *adjusted* income or consumption, not to the initial variable, personal consumption expenditures. In 1986, for example, the ISEW inequality index stood at 112.8. Personal consumption divided by 1.128 gave us a "weighted consumption" figure of $1024.4 billion (in 1972 dollars), 11.3 percent less than the unadjusted $1155.5 billion. But when this 131.1 billion reduction is finally carried through to the Index of Sustainable Economic Welfare, ISEW, which was put at $822.1 billion, it represented a downward adjustment not of 11.3 percent but of 13.8 percent from a value of ISEW that would otherwise have been at $953.2 billion.

Second, and of even greater importance in terms of magnitude, I must question the arbitrary and extremely volatile nature of the index itself. Relatively small changes in the distribution of income generate large movements in the index and consequently have very great effects on ISEW and proportionately still larger ones on its rate of growth.

The index of inequality, it may be recalled, is calculated by averaging the ratios of the percentage of income received by the top quintile to the percentages received by each of the quintiles. From 1968 to 1986 the share of the lowest quintile fell from 5.6 percent to 4.6 percent and that of the second lowest from 12.4 percent to 10.8 percent. These declines generated an increase of 22.6 percent in the inequality index, from 92.0 to 112.8 and hence an 18.4 percent reduction, amounting to 213.1 billion, in personal consumption. But as pointed out above, this comes to an even larger proportion, 20.6 percent, of what ISEW would otherwise have been. With the inequality adjustment, per capita ISEW rose from 3189.7 to 3402.8, or 6.68 percent, which came to only 0.27 percent per year. By contrast, conventional per capita GNP grew by 68.4 percent, or 2.20 percent per annum.

Without the inequality adjustment, per capita ISEW would have risen by 25.9 percent, or 1.24 percent per annum, over four times as fast as the unadjusted measure, making up fully half of the difference from GNP per capita growth. I dare say that with a less volatile inequality index, properly applied to the final unadjusted measure of sustainable welfare, the difference between conventional and adjusted measures of growth would have similarly been much less.

I have some further problems with the inequality index, although quite where, on balance, their solution takes us is not entirely clear. It is acknowledged that ISEW deals with before-tax rather than after-tax income and ignores various welfare benefits such as food stamps and Medicaid, which are not reflected or not reflected fully in the official measure of personal consumption. A serious problem going in the other direction is the failure to include capital gains and losses, unrealized as well as realized. It is well-known that the very rich receive very large portions of income from capital gains while the poor receive virtually none. The measures of the size distribution of income employed in ISEW are then highly suspect. Indeed, it should, ideally, not work with a distribution of income at all, but rather one of consumption, since welfare is, properly, tied largely to consumption.

ISEW appropriately subtracts expenditures for consumer durables and then adds back an imputation for the services of these durables. The imputation for services, however, is crude and outrageously low. It is taken simply as 10 percent of the stock of durables. Thus, in 1986 for example, $212 billion in services are added. The more reasonable way to estimate the value of a flow of services from capital would be to add estimates of annual depreciation--the amounts of capital being transformed into services--and imputed earnings, based on the real rate of interest. Such a procedure, judging from my TISA calculations, would yield estimates of services close to 90 percent of the value of current expenditures for durables, rather than the less than 40 percent in ISEW.

A similar problem emerges in ISEW's estimates of the value of the services of streets and highways. Again, the assumption that these are 10 percent of the value of capital invested has little to commend it.

What is worst about all this is that it introduces a systematic, downward bias in estimates both of ISEW itself and of its rate of growth. ISEW entails the subtraction of large and rapidly growing streams of investment and the addition of (incorrectly) much smaller streams of capital services. On consumer durables and services alone, noting the effects on the trend from 1962 to 1986 is again instructive. ISEW subtracts $54.7 billion dollars of expenditures on consumer durables in 1962 and $212.0 billion in 1986. It adds back only $22.7 billion of services in 1962 and $79.8 billion in 1986. Growth is thus reduced by $102 billion over that period. In relative terms, the growth in ISEW over this period is consequently reduced by some 7.5 percent. An appropriate imputation for the services of consumer durables would have contributed little or nothing to slowing ISEW's rate of growth.

A similar, downward bias to the rate of growth of ISEW is introduced by the technique for calculating the additions and subtractions with regard to health expenditures. Using a 1950 base, so that these items are both zero for that year and then grow in proportion to the increments of expenditures, has the consequence of making the addition for public health expenditures and the subtraction for private expenditures larger proportions of weighted personal consumption (or of ISEW) in later years than in earlier years. Since the subtraction for private expenditures is larger in magnitude, the net effect is a disproportionate reduction of ISEW in later years.

The correction for advertising is arbitrary but essentially unjustified to begin with. The main point is that by the anomaly of the definition of GNP and its components in terms of final product, advertising expenditures, which overwhelmingly involve purchases of one firm, such as General Motors or AT&T, from another, such as the New York Times or CBS, are not counted to begin with. It is true that if GM spends more advertising on cars this may raise the price of cars and hence nominal GNP, but the price deflators will then be higher and, since neither the quantity nor quality of cars has changed, there will be no change in real GNP. Similarly, of course, there will be no change in *real* consumption expenditure for cars, and the advertising expenditures themselves are not purchases directly by consumers and are not counted in consumption. Thus, neither Zolotas, nor ISEW, which copied him, are warranted in making a subtraction for wasteful advertising expenditure because, however wasteful they may be, they were not in the measures of GNP or consumption to begin with.

It may be superfluous at this point for me to add that, if we were to subtract wasteful advertising expenditures as not contributing to welfare, restricting this to national advertising seems quite arbitrary. I might rather argue that national advertising, going in considerable part to national television and other media services, involves a fair amount of uncounted consumption. It should perhaps then be, at least in part, added rather than subtracted to get a measure of welfare. Why, after all, count as consumption the movie seen in a movie house, or the rented video-cassette, paid for directly by the consumer, and yet exclude the movie seen on home commercial television and paid for by advertising?

I am in accord with the subtraction of commuting costs in moving from a measure of consumption to one of truly final product, which would offer a better index of welfare. I again, however, have a problem with the calculation of commuting costs in ISEW. The proportion of travel costs related to commuting to work is based on mileage estimates, which is reasonable. But this ratio is applied to personal consumption expenditures for user-operated transportation, which is unreasonable. Recall that ISEW does appropriately move from consumption expenditures to consumption services. The appropriate imputation for commuting costs must involve not items such as expenditures for purchases of automobiles but an estimate of the services of automobiles.

Because of the general growth in expenditures, the value of services, correctly calculated, since it involves largely depreciation, an average of previous lesser expenditures, will tend to be somewhat less. This suggests that the commuting subtraction in ISEW tends to be too large. My TISA estimate for 1981 was $13.3 billion (1972 dollars) while the ISEW estimate was $29.0 billion. This difference is greater than is likely to be accounted for by the difference between current expenditures or investment and the services of capital, and there may have been other factors, as well, contributing to it.

I find ISEW's estimates of costs of urbanization probably excessive. I suspect, in fact, one could make a good argument that urbanization has substantial benefits that may outweigh the costs.

ISEW bases its estimates of urbanization costs on increases in the ratio of the value of land to the total value (land and structures) of residential property. It is not clear why this should relate at all to costs of urbanization. The ratio of land value to the total has probably gone up generally, in rural areas as well as urban. This may be expected if only because land on Earth is finite and essentially fixed in amount. As, with increasing population and accumulation of reproducible capital, the quantities of other factors of production rise, it is to be expected that the marginal product of and value of land, the fixed factor of production, will rise. I fail to see that this has much to do with urbanization. The phenomenon would occur if all of the population lived in rural areas.

To the extent land values rise more than proportionately in urban areas, it may occur precisely because living is more desirable in urban areas. Even with all the reported crime and congestion, many people find the New York area desirable and pay enormous rents to live there. Perhaps it is the theaters, the restaurants, the throb of city life. Perhaps it is the opportunity to meet more people. Perhaps it is the variety of services available in a large metropolis but not to be found back on the farm. Having been brought up in New York and lived most of my life in the Chicago area, I am not one to think my welfare would be better in a small town. I might argue then that the fact that land values are higher and rents are higher may reflect the fact that many people think urban living is better.

The costs of water and air pollution turn out to be rather minor in ISEW and air pollution costs are estimated to be declining. Here I believe arbitrary assumptions as to trends in regard to water pollution and a misuse of flows instead of stocks in regard to air pollution may well have contributed to *under*estimating the increasing costs.

ISEW anchors its time series on air pollution costs to a $30 billion (1972 dollar) figure for 1970. This in itself may well be low because of exclusion of some costs of illness as well as all of any costs of early mortality. (I do not share ISEW's reluctance to put a value on human life; indeed, I should think it vital in any measure of welfare.) My prime methodological quarrel, though, is with construction of the time series, which bases movements from the 1970 bench mark on an index of the annual *flow* of pollutants into the air. But surely it is the stock of pollutants in the air, not what has been added in one year, which relates meaningfully to costs of air pollution. The annual flow of additional pollutants may be diminishing while the total stock of pollutants in the air is still rising. This last will depend upon whether the additional pollutants are or are not matched by decreases due to natural forces or environmental cleanup. Without knowledge of what is happening to the quality of air--the stock of pollutants--I do not have a handle on what is happening to the costs of air pollution.

I am bothered by the estimates of the value of land loss primarily because I do not see companion estimates for the value of land gain. If land is taken from agriculture and put to more profitable (and presumably more productive) use, I fail to see that as a net loss to national wealth, the quality of life or economic welfare. Much of the removal of land from agriculture reflects, I should think, vastly increased agricultural productivity, so that less land, as well as fewer farmers, are needed to feed our population, and even feed some of the rest of the world.

I must also reject ISEW's objection to calculating present values by discounting the value of future losses--and future benefits. If one were to calculate the value of the loss of farm land to soil erosion or to urbanization as the simple sum of the infinite stream of lost farm products, that sum would come to infinity, or would be bounded only by the end of time, or more proximately, I suppose, the end of life on earth. Perhaps at that I should accept a shorter horizon, as earth dwellers may eventually find land on other bodies in the universe. We get into all kinds of nonsense though, if we do not distinguish properly between current and future values and between flows and stocks.

Failure to do so generates some confusion in the discussion of depletion on non-renewable resources and environmental damages. The correct way to handle these variables is to adjust our measure of income or sustainable welfare for the loss of capital. If we can calculate the value of these capital losses we can recognize them in the measure of net capital growth. This recognition will remind us of the necessity then of including in net capital growth all of the related--or unrelated-- gains that may be taking place.

With depletion of non-renewable resources, ISEW would appear to come to a reasonable procedure by rather devious reasoning. Disinvestment in inventories of resources under the ground is after all not different in its implications for sustainable resources than any other disinvestment in inventories, which will be recognized in the net capital growth variable. ISEW makes a subtraction for this deple- tion but apparently includes extraction costs. This is not correct, as the current incurring of extraction costs is not an exhaustion of capital and has no effect on the sustainability of consumption or welfare. The ap- propriate subtraction is the value of the resources themselves. It is this that future generations will have lost if we use them up.

The discussion of changing resource prices with regard to ISEW appears to miss the point made by economic theorists. First, whatever are expected future prices, they are reflected in current prices. The value of the current loss in wealth due to depletion is then the value of the depleted resources at current market prices. A social planner--or perhaps the controller of a cartel--may claim to know better than the market the "true" value of these resources, but history indicates that those who bet against the collective wisdom of the market do so at con- siderable risk. They should be sure that they really know something that the market does not.

Danger of intervention to correct market behavior regarding pre- sumably non-renewable, depletable resources are suggested by the im- plications of the actual behavior of resource prices. Economic theory suggests that rational owners of resources will supply them to the point that they have depressed current prices so that they are sufficiently below expected future prices to make the marginal return from current extraction and sale equal to the return from leaving the resources in the ground and extracting them in the future. Current prices must then be such that expected future prices exceed them by the rate of in- terest (or generally the net return to capital), that is, what could be received by extracting and selling the resources now and investing the proceeds.

If resources are truly non-renewable, we should expect competitive market prices then to be rising and, externalities aside, the optimum amount of depletion to be taking place. If one believes that depletion is taking place at a rate faster than optimum, that we are improperly using wealth we should be leaving for the future, one must believe that prices are not expected by those controlling the markets to rise at a rate sufficient to justify them saving the resources one thinks they should be saving.

Articulating such a belief against the views of market participants, who are "putting their money where their mouths are," may denote superior knowledge or a rate of time discount different from (lower than) that indicated by market rates of interest. In the latter case, by the way, one should try to bring about more saving and investment, but not necessarily in the form of depletable resources. There is also the possibility, though, that the market anticipates correctly that the resources in question are not entirely non-renewable, that substitute resources will be developed or that new technologies and new needs will reduce the future demand for and value of the resources. Prices may not be rising enough and may not be expected to rise enough to bring on greater conservation precisely because expectations are (correctly) such that more conservation is not economically justified and therefore is not needed.

The tie-in of this reasoning to the issue of accounting for sustainable welfare then is first the recognition that the current loss in wealth need not take into account future prices; they are, as best we can know them, already reflected in current prices. But second, it indicates that along with recognizing current depletion as disinvestment, we should include the value of the discovery of new resources, or the development of new technologies that make new resources valuable, as investment. If these are properly entered into ISEW's net capital growth, we may find that on balance resource use and development are reducing sustainable welfare considerably less than thought, if indeed at all.

Environmental damage costs should similarly be calculated as the rate of reduction in the value of our environment. ISEW's calculation of this as $0.50 per 5.8 million BTUs consumed would then appear arbitrary and hard to defend. The environment may well be deteriorat-

ing for reasons that have little to do with energy use. It may be in part
self-restoring as damage escapes the Earth's atmosphere. Or we may be
taking measures to restore it. In any event, the simple linear equations
of energy use and environmental damage, let alone with particular, arbitrary and unchanging coefficient, is hard for any economist to accept.
I must note that the environmental damage term, to make matter
more troublesome, is the single largest subtraction in ISEW, coming to
no less than $258.7 billion in 1986, thus reducing the measure of sus-
tainable welfare, again $822.1 billion, by no less than 23.9 percent of
what it would have been without the subtraction.

A final ISEW adjustment, for the change in the new international position of the United States, makes good sense in principle, but the
accuracy of the measure is very much in doubt. This addition to the
index of sustainable economic welfare essentially represents net foreign
investment, the increase in the value of U.S. assets in foreign nations
minus the increase in the claims of foreigners on U.S. assets. The difficulty is that a major portion of these assets is valued at original cost
rather than current market value. I refer in particular to the direct investment component.

The error here becomes especially important because of its differential impact on U.S. and foreign assets. Much of U.S. investment
abroad was made many years ago, when prices were low. Their current
market value is hence much more than their original cost. Foreign
claims on U.S. assets, to the contrary, were largely acquired relatively
recently. U.S. claims on foreign assets thus tend to be considerably understated as compared to foreign claims in the U.S. The net international position of the U.S. tends therefore to be considerably better than
usually indicated. Paul Pieper and I have indeed argued that bringing
assets and liabilities to market value would largely if not entirely eliminate the loudly and frequently proclaimed status of the U.S. as the
"world's greatest debtor nation."[2]

In terms of changes in the international investment position of
the U.S., included in ISEW, corrections to the dollar market value of
U.S. direct investment abroad would in recent years generally reduce
the disinvestment reported in ISEW. In 1985 and 1986, where ISEW reports negative figures of $49.6 billion and $63.4 billion, disinvestment
numbers from one set of Eisner and Pieper estimates of the adjusted
measure of the U.S. international investment position would come to
only $28.7 billion and $19.1 billion, respectively. The differences related
largely to gains in the dollar value of U.S. direct investments abroad as

a result of application of the higher value of foreign currencies (depreciation of the dollar) to the larger market values of these investments. Substitution of the adjusted numbers for those currently in ISEW, by raising the more recent figures, would have some significant effect of increasing ISEW rates of growth.

By way of conclusion, I may express some reserve at the tenor of the presentation of ISEW, that sustainable economic welfare is somehow not as great as suggested by conventional measures of GNP or consumption, and that matters are getting worse, or at least not getting better as fast as conventional measures of income and product per capita might suggest. I do not believe that one should approach the effort to find expanded national accounts that give a better measure of economic activity or of "welfare" with the preconception that welfare may "really" be less or that its rate of growth or improvement is in fact less than suggested by conventional measures.

Our essential aim should be to get measures that more fully reflect the elements augmenting or diminishing welfare. We may then be better able to devise and implement policies that will contribute to this welfare. My own work suggests that adjusted and extended measures will be making substantial additions in the way of non-market activity in the home and government as well as subtractions of intermediate products such as police and defense services. My Total Incomes System of Accounts GNP is in fact considerably larger than the Bureau of Economic Analysis GNP, but this is of not much greater significance than saying that people's heights measured in inches are greater than their heights measured in feet. A more important judgment would be that rates of growth in the adjusted measures are different from those in the conventional measures.

Here, though, considerable caution is in order. There are some systematic factors to which one can look. A period of sharply increasing military expenditures, such as in the 1980's will contribute to a larger rate of growth of conventional measures, which include them, than of adjusted measures which treat military services as intermediate. A period of movement from non-market to market labor, effected by the very great movement of women from home to jobs over the last several decades would also make conventional measures, which include market but not non-market product, grow more rapidly. Successful activity to improve the environment would, however, tend to raise adjusted measures more than the conventional ones.

In terms of overall comparisons, as noted by Nordhaus and Tobin, and confirmed in my own TISA, conclusions are extremely sensitive to choices of deflators and their implications for changes in productivity of non-market labor and changes in the real contributions of the new elements in the expanded accounts. This led Nordhaus and Tobin to report that their MEW could not be used to prove that postwar growth in GNP or NNP per capital was a mirage, and that economic welfare was not in fact increasing, perhaps increasing at close to what was suggested by conventional measures. My own work with TISA brings me to a similar tentative conclusion.

The suggestions in the ISEW accounts and the discussion of them that in fact the growth in sustainable welfare has been significantly less than indicated by conventional measures stem, as I have indicated, from a number of major doubtful assumptions and procedures. Corrections on these matters would appear to force at least an agnostic position similar to those taken by others working with adjusted and expanded accounts.

This is not to say that accounts of this kind cannot be extremely useful, indeed vital, in the evaluation of factors contributing to economic welfare, and in the formulations of policies that will increase it. It is in that sense that ISEW and efforts of its kind are very much to be welcomed.

Chapter 4

THE ISEW FROM A NATIONAL ACCOUNTING PERSPECTIVE

Carol S. Carson, Director
Bureau of Economic Analysis
and
Allan H. Young, Chief Statistician
Bureau of Economic Analysis

This essay is in four parts. The first part briefly considers the prospects for a measure of welfare, such as the ISEW developed by the Economic Welfare Study Group, becoming a key aggregate in national economic accounting and in the formulation and assessment of government policies. The second part takes issue with some aspects of the content of the ISEW. The third part considers how the revised United Nations System of National Accounts will provide an improved basis for considering some of the societal problems addressed in the ISEW measure. The fourth part, although not central to the discussion, takes issue with several points and provides some additional background.

Note: The authors have extensive backgrounds in the development, preparation, and use of the official national economic accounts of the United States. It is from this perspective that the Study Group invited them to comment on the ISEW measure. Carol S. Carson is the Deputy Director and Allan H. Young is the Director of the Bureau of Economic Analysis of the U.S. Department of Commerce. In addition, Mrs. Carson is a member of the expert group that is revising the United Nations System of National Accounts. The views expressed are their own and do not represent an official position of the Department of Commerce.

Will the ISEW Become a Key Aggregate?

The Study Group concludes its paper with the question: "Are the policies of our government going to be guided by GNP or by ISEW or some other measure of sustainable welfare?" If one interprets the question in a broad sense, it is whether the government will be guided by considerations of the full range of costs and benefits. Clearly the welfare of society occupies the central role in the process of governance. Even though the process at times unduly favors the short run over the long, or market costs and benefits over nonmarket, or both, our answer to the reformulated question is essentially "yes." Two interesting illustrations of how the process of governance has taken into account in a substantial way both market and nonmarket costs and benefits may be found in the ISEW component data. As the Study Group points out, the data suggest that government policies concerning air pollution and auto safety have contributed to an increase in per capita welfare.

If one interprets the question in a narrow sense, it is whether the ISEW or some other single-dimension aggregate measure of sustainable welfare would be useful in guiding, shaping, or choosing among government policies. Here, although we share the concerns of the Study Group, the answer is a qualified "no." The qualification, which is an important one, is placed on the answer because clearly the construction and advancement of the ISEW is a useful endeavor. Much as did earlier work by Tobin and Nordhaus and others, development of the ISEW sensitizes and keeps before society the fact that not all old problems are fully solved and that new problems arise that must be addressed if welfare is to be protected and extended in a dynamic society. In this indirect manner, the ISEW and measures like it help guide government policy.

We believe that a single-dimension aggregate measure of sustainable welfare will be of little direct use in guiding, shaping, or choosing among government policies because the factors determining welfare cannot be reduced and combined into a single measure that would command widespread agreement and acceptance. In this respect, a measure of welfare differs from the GNP.

Looking back, widespread agreement to, and acceptance of, the GNP and the national income and product accounts grew not so much out of their role in planning in World War II as out of their role in implementing the Full Employment Act of 1946. That Act codified a societal consensus that evolved out of the experiences of the 1930's. It assigned the federal government a responsibility for maintaining full employment, and measurement of output was central to accomplishing this goal. Given that the goal was in terms of market employment, the suitable measure of output was one that adhered rather closely to the market boundary, and hence GNP and the accounts became a key ingredient in post-World War II policymaking.

Looking ahead, we do not see a consensus as to goals, concepts and definitions, and basis for measurement that would permit any one single-dimension aggregate welfare measure to play a comparable role in guiding, shaping, or choosing among government policies. We do see the potential usefulness of a detailed accounting approach--the satellite accounts taken up in our third part--for dealing more completely with a broad range of societal problems than is possible with the present national economic accounts.

Comments on the Content of the ISEW

In this section we make two general comments about the contents of the ISEW and then critique some of the components. The general comments lay some of the groundwork for the following section about the United Nations System of National Accounts.

General Comments

The first general comment is that the ISEW shows some symptoms of unduly turning its back on the rest of the world. First, the long-term environmental change (component U) is calculated on the assumption that the amount of environmental damage is directly proportional to the consumption of fossil fuels and nuclear energy in the United States. Yet if consumption of the fossil fuels and nuclear energy is to be the indicator, it would seem that world-wide consumption, not just U.S. consumption, must be brought into the calculation. Possible climate change and stratospheric ozone depletion, for example, are global issues, and the United States and other nations at the Paris Summit in July 1989 recognized them as requiring international cooperation. Second, the ISEW design does not reflect any explicit consideration of international comparability. As we see it, however, comparability is an important criterion; not only is there general interest in comparisons across countries, but increasingly policy is being discussed, if not formulated, on a multinational basis. In fact, one reason that GNP and similar aggregates are used as widely as they are is that, over the years, standard concepts and methodologies have been forged that facilitate comparisons across countries. It may well be that a single index of economic welfare is inappropriate because what would be considered to merit inclusion would vary from country to country--at least that was the conclusion of United Nations Statistical Commission a little over a decade ago.[1] However, at least some components seem to be amenable to standardization, and we believe that, if measures such as the ISEW are to be proposed, comparability should be among the criteria applied in selecting elements.

The second general comment relates to the relationships of the components. First, some of the components do not appear to be fully consistent on a conceptual level. For example, streams of services are added only for some government equipment and structures--namely, highways and streets (component G); only these are considered as adding to economic welfare. Yet for the net capital growth (component V), "capital" includes *all* government structures and equipment--even including military. If only streets and roads, among the government's expenditures on equipment and structures, are considered to yield services that contribute to welfare, why are the full range of the government equipment and structures considered necessary to equip the labor force and the excess counted as adding to welfare?

Second, the "plus-minus" structure in which the ISEW is calculated does not facilitate, and in fact may impede, the recognition of tradeoffs in the real world between activities as represented by some components. For example, driving heavier cars may help reduce the economic loss from automobile accidents (in component N) but increase the consumption of fuel and thus add to the long-term environmental damage (component U).

Third, the dollar dimension in the "plus-minus" structure that starts with personal consumption expenditure (adjusted for distributional equity) imposes a stringent requirement on the components. Each component should not only register an appropriate change over time if viewed as an index, but should also be weighted into the total in a way that is consistent with the market value to consumers. National advertising (component K) is one of the components that can be questioned in this respect. Payments by companies to newspaper publishers, television networks, and other media for space and time to advertise their products represent purchases by business, not purchases by consumers. Although the costs of the advertising are presumably passed along to consumers in the price of the advertised products, the consumer does not explicitly put a market value on the advertising. Further, it should be noted, advertising revenues cover the costs of much of the television programming, for example. Should a value for television entertainment provided free to consumers be added back to the ISEW?

Comments on Specific Components

For two components, we question the appropriateness of the concept or its implementation. These components are of particular interest because they are major contributors to the decline in ISEW in the 1980's. Next, we will mention a set of data that would appropriately broaden the scope of the pollution components. Finally, we discuss another component that is a major contributor to the decline in the ISEW in the 1980's. We believe that this component, like the first two we discuss, unduly depresses the ISEW as a measure of economic welfare, but it is difficult to say by how much.

Index of distributional inequality. The Study Group attempts to deal with the long-recognized need to take income distribution into account when considering economic welfare. However, both the statistical and conceptual basis for the distributional inequality component (component C) of the ISEW are very weak. The Study Group briefly notes the two reasons for this. First, the distributional inequality component is based on before-tax income data. The Study Group calls for a thorough study to determine an appropriate after-tax measure that includes transfers and other, hidden benefits. For this essay, we are willing to grant that before-tax distributions of Census Bureau money income may provide a basis for a rough-and-ready approximation to a suitable measure.

Second, there is no approach to combining distributional equity and aggregate welfare in a single measure that commands general agreement. The Study Group sets forth its own approach. The approach taken is to create an index of income inequality and then to divide the index into personal consumption expenditures in order to allow for the effect of changes in the distribution of income upon welfare.

The approach taken by the Study Group may be written as

$$W = \frac{C}{I^A}$$

where W equals welfare (before the subsequent plus-minus adjust-ments), C equals consumption, I equals the index of income inequality, and A equals a constant. The percentage change in W is then approxi-mately

$$\Delta \ln W = \Delta \ln C - A \; \Delta \ln I.$$

Thus the approach depends on the value of A and the particular form of I that is chosen.

The Study Group assumes that A is equal to 1.0. Thus welfare remains constant if a 1-percent increase in I is offset by a 1-percent in-crease in C. However, no justification is given for taking A to be equal to 1.0 instead of some other value.

The index of inequality calculated by the Study Group, designat-ed $\tilde{I}$, is the ratio of the average income of the highest income quintile to the harmonic mean of the average income in each of the five quintiles:

$$\tilde{I} = \frac{Y_5}{\left[\frac{1}{5} \left(\frac{1}{Y_1} \; \frac{1}{Y_2} \; \frac{1}{Y_3} \; \frac{1}{Y_4} \; \frac{1}{Y_5} \right) \right]^{-1}}$$

and

$$\Delta \ln \tilde{I} = \Delta \ln Y_5 - \Delta \ln \tilde{Y}$$

where Y_i is the average income of the ith quintile and $\tilde{Y}$ is the harmon-ic mean of the Y_i.[2]

$\tilde{I}$ is only one of many possible indexes of inequality. An equally plausible index, designated $\bar{I}$, would result from use of the average in-come of all recipients in the denominator instead of the harmonic mean of the quintiles,

$$\bar{I} = \frac{Y_5}{\overline{Y}}$$

and

$$\Delta \ln \bar{I} = \Delta \ln Y_5 - \Delta \ln \overline{Y},$$

where $\overline{Y}$ is the average income of all recipients and is equal to $\Sigma \; Y_i \, / 5$.

The ISEW is quite sensitive to the choice of I, assuming the value of A continues to be taken as equal to 1.0. As calculated by the Study Group, the ISEW declines 2 percent from 1980 to 1986. If I is substituted for I, the index increases 7 percent in this period.[3]

To sum up, the Study Group has offered no basis for choosing A and I. Under these conditions, we do not consider the attempt to include distributional equity in an aggregate welfare measure to be a step forward.

Consumer durables--services and expenditures. In constructing the ISEW, the Study Group followed a procedure that is rather common--substitution of a measure of the services of consumer durables (component F) for expenditure on consumer durables (component I). However, we believe that the measure of the services calculated by the Study Group for use in this procedure is unreasonably low and, accordingly, the net effect of subtracting expenditures and adding services unduly depresses the ISEW. In the 1980's, the amount by which expenditures exceeded services grew from about $76 billion in 1980 to $132 billion (1972 dollars) in 1986. Thus the net effect of the substitution was one of the largest contributors to the decline of the ISEW in recent years.

The literature on the difficulties of calculating the value of services of consumer durables is large, and several different methods of calculation have been used by researchers.[4] It is possible that the Study Group was attempting to implement what is known as an "opportunity cost measure." This is suggested by the fact that they derive a rate of return on an alternative investment and apply that rate to the stock of consumer durables to obtain an imputed value.[5] When others apply the opportunity cost method, the service value of durables consists of such an imputed value *plus* depreciation. However, the Study Group's estimate of services is less than depreciation alone. In other words, the value of the services as calculated by the Study Group is less than the estimate of the value of the wear, tear, and obsolescence that takes place in a year. This relation holds for the whole time period shown in the Study Group's table A.1.

Table B.4.1 is for the year 1972, so that the Study Group's estimates in 1972 dollars can be compared with some other estimates that are based on the estimates of the stock of consumer durables prepared by the Bureau of Economic Analysis, some of which are in current dollars.[6] The table highlights how much lower the Study Group's esti-

Table B.4.1. Services of Consumer Durables
and Related Estimates, 1972
(Billions of dollars)

	Study Group (1)	Katz and Peskin (2)	Ruggles and Ruggles (3)	Eisner (4)
Expenditures		111.1		
Net Stock		421.3		
Depreciation		76.5		
Services	42.1	142.0	121.3	94.1
Ratios:				
Services/expenditures	0.38	1.28	1.09	0.85
Services/depreciation	0.55	1.86	1.59	1.23

Col. 2: Arnold J. Katz and Janice Peskin, "The Value of Services Produced by the Stock of Consumer Durables, 1947-77: An Opportunity Cost Measure," 60 *Survey of Current Business* (July 1980): table 9. The estimate of services is the sum of the net return, depreciation, repairs and maintenance, and personal property taxes.

Col. 3: Richard Ruggles and Nancy D. Ruggles, "Integrated Economic Accounts for the United States, 1947-80," 62 *Survey of Current Business* (May 1982): table 1.40. The estimate of services is based on the Katz and Peskin estimate, but omits the maintenance and repair component.

Col. 4: Robert Eisner, *The Total Incomes System of Accounts* (Chicago: University of Chicago Press, 1989), table 6. The estimate of services is the sum of gross imputed interest, depreciation, personal motor vehicle licenses, and personal property taxes. The estimate of net stock differs from the others by the inclusion of all, rather than 20 percent, of the stock of tires, tubes, and auto accessories.

mate of services is than the estimate of annual depreciation. It also shows that the Study Group's estimate of the value of the services of consumer durables is much lower than any of the other estimates, each of which is a variant of an opportunity cost measure.

We do not wish to argue the merits of one of these measures over the others. However, we believe that it is instructive to note that if depreciation on the constant-dollar stock--the element common to all of them--is substituted in the ISEW for the Study Group's estimate of the services of consumer durables, the decline in the ISEW from 1980 to 1986 is wiped out.

Pollution.   Water pollution, air pollution, and noise pollution in the ISEW (components O, P, and Q, respectively) measure damage--indeed the damage that occurs despite efforts to avoid or counter it. The ISEW does not recognize that there are expenditures to abate and control pollution.

The Bureau of Economic Analysis makes estimates of such expenditures for all sectors within a framework consistent with the national income and product accounts. The series is available for 1972-87; table B.4.2 provides an overview. It shows pollution abatement and control (PAC) expenditures by sector. The spending by the personal sector is all consumption. The spending for durables are for motor vehicles emission abatement devices; the spending for nondurables is for the operation of those devices. The spending by business and government includes both current and capital spending. The estimates have additional dimensions: They are broken down by type of media--air, water, and solid waste--and into spending for abatement, regulation and monitoring, and research and development.

We think it would be consistent with the goals of the ISEW to take some of the PAC expenditures into account--at least those in personal consumption. When converted to 1972 dollars to be consistent with the rest of the ISEW, the PAC expenditures in personal consumption would increase from about $3 billion in 1980 to about $5-1/2 billion in 1986, thus depressing the ISEW slightly over the period.[7]

Net international investment position.   The Study Group takes the view that reliance on foreign financing of capital is undesirable because it sets in motion future transfers of income from the United States to the rest of the world. In constructing the ISEW, the Study Group accounts for this effect on welfare by deducting the change in the

Table B.4.2. Constant-Dollar PAC Spending, by Sector

| | Millions of 1982 dollars | | | | | Percent change | | | | | |
| | | | | | | | Change from preceding year | | | | |
	1983	1984	1985/r/	1986/r/	1987/p/	1972-82 average annual rate	1983	1984	1985/r/	1986/r/	1987/p/
Pollution abatement and control.........	60,007	64,713	68,121	71,800	71,366	3.0	4.0	7.8	5.3	5.4	-0.6
Personal consumption..................	9,731	10,565	11,336	12,228	10,333	9.8	17.0	8.6	7.3	7.9	-15.5
Durables........................	6,060	6,893	7,518	8,196	7,377	19.4	21.6	13.7	9.1	9.0	-10.0
Nondurables.....................	3,671	3,673	3,818	4,032	2,957	3.3	10.1	.1	3.9	5.6	-26.7
Business............................	38,124	41,078	42,905	44,407	45,519	2.7	3.7	7.7	4.4	3.5	2.5
On capital account...............	12,898	14,561	14,832	14,490	14,590	.7	-4.0	12.9	1.9	-2.3	.7
Motor vehicle emission abatement..	3,231	4,335	4,615	4,456	4,284	20.9	20.6	34.2	6.5	-3.4	-3.9
Plant and equipment.............	7,615	7,905	7,975	7,699	8,182	(*)	-14.9	3.8	-.9	-3.5	6.3
Other..........................	2,052	2,320	2,242	2,335	2,124	-5.3	13.8	13.1	-3.4	4.1	-9.0
On current account...............	25,226	26,517	28,074	29,918	30,929	4.2	8.1	5.1	5.9	6.6	3.4
Motor vehicle emission abatement..	2,619	2,661	2,745	2,824	2,129	7.7	6.1	1.6	3.2	2.9	-24.6
Plant and equipment.............	14,998	16,173	16,788	17,886	19,466	3.8	6.5	7.8	3.8	6.5	8.8
Public sewer systems/1/..........	5,475	5,649	6,016	6,691	7,081	5.8	6.1	3.2	6.5	11.2	5.8
Other/2/........................	2,133	2,034	2,525	2,517	2,253	-.8	31.5	-4.6	24.1	-.3	-10.5
Government...........................	12,152	13,070	13,879	15,165	15,514	.7	-3.6	7.6	6.2	9.3	2.3
Public sewer system construction....	5,551	6,387	7,005	7,774	8,256	-1.1	-9.7	15.1	9.7	11.0	6.2
Other/3/............................	6,601	6,683	6,874	7,391	7,258	2.8	2.3	1.2	2.9	7.5	-1.8

r Revised.
p Preliminary.
* Less than 0.1 percent.
1. Spending to operate public sewer systems is classified in the national income and product accounts as business spending. Construction of public sewer systems is classified in the national income and product accounts as government spending.
2. For this table, private purchases for research and development are included with business pollution abatement spending on current account.
3. For this table, spending for government regulation and monitoring and for research and development are included with government pollution abatement spending.

Source: Survey of Current Business, June 1989.

net international investment position (component U). This approach represents a polar case in that it does not allow for any benefits from foreign investment. Further, the use of changes in the net international investment position overstates the inward flow of investment from 1982 to 1986.

The approach taken by the Study Group rests on the assumptions that foreign investment has been an alternative way (alternative to domestic saving) of financing total investment and that part of a fixed amount of GNP is transferred to the rest of the world. This approach is one polar case. The other is that foreign investment represents an addition to total investment and that the additional investment works to enlarge GNP and thus to create additional income, some of which is transferred to the rest of the world. To the extent that this latter case represents reality, the negative effect on welfare should be considered to be less than that estimated by the Study Group.

The change in the net international investment position consists of the net capital flow and various adjustments to the position, most of which are for changes in exchange rates and prices. It is only the capital flow from abroad that is available to finance investment. From 1982 to 1986, the net capital flow was about 25 percent smaller than the change in the net international investment position. Consequently, even assuming the polar case, the effect on welfare in recent years would be less than that calculated by the Study Group.

The United Nations System of National Accounts

In this section we develop the thesis that the United Nations System of National Accounts (SNA), as it is being revised for approval in the next few years, provides a better framework than the NIPA's for dealing with many of the issues that underlie the concern of the creators of ISEW and that this framework overcomes some of the ISEW's shortcomings. The SNA has several attributes that are the source of its analytical potential: (1) it is comprehensive, integrated, and plays down the single-aggregate approach; (2) it is designed for use by countries around the world; and (3) it explicitly takes into account, by the provision of satellite accounts, the need to develop alternative concepts and definitions. We will highlight these attributes and several specific features in the overview of the SNA that follows.

The SNA: Structure and Purpose

The SNA is a comprehensive framework for recording estimates of the macroeconomic flows and stocks of the economy.[8] The SNA includes accounts that in the United States are called the national income and product accounts (NIPA's) and input-output accounts, both prepared by the Bureau of Economic Analysis, and the flow of funds accounts and balance sheets, both prepared by the Board of Governors of the Federal Reserve System. (The SNA does not include balance of payments accounts, which are considered a separate system. Nonetheless, because the presentation of foreign transactions in the SNA may be viewed as an embryonic balance of payments, harmony between the two systems is evolving.) In addition, the SNA includes a set of accounts that record changes in the prices of balance sheet items and other elements, such as destruction in natural disasters or mineral discoveries, that "explain" changes in the economy's net worth from one period to the next. Because such accounts are not prepared in the United States and because U.S. balance sheets are not complete, the SNA provides fuller coverage than the U.S. accounts.

Further, the SNA is an integrated framework--that is, the several subsets of accounts use the same concepts, definitions, and classifications. The U.S. accounts are less integrated, and thus do not facilitate, to the same extent as the SNA, analyses that draw upon estimates of consumption and investment, real and financial transactions, stocks and flows, etc. Although the NIPA's and input-output accounts are integrated and the NIPA's and balance of payments are reconciled by a few regularly published conceptual and statistical items, the NIPA's and flow of funds are less transparently reconcilable.

Also, the SNA presents a set of accounts that record the stocks and flows for each major economic group (called a sector). This structure facilitates analyses that treat a sector's multiple roles in the economy. For the household sector, for example, the structure facilitates analysis of the household as a producer, income recipient, consumer, saver, and holder of assets. The usual presentation of the U.S. accounts is more consolidated, although the separate sector accounts can be derived.

Consistent with these structural characteristics, the SNA plays down the role of any single aggregate such as GNP or its counterpart GDP (where "d" indicates domestic, referring to territory, rather than "n" for national, referring to the residence of the owner). First, the

SNA aims to provide a complete, albeit simplified, picture of an economy, so that provision of aggregates is not its sole, or even its main, purpose. Second, the SNA does, of course, provide aggregates--summary indicators of the economy from a particular point of view. However, because the SNA is comprehensive, it covers more than production. Thus, for the SNA even more than for the NIPA's, a summary measure of production, such as GNP, is only one of a number of aggregates to be used for macroeconomic analysis and comparisons over time and space.

The purpose of the United Nations in developing and maintaining the SNA is two-fold: 1) To provide the basis for international reporting of information needed by international organizations for operational purposes--for example, when setting borrowing terms, determining eligibility for assistance, and assessing contributions--and (2) to provide guidance to national statistical agencies designing or improving their own sets of economic accounts. Most countries with market economies follow the SNA. In the latest edition of the United Nations compilation of economic accounts estimates, almost 150 countries reported on the basis of the SNA. Thus, the SNA underlies the largest body of comparable national accounts estimates available. Further, even before the dramatic changes in Eastern Europe, many countries with centrally planned economies, which previously had prepared their economic accounts following a system based on Marxist principles, were preparing SNA totals and were interested in doing more with the SNA.

Satellite Accounts

The SNA in use today is over 20 years old, and it is undergoing a thorough review and revision. The process dates back to 1975, when the United Nations began a study of countries' experience in compiling and using the SNA. Subsequently, it was decided that the revision should update, clarify and simplify, and harmonize the SNA with other international guidelines. The updating was to reflect new economic institutions, statistical developments, and new analytical applications.

The recommendations for the revision will be discussed around the world in 1990; final agreement on a revised manual to describe and explain concepts, definitions, accounting structure, and other aspects of the revised system is expected in 1993. One of the recommendations that is especially relevant to the concerns of the Study Group that prepared the ISEW is the emphasis on "flexibility," which is implemented in part by the concept of satellite accounts.

At their present stage of evolution, satellite accounts cover a range of approaches. Some may be only an additional table. Others provide alternative constructs in a presentation like the central framework of the SNA to give a different picture of the overall economy. Still others provide a full picture of one field within the overall economy.

A table that presents estimates of the value of services provided by households for their own consumption illustrates the first approach. Continuing this illustration, the second would include these estimates in a presentation like the central framework, which would show--in addition to the consumption of these services--the imputed income associated with these services, the enlarged consumption and income totals, and perhaps some nonmonetary data drawn from time-use surveys.

The third approach--providing a full picture of one field within the overall economy--is an important development in national economic accounting. First in France and more recently in other European countries and in Canada, satellite accounts have been or are being prepared in fields such as health, education, environment, research and development, tourism, and agriculture. As mentioned earlier, the Bureau of Economic Analysis has prepared estimates of pollution abatement and control expenditures for a number of years, and these may be considered as first steps toward a satellite account on the environment.

The essence of these satellite accounts is the following set of characteristics:

- They are purpose-oriented.

- They are articulated with, but may depart from, the central framework.

- They feature expenditures for the field as the principal aggregate of the account.

- They delineate transactions and transactors relevant to the specific field, but the classifications of transactions and transactors are internally consistent.

- They are in the form of tables that answer three questions:

  - Who is producing, and what are the means of production?
  - Who is financing?
  - What is the result of the expense, and who is benefiting from or using the result?

- They encompass nonmonetary data--for example, relating to production, such as the stocks of equipment and number employed, or to beneficiaries, such as the number of persons-- when relevant.

The purpose-orientation is the key to the analytical role of these accounts. Heretofore, the economic accounts were largely organized in relation to production--the goods and services produced and the incomes earned--and used a sector breakdown. For a satellite account, the criterion for a transaction's inclusion is linkage to the purpose, not its relation to production. By cutting across sectors and incorporating additional information to provide a full picture of a function or area, satellite accounts provide a needed new dimension to the central framework.

A satellite account for health illustrates some of the strengths of these accounts. It would include not only the services purchased in a hospital by a patient, but also the services rendered free of charge to employees by a company doctor and the expenditures on health research in government laboratories. Satellite accounts are particularly useful in cases such as health when the goods and services involved are diverse in terms of their classification in the central framework--in the health example, as personal consumption expenditures, intermediate purchases by business, and government purchases. Similarly, they are particularly useful when the sector financing the expenditure is not the sector using or benefiting from the goods and services. Further, they allow a classification other than the one that is primary in the central framework; for example, the government expenditures of health research may have appeared in the central framework classified as research expenditures, but can be classified as health expenditure in the satellite accounts.

The strengths of satellite accounts--cutting across sectors and incorporating information either not in, or not easily accessible in, the central framework--makes them particularly suited for dealing with some of the major societal problems of today and the future.[9] It seems very likely, for example, that a health satellite account would have helped the Study Group define measures of health expenditures by households and by government that more closely approximated their desired separation of defensive expenditures from those that contribute to welfare.

Other Features

Several other recommendations for the revised SNA are relevant to particular concerns that the Study Group dealt with in constructing the ISEW.[10]

Consumption and consumption expenditures.   The revised SNA, it is recommended, will distinguish between consumption, defined as acquisition of a good or service for the satisfaction of a need or want, and consumption expenditure.   This distinction had been discussed for many years in connection with the development of welfare-oriented measures, with reconciliation of the SNA aggregates with those found in the economic accounting systems used by centrally planned economies, and with studies that make comparisons across time and countries in the face of differences in the public-private mix, such as for health services.

The distinction will be achieved by showing " individual" and "collective" components of consumption expenditure (that is, expenditure other than for durable goods and structures) for government and nonprofit institutions.   Household final consumption expenditure would have five components:

1. Household final consumption expenditure

2. Government final consumption expenditure
    a. Individual
    b. Collective

3. Nonprofit final consumption expenditure
    a. Individual
    b. Collective

Individual consumption refers to goods and services acquired by households for exclusive use of the household, and collective consumption refers to services provided to the community as a whole.

The separation of expenditures by government into individual and collective is to be made by reference to a classification of the functions of government. Specifically, government consumption expenditures (except that on general administration and research) in the following categories would be considered as individual: all of education, health, social security and welfare, sport and recreation, and culture and parts of provision of housing, collection of household refuse, and operation of transportation systems. Thus, household consumption exceeds household consumption expenditure to the extent that there are government and nonprofit institutions expenditures for goods and services in the categories designated as individual.

Services of consumer durables. The logic of treating refrigerators, cars and other consumer goods that last several years as investment and calculating an estimate of the services they provide to be included in consumption has long been argued. However, the recommendation is that the SNA continue to treat expenditures on, rather than services of, consumer durables as part of consumption. In recognition of the analytical interest in the stock of durables and in the depreciation of that stock, the balance sheets of the SNA are to show these items, with detail by type of durable, as memoranda items. Thus, analysts would have the data needed to build an opportunity cost measure of services by applying a rate of return, but the choice of the rate of return--the most controversial element--would be left to the analyst to make in the context in which the estimates would be used.

Natural resource accounting and accounting for the environment. At present, how natural resource accounting and accounting for the environment will fit into the revised SNA is still an unresolved, but very live, issue. Especially since the early 1980's, the international organizations sponsoring the revision of the SNA have made a substantial effort to develop environmental accounting. For example, the United Nations and World Bank held several joint workshops, and drawing on this work, the United Nations Statistical Office has outlined an approach in which environmental accounts would be SNA satellite accounts. The objectives of these accounts are listed below to illustrate the scope of the discussion.

- Measure expenditures for environmental protection;

- Assess the costs and benefits of environmental activities, processes, and effects, and account for "defensive expenditures" and the depletion of natural resources;

- Measure environmentally adjusted income and product (that is, derived by deducting from gross output not only the traditional intermediate consumption but also expenditures on environmental protection now included in final consumption), sustainable income and product (that is, derived by deducting, in addition, the environmental costs to assets that are now included in cost accounting), or both;

- Link physical resources with monetary accounting.

There has been agreement that the new manual should stress that GDP is not a measure of welfare and that care should be taken in interpreting the accounts. More specifically, the new manual is to discuss the interpretation of the main aggregates, such as GNP and GDP, in relation to environmental degradation, depletion, and defensive expenditures. So far, however, there has not been agreement on a recommendation to include the United Nations or any other suggested framework for a satellite account in the new manual. The argument that has prevailed is that too many questions of identifying, defining, and measuring environmental issues are as yet unresolved.

Work in environmental accounting continues. For example, the International Association for Research in Income and Wealth recently had planned a special conference on environmental accounting. Also, the United Nations is working on a draft handbook to attempt to clarify conceptual issues and procedures, and plans are being made to test the proposed methodology for satellite accounts in several countries. At the same time, interest in environmental accounting continues to grow. It is not improbable that progress in accounting and growing interest together will lead to a preliminary or experimental set of international guidelines for environmental satellite accounts by the time the new manual is finalized.

Summing Up

There are two recognized approaches to presenting measures of social and environmental forces that bear upon economic welfare. One is to use the estimates of imputed or actual additions and subtractions to GNP or some other economic accounts aggregate to compile an alternative aggregate. The other is to present the additions and subtractions "below the line" or in supplementary tables, allowing a user to design an aggregate reflecting particular values or uses if one is needed.[11] We presented a view in the first section about the use of a single aggregate that hinted at our preference. This view is reinforced by a belief that the SNA, especially as it will be revised in the next few years, has a number of structural characteristics and features that will facilitate a broad range of analyses and policymaking, including those of the kind that concern the Study Group. Support is building for the Bureau of Economic Analysis to modernize and extend the U.S. system of economic accounts by moving to the SNA. For example, in January 1990 the Chairman of the Council of Economic Advisers introduced a multi-year statistical initiative to improve federal statistics. One of the recommendations was that the United States move to the SNA by the mid-1990's.[12] Satellite accounts will play an important role in the modernized and extended system, and it seems to us that progress in measuring and analyzing a number of the Study Group's concerns could be made in the framework of satellite accounts.

Comments on the Setting for the ISEW

In the paper by the Study Group, the first several sections, beginning with "GNP and Related Measures" up through "Nordhaus and Tobin's Findings Considered," provide the setting in which the ISEW was offered. Even though the viability of the ISEW is not affected, we feel we need to take issue with two points in those sections. In general, our comments suggest that the Study Group unnecessarily sets up GNP as a clay pigeon.

Taking Issue

Recognition of GNP for what it is. The section "Measurement of Economic Welfare - Background" begins "Economists have long recognized the need for a measure of economic welfare other than GNP." That sentence could be interpreted as saying that some economists thought (or even still think) that GNP is a measure of welfare. That interpretation is encouraged by the next sentence, which comments that it was only by the time of the 1971 Conference on [Research in] Income and Wealth that it "became clear" that many users considered that the emphasis on market transactions in GNP led to too narrow a perspective for the measurement of economic and social performance. It seems useful, therefore, to document economists' views at key dates in the history of GNP and related measures to indicate what they have recognized and for how long.

The Study Group, in the section on GNP and Related Matters, notes that the Commerce Department began reporting measures of the product of the economy in 1934. That report was prepared under the direction of Simon Kuznets, a pioneer in developing national income and product estimates. In describing the uses and abuses of the measures of national income, the report noted that when the total of income paid out is adjusted for changes in the price level and calculated per capita, "the result is illuminating of movements in the nation's economic welfare." But, the report cautions, this and the several other uses mentioned are valuable only if the results are interpreted with the full realization of the definition of the measure: The estimates primarily cover the market economy (specifically excluding the household services by family member and services of consumer durables), are valued at market price, which is affected by income distribution, etc. Further, it goes on to say that additional problems are encountered when the estimates are interpreted from the point of view of economic welfare: Welfare cannot adequately be measured unless the personal distribution of income is known and account is taken of the cost of earning income. Therefore, the report concluded, welfare can scarcely be inferred from national income as defined.[13]

A report on approaches to economic accounting made by the United States, Canada, and Great Britain in 1944, referred to by the Study Group, describes the fundamental purpose of national income statistics. That report notes the following:

> This (accounting) approach to national income statistics perhaps tends to minimize the importance to be attached to any single series, such as national income, and to emphasize the interrelations among different types of transactions. It may be contrasted in particular to the welfare approach to national income measurement, which seeks to obtain a unique series, fluctuations in which may be accepted as a measure of changes in economic welfare. The proposals, however, do not suggest the elimination of any data analysts may consider useful in the measurement of welfare.[14]

Finally, for an overview of how and when the movement to develop broader measures developed, it is useful to refer to F. Thomas Juster (and associates), who has pioneered a theoretical framework for the measurement of well-being.

Concern among economists with the measurement of material well-being dates back to the early 1900s . . . The
major conceptual work in defining the boundaries of material well-being, as reflected by the concepts of National
Income and National Product, . . . is attributable to work by
Simon Kuznets, Milton Gilbert, and George Jaszi during
the 1930s and 1940s . . . Starting late in the 1950s and continuing through the 1960s and 1970s, a set of critiques of
the Income and Product(s) Accounts began to surface.
These critiques centered on issues of analytical relevance
and appropriate boundaries, and warrant being associated
more with a label like Social Accounts than that of
Economic Accounts.[15]

Use of GNP per capita in international comparisons. In the introduction to chapter 1, the Study Group first explains income and
product totals and then makes the transition to per capita measures
with the following statement:

Measuring output per person is certainly preferable to
using a national total if one is seeking to make welfare
comparisons. Unfortunately, this practice also lends legitimacy to the use of national income as a measure of economic welfare. As a result, many of the economic policies
of developing nations are aimed at increasing per capita
GNP--despite all the caveats made by economists that
GNP is not really a measure of economic welfare.

This statement seems questionable to us on several grounds. To
say that using GNP or some other aggregate on a per capita basis lends
legitimacy to the use of such measures as a measure of economic welfare is tantamount to saying that any attempt to remedy obvious defects
leads to greater misuse. Also, it is unclear to us what it is that the
Study Group identifies as causing--thus justifying the phrase "as a result"--economic policies to be aimed at increasing per capita GNP.
Certainly, it is not the availability per se of the measure; as we explore
below, it seems to us that the current lack of a more appropriate measure is the cause and that better approaches are actively being sought.

It is useful to take a quick look at the context in which GNP per
capita is presented by the World Bank. The World Bank is particularly
relevant to this discussion because its stated purposes is "to help devel-

oping member countries to improve economic and social conditions so that their people may live better and fuller lives."[16]

First, GNP per capita is presented in a way that clearly labels it for what it is. Even a booklet for nonspecialists, such as *The Development Data Book*, notes: "GNP per capita helps measure the material standards and well-being of a country, but it does not show whether all people share equally in the wealth of a country or whether they lead fulfilling lives."

Second, in this booklet as well as in the more sophisticated *World Development Report, 1989,* GNP per capita is but one of several indicators presented. Others include life expectancy at birth, primary school enrollment rate, merchandise exports, daily calorie supply per capita, and energy consumption.

Third, GNP per capita is used in international comparisons in part because it is widely recognized, if not completely understood, and is calculated in more or less the same way in many countries. This point was made earlier in suggesting that international comparability needs to be taken into account when developing policy-oriented indexes and measures. International organizations have examined the possibility of using other indicators both operationally and analytically. They reexamine these possibilities from time to time, but so far have decided that these indicators tend to be qualitative and not amenable to standardization that is needed for these operational purposes. In the meantime, as noted above, the international organizations are actively pursuing improvements, including the development of environmental accounting.

Updated Information

The section "GNP and Related Measures" opens by saying that an understanding of the origins and composition of GNP is important background, which is certainly true. However, background summaries are treacherous: The next paragraph makes too big a leap and is probably misleading. It refers to the initial statistics on net product--an aggregate--as being reported in 1934. It then jumps to the mobilization for World War II, using a quotation of Richard Ruggles to say that the consequent demand for data shaped *the accounts*. The point we want to make is that the product aggregate changed little during the 1940's; it was the accounting structure into which the product estimates were placed that evolved. Ruggles' paragraph from which the Study Group quoted closes in a way that confirms our point: "The emphasis thus shifted away from the earlier focus on national income aggregates to the estimation of how income was generated, received, and spent by the various sectors."[17]

In describing the evolution of the U.S. economic accounts, the same section notes that the system of accounts was supplemented in various ways and revised in 1958 and 1965, although it remained basically unchanged.   To be sure, the system has been basically unchanged, but it is probably misleading not to mention the comprehensive (or "benchmark") revisions in 1976, 1980, and 1985.   At the time of these comprehensive revisions, the Bureau of Economic Analysis reviews the definitions and classifications of the NIPA's and incorporates changes so that the accounts depict in an analytically useful way the evolving institutions in the economy and the economic activities in which they engage.   Further, preparation of another comprehensive revision for publication is underway.

In the section "Measurement of Economic Welfare--Background," reference is made to work done by the Bureau of Economic Analysis on non-market activity, raising the prospect that when the Bureau "completes the work" the United States will be closer to an officially recognized measure of economic welfare.   Since the preparation of Richard Ruggles' account, on which the Study Group relied, this work was abandoned; the decision to discontinue the work was made in the late 1970's in a period of budgetary constraint.   The work was quite useful, and in some areas it laid a foundation upon which others have built.[18]

Chapter 5

SOME REFLECTIONS ON THE ISEW

Robert R. Gottfried, Associate Professor
The University of the South, Sewanee, Tennessee

The ISEW authors have undertaken an ambitious and important project: the creation of an aggregate index which not only measures welfare better than either the GNP or MEW but which also considers welfare's sustainability. They have succeeded to a large degree. As the authors rightly point out, any such attempt at best will turn out to be imperfect. However, given the widespread *de facto* acceptance of GNP figures as a measure of welfare the authors' careful effort to produce an index better reflecting national well-being deserves applause.

In this vein this authors' comments attempt to support and strengthen the work represented by the ISEW approach. The first section of this essay offers some general reflections, particularly on the treatment of capital, natural capital, and sustainability. The second section considers additional questions raised by individual columns.

General Reflections

Overall Methodology

Following previous works the authors take as their starting point the data for consumption inasmuch as consumption may be the component of GNP which most closely measures welfare. However, this study and the previous works may be hampered in that they take the GNP framework as given. As is widely recognized, this framework measures economic activity, not welfare. Therefore, it might be worth reflecting for a moment on how welfare has been treated in economic theory and on the implications this treatment might have for an ISEW.

Microeconomic theory generally considers utility to be a function of the combination of goods and services consumed. The higher the level of disposable income (after-tax income), the more goods and services an individual can consume now or in the future (via savings). Consumption depends, however, not only on the level of income but also, among other things, on one's wealth. All other things equal, wealthy people buy more goods and services, given a certain level of disposable income, than do less wealthy individuals. In other words, welfare appears to be a function of both one's level of disposable income (a flow of dollars per year) and one's wealth (a stock of valuable assets). Aggregate disposable income and wealth, in turn, determine aggregate welfare.

Inasmuch as the ISEW is concerned with sustainability, the index attempts to measure society's ability to pass a given level of welfare on to future generations. Accordingly, it considers the stock of capital (the nation's wealth) being handed down to future generations and to the current generation in its later years, as well as the longevity of that capital. If sustainability also implies less vulnerability or risk, then greater capital also may provide a margin of safety which affects welfare.

Thus, aggregate welfare depends in some way on disposable income and capital. This seems to agree with common sense. If one assumes that welfare is a linear (additive) function of these two variables, one obtains:

$$\text{welfare} = Y_d + K, \quad \text{where } Y_d = \text{disposable income}$$
$$K = \text{capital}$$

Disposable income either can be produced domestically or can be received as transfers of income from abroad in the form of foreign aid grants. In the latter case that component of income may not be sustainable. So,

$$\text{welfare} = Y_n + Y_t + K, \text{ where n and t stand for the source of income,}$$
$$\text{national and transfer respectively}$$

Disposable income can either be consumed or saved, so $Y_d = C + S$, where C represents consumption and S savings. When using historical data, savings and investment are always equal, as the macroeconomic section of any introductory economics text will attest. So, welfare $= Y_n + I + K$

$\qquad = C_n + C_t + I + K$, were I is investment.

That is, welfare depends upon the level of current consumption and the resultant new amount of capital stock. To the extent that foreign transfers resulted in capital investment, then part of the unsustainable income from foreign transfers has changed into a sustainable source of future income. However, as a result, future income could be affected by subsequent foreign debt payments, vulnerability to the vagaries of export markets, and profit repatriation. These considerations could suggest decomposing investment into foreign and domestic-owned investment in an attempt to measure sustainability. Sustainable welfare also would require taking into account the presence of C_t in some way. This could be of particular importance in developing countries. Finally, should the above approach be valid, an index of aggregate economic welfare includes the stock of capital, not only net additions to the stock, or investment. The question remains as to whether or not the ISEW index should measure capital and investment in terms of the stock of capital and changes in it, or in terms of changes in the flow of services from the changing capital stock.

Nonrenewables. Natural Capital and Sustainability

When the discussion turns to sustainable welfare, environmental and resource questions, as well as the problem of time, immediately come to the fore. As seen below, considerations of sustainability and of how best to treat "natural capital" over time provide some guidance as to whether the capital stock should be measured in terms of its total value or in terms of the annual value of the services it provides.

Resource extraction and environmental degradation exert an influence over both present and future generations. The usual economic analysis utilizes interest rates to guide the rate of nonrenewable resource extraction and to value the effect of future environmental impacts on the current generation. The ISEW authors regard discounting future effects of present policies as socially unacceptable and therefore call for a zero discount rate. The subject of whether discount rates should be lower for efficient intergenerational allocation of resources and/or for intergenerational equity is a controversial one. Suffice it to say here that the authors have substantial support in the discipline for such a stance.

Hartwick and Olewiler (1986) point out that a constant level of consumption over generations (a prerequisite for sustainable welfare, according to some), given a constant population, implies an optimal savings rule that all resource rents be reinvested. This will occur if nonrenewable resource decision-makers utilize a zero discount rate.

Thus, the authors would appear to have some support, from the sustainability standpoint, for utilizing a zero discount rate and seeking a means for calculating the proportion of the rent on resources which should be reinvested in order to maintain a constant consumption level. In theory, to the extent that these rents *were* reinvested the future would be compensated for having less resources passed on to them. Aggregate welfare would remain unchanged. To the extent that these rents were not reinvested, however, society would lose. Thus, rather than subtract the resource rent as a matter of course, as suggested by the ISEW authors, it may be more appropriate to subtract the proportion of the rent not reinvested. Page, for instance, asserts that perhaps ninety percent of resource extraction is used for short-lived consumer goods.[1] Therefore, one could subtract ninety percent of the rents in the ISEW to reflect the loss of opportunity to the future. If the authors' concept of sustainability allows per capita consumption to rise over time, not remain constant, this would imply an increase in investment and saving now over that necessary to maintain a constant level of consumption. This author is not sure what this implies for the proportion of rent that would have to be invested. At first glance it would appear to approach 100% of rents. Exactly why the authors subtract 100% of the *total value* of minerals for welfare accounting purposes remains unclear to this writer.

As the authors note, a *financial* fund to compensate future generations will not compensate them adequately. Only by converting a proportion of the extracted resources into productive capacity can they compensate coming generations. A fund the value of which is rising at the same rate as resource prices in theory could enable future generations to buy the scarcer resources for capital formation. Meanwhile, however, society has wasted the previous resources. Converting resource rent into productive capital is equivalent to reinvesting a portion of the resource itself. Merely putting this rent into a fund allows these resources to be put to nonproductive uses and "lost" to future generations. Yet, even capital depreciates and lives a relatively short life. Thus, it fails to represent complete compensation to future citizens for the loss of options due to current resource extraction.

El Serafy's analysis and the above share a common shortcoming in that they fail to account for the environmental degradation caused by resource extraction and processing. Ecosystems provide a great deal of goods and services to society, as the ISEW authors note in their treatment of wetlands. As such, ecosystems constitute part of national wealth. Resource extraction decreases the amount of services rendered free to the economy by damaging these productive assets. Thus, the present should compensate future generations for the loss of these assets, as well as for the loss of nonrenewable resources.

The compensation for this lost capital provides an interesting set of issues. First, the ecosystem provides a variety of goods and services in differing amounts and longevities. The value of the ecosystem thus may vary over time depending upon the uses to which it is put. Second, if one attempts to obtain the present value of this potentially very long-lived productive asset at a zero discount rate, one merely needs to add up the annual values. Of course, this results in an infinite present value. As Hemingway once said, "A thousand years makes economics silly..."[2] For this reason it would appear more reasonable to deal with the annual services natural capital provides rather than with a changing stock of capital. Additions to or subtractions from the capital stock, as in ecosystem destruction, then appear as additions to or subtractions from the annual flow of capital services. The value of the annual services from natural capital will change as the demands placed upon that capital change over time. Thus, in general the ISEW authors appear to be on the right track in their treatment of this component of national welfare. Consistency, then, requires the use of services as the measure of man-made capital and investment as well. However, as noted in the detailed comments on specific columns below, the authors do not treat capital consistently. Sometimes they deal with capital services and sometimes with changes in capital stock. All capital-related columns should provide data on capital services, so that total capital services (higher or lower than the previous year) are reported.

Finally, the ecological understanding of "stability" provides some guidelines as to other factors that would be well to include in some way in the ISEW. Ecosystem stability consists of three aspects. First, ecosystems are *persistent*, or "stable," if the system remains constant over time; e.g., if biomass production maintains a constant level over time. Second, ecosystems exhibit *resistance* if they can withstand disturbance or change, whether regular or irregular. Third, ecosystems demonstrate *resilience* when they are able to recover from change. The latter two characteristics only can be measured after changes have occurred.[3] Taken a slightly different way sustainability also can imply the need to maintain flexibility of response in the face of uncertainty.

Sustainability as considered in the ISEW document refers primarily to the persistence of welfare. One could ask "How resilient and resistant is our welfare?" This could involve seeing how well the economy reacted to disturbance, as in the OPEC-induced changes of the 1970's and the drought of 1988. Would other patterns of production or of capital stock (e.g., more or less natural capital) have permitted a more rapid recovery or less disturbance in welfare? For instance, one could analyze input/output relationships in the economy, seeking industries or industry groups exhibiting low resistance and/or resilience, calculating the probabilities of disruptions in those areas and the national effects of disruption.[4] If other economic configurations could have provided more sustainability, how much would people have been willing to pay to achieve that sustainability? In the case of the drought, for instance, how much would society have been willing to pay annually to induce farmers to move to an agriculture less vulnerable to drought?[5] This could be a measure of annual loss of sustainability. Alternatively, one could consider the cost of making these structural economic changes.

Page points out that, as nonrenewable resource extraction increases, the future receives increased risk due to the increase in wastes and the decrease in available resources.[6] Society depends upon technological change to overcome the declining resource base. However, because society cannot *know* that the required technology will be developed or will come on line in time, and because technological change often presents uncalculated and perhaps unmanageable side effects, current generations pass on increased risk to future generations. How much extra risk does society encounter? How can this increased risk be factored into an index of aggregate welfare? Should risk be calculated in absolute terms or be considered relative to the minimum amount of risk that society could expect to achieve (for instance, perhaps under a renewable-energy-based economy with maximum recycling)?

Of course, these aspects of sustainability probably will take awhile to incorporate in an ISEW. This author offers these speculative comments with the hope that they will spur discussion of the broader context of sustainability.

Before proceeding to detailed comments on each column it might be worth exploring briefly the applicability of the ISEW approach to developing countries. One should be able to apply the general approach anywhere. However, data limitations will prove far more troublesome abroad. Income distribution figures, particularly up-to-date ones, either can be difficult to find or are nonexistent. Given the large income inequalities often occurring in developing nations data availability may serve as a large constraint on using the ISEW. Similarly, the services of household labor will loom particularly large in such an index. Such figures often will be difficult to obtain. They may have to be imputed from occasional site specific studies. Developing countries often lack environmental data, although again, because these countries generally have much lower levels of capital and rely much more obviously on their natural resource base than do developed countries, these data are of crucial importance. Finally, the question of sustainability as resistance and resilience, the ability to handle change, assumes great importance in smaller, poorer countries often at the mercy of international economic and political trends. Thus, application of the ISEW methodology in developing countries in general may require imagination and creativity. Nevertheless, it would be worth the effort.

Detailed Comments

Rather than comment individually on all columns the author wishes to express here his appreciation of the care and creativity the ISEW authors have shown in their treatment of many difficult areas, particularly those concerning the environment. The subsequent comments by column represent some suggestions for possible improvements.

Columns C and D. Index of Distributional Inequality and Weighted Personal Consumption.

The authors correctly point out the difficulties involved. This author agrees with the necessity of including equity considerations. Precedents do exist for weighting income. The GNP implicitly places equal weights on all individuals. In the benefit/cost literature and the related project evaluation literature some authors will allow for groups to be given larger weights and others smaller weights according to weights usually established by policy-makers. For instance, if government policy targets low-income groups, benefits accruing to them could be weighed more heavily than those received by upper income groups.

It would be helpful if the ISEW authors could discuss the rationale for the index they utilize. Why is this index preferred to some other? For instance, how does this result differ from assigning weights to each decile (where the sum of the weights equals one), multiplying each decile's share of consumption by the weight, and then summing the results? Which is preferred theoretically?

Further, how critical is the choice of the base or reference quintile? What would happen if, instead of taking the difference between each quintile and the richest, one were to take the difference between each quintile and the poorest? or an intermediate quintile? How sensitive is the index, and the overall results, to the choice of base quintile?

Column H. Public Expenditures on Education and Health (Consumption).

How do the authors treat primary and secondary education? It would appear that much of this education would constitute human capital formation. Yet, there appears to be no discussion or treatment of this question in the document or the index itself. Should this component be included, it might be possible to adjust these expenditures by changes in the literacy rate or some similar figure to correct for quality changes in primary and secondary education.

It should be noted that the authors claim to have omitted any estimates of human capital from changes in the stock of capital. However, by adding the portion of public health expenditures assumed to add to social welfare, it would appear that they could be including human capital formation here. Note that this would represent additions to capital, not services from capital.

Column J. Private Education and Health Expenditures.

Comments on health similar to those for Column H.

Column M. Cost of Urbanization.

As the authors correctly point out earlier in their paper, increasing land prices represent increases in the growing demand for a fixed resource. Urban land prices, according to land theory, are determined by many factors, particularly the demand for structures and the cost of construction. Thus, higher housing prices cause land prices to rise, not vice-versa. Rather than calculate changes in housing costs due to changes in land prices, it would be more appropriate to analyze the proportion of the increased demand for housing which is due to population growth. This effect could be entered into a model of the housing market to determine population's effect on housing prices. One then could determine the amount by which the price of land has risen due to the increment in housing prices. The two increases in prices would be the total effect of population growth on housing prices. Of course, in more general terms using econometrics one could attempt to measure the impact of population growth on prices in general, or on a group of basic commodities.

Column N. Damage from Auto Accidents.
Would this be included in Nordhaus and Tobin's urbanization adjustment measure (urban wage differentials)? Would this capture changes in the consumer durable and capital stock? If so, a measure of lost annual services might be preferable. Cumulative effects, adjusted for average vehicle life, would have to be utilized in a manner similar to the authors' treatment of wetland loss.

Column O. Water Pollution.
If damages can be divided into effects on flows (loss of annual recreation services, increased dredging costs) and stocks (lost capital capacity, as in damage to turbines and in decreased dam life due to sedimentation), this distinction would clarify the type of damage and permit converting the figures to loss of capital services as appropriate.

Column P. Air Pollution.
Comments similar to those for water pollution. Care needs to be taken to avoid duplication between effects of air pollution on the quality of urban life (part 5 of this component) and Column M, Cost of Urbanization, where urban land values and housing prices are affected by air quality.

Columns R and S. Loss of Wetlands and Farmland.
Given the state of data availability, the authors do an excellent job in this area. Here they deal with capital changes in terms of annual, cumulative loss of capital services. This should be the approach used in general for capital.

Column T. Loss of Nonrenewable Resources.
For sustainability to occur, the resource rents from resource extraction should be reinvested in capital (not financial assets, but machinery, equipment, etc.--see general comments in the preceding section). If the rents were invested, then capital services would be higher due to new capital formation. How should one treat the addition of productive capital arising from the extraction (and loss) of nonrenewable resources? Perhaps considering the process in terms of a double-entry type of bookkeeping system might help.

If one follows the mainstream economic view that capital and nonrenewables are perfect substitutes, the capital formation proceeding from the adequate investment of resource rents would offset the loss of the nonrenewable resources. Thus, the increase in capital services would be a form of credit. An annual debit of equal size could be subtracted in column T to show that welfare has remained constant. As the capital depreciates and its services eventually cease, the annual debit similarly would decline and go to zero.

If resource rents were not reinvested, which generally appears to be the case, then society would not receive the additional capital necessary to maintain persistent production. The ISEW would show a debit without an offsetting credit. In this case the services of the additional capital stock which would have resulted from investing resource rents could be subtracted from this column on a decreasing basis for each year of the average expected life of new capital. Should depletion of the resource base be considered to increase risk (as discussed above), the debit could be increased somewhat to reflect the greater risk. The approach suggested here would be more in keeping with that suggested in this essay than that suggested by El Serafy.

If one believes that capital cannot substitute totally for nonrenewables, one could continue some portion of the annual debit as a constant after capital services have ceased. This would reflect the fact that, because the resources no longer are available and neither is the compensating capital, to that extent new capital services would appear to offset the annual debit and minimize the decline in welfare. In the absence of recycling, capital formation to replace depreciation would require resource extraction and thereby would add to the annual debit as well as to capital services. This would result in a decline in welfare *despite* capital formation. Should depletion of the resource base be considered to increase risk (as discussed above), the increases in capital services due to the investment of resource rents could be reduced somewhat to reflect the increased risk.

Column W. Net International Position.

Being a net debtor is particularly a problem if the borrowing country does so for consumption purposes, not if it borrows for capital formation. The latter generates income which can be used to pay the lender. The U.S.A. grew in its early years by just such an arrangement. Thus, this measure would not signal weakness necessarily in developing countries while it might, though not necessarily, for developed countries.

A preferable measure of sustainability in this vein instead might be the ratio of international debt service to export earnings. The more that export earnings must be used to pay international debtors the more drag the international indebtedness places on the economy. Also, higher ratios make the economy more vulnerable to disruptions in its ability to earn foreign exchange. Thus, as a measure of sustainability this proxy appears to have a clearer meaning than that utilized in the ISEW because it raises issues of resistance and resilience of the economy. However, in the case of the U.S.A. its application may be a bit less suitable due to the fact that much foreign debt is owed in dollars, not foreign exchange. However, in this author's opinion its interpretation is still clearer than that of the net international position. Further thought is required as to how to utilize this type of measure within the ISEW framework.

Columns E,F,G,H,J,O,R,S,U,V.

These columns bear the brunt of the problem of how to treat capital. This author has asserted that services from the entire capital stock should be reported every year in order to make clear the level of welfare. Columns E, F, G, R, and S report capital in terms of annual services. Columns H, J, O, U, and V, on the other hand, report changes in the capital stock. Regardless of whether one accepts the authors' viewpoint these columns should treat capital consistently by choosing one or the other approach.

Chapter 6

MEASURING LOCAL ECONOMIC WELL-BEING: PER CAPITA INCOME AND LOCAL ECONOMIC HEALTH

Thomas Michael Power, Professor and Chair
Economics Department, University of Montana, Missoula

1. Introduction

Economic policy is not only (or, even, primarily) made at the national level. Each small city, rural area, region, state, and multi-state area has its own groups of public and private "promoters" who seek to stimulate the quantitative expansion of the local or regional commercial economy. These groups are engaged in a national, even international, competition to attract a larger amount of capital, labor, and other resources to their areas. These local and regional economic efforts and policies have as real an impact upon the social and natural environment as any national policy. In fact, it may be that most public economic policy is actually made and implemented at this decentralized level.

Because of this, it is important to look at how economic welfare is measured at the local level and how that measurement influences local economic policy. The problem of misleading economic indicators is not limited to national measures like GNP. This chapter will explore both the unique problems associated with local measures of economic well-being as well as problems similar to those associated with national indices of economic welfare.

2. Conventional Measures of Local Economic Health

On the state and local level the summary statistic regularly used to indicate the relative economic well-being of a local area is per capita income, total personal income divided by the size of the local population. When per capita income is below the national average or its growth is lagging behind the national growth rate, this is taken to indicate that something is lacking in the local economy and various local development policies are suggested to correct the situation. Since close to two-thirds of the states have per capita incomes below the national average, including most nonmetropolitan areas, this statistic paints a rather negative picture of most of the geographic area of the nation.

Typically, this summary statistic is also used to suggest a particular set of public policy measures: If average incomes are low, recruitment of new high wage firms appears as a fairly direct solution. If successful, it is casually assumed, such recruitment efforts would boost average earnings which the per capita income statistic has demonstrated are too low. In addition, such job recruitment, even if it does not bring in unusually high paying jobs, would, it is assumed, reduce unemployment and provide more job opportunities for multiple family members and in these ways boost average family income.

Given the important role that per capita income has played in both measuring local economic well-being and in suggesting appropriate economic development policies, it is vital to understand just what this statistic actually measures and what the various forces are that determine its level at the state or local level.

The problems with using per capita income as a measure of local economic well-being partly parallel some of the problems associated with the use of GNP to measure national economic welfare. But the measurement of local economic welfare in the context of a national economy with mobile capital and population raises an additional layer of complications and problems of interpretation.

3. Per Capita Income: Its Intuitively Obvious Interpretations and Their Conceptual Problems

Since the average income available per person to support consumption expenditures would seem to determine household access to necessary and desirable goods and services, one might expect it to give us some indication of at least the potential economic welfare of the population.

"Potential" is used here because measures of average income ignore the actual distribution of that income. As chapters 1 and 2 have
made clear, income can be relatively concentrated in the hands of a sub-
set of households in a way that makes average income a rather misleading indicator of the general well-being of the total population
while actually damaging overall economic welfare. But this distributional problem with interpreting per capita income is *not* the focus of
this paper.

There are problems with the conceptual underpinnings of the familiar interpretation of per capita income and with the efficacy of the
policies derived from its interpretation. The policy problems are tied to
the extent to which job recruitment and creation actually impact average wages, incomes, and unemployment rates. In a mobile economy
where workers can shift to where incomes and employment opportunities are greatest, job creation may well not have the assumed effects
on local economic well-being. Immigration and/or reduced outmigration may put downward pressure on wages and boost unemployment
rates. This practical aspect of policies aimed at boosting per capita income has been discussed elsewhere.[1]

It is the conceptual issues associated with the interpretation of
per capita income statistics that are the focus of this paper. These conceptual problems are divided into two groups. First is the possibility
that geographic differences in per capita income reflect not real differences in economic well-being but compensating differentials associated
with regionally specific characteristics that directly affect economic
well-being while offsetting the differences in average money income.
The second set of problems in interpreting differences in per capita income is associated with the way voluntary and, assumedly, welfare-en-
hancing, household decisions rather than external economic forces affect the level of per capita income.

There is plenty of reason to suspect the conventional economic
interpretation that per capita income differences reflect real differences
in local economic well-being that can be effectively eliminated through
local job creation programs. In the first place, per capita income differences between areas have persisted throughout this century. Despite
massive shifts of labor, capital, and industry between regions, significant differentials can still be found. Connecticut, New Jersey, and
California have had per capita incomes fifty to one hundred percent
higher than those in Mississippi, South Carolina, and Arkansas for fifty
years or more despite the industrialization of the South and massive
migration both from and to the South and West.[2] Although those dif-

ferences have narrowed over time in the past, they have also, more recently, grown.[3]

This suggests that whatever the determinants of these differences, they are not due to short run labor market disequilibria. Local surplus labor supplies or excess labor demands are not likely explanations in a mobile economy for a phenomenon this persistent. This raises the possibility that the differences in per capita incomes are not tied to disequilibrium at all and may be unrelated to actual differences in local economic well-being. If that is the case, the current use of those statistics to guide local economic development policy could be misguided.

4. Per Capita Income: The Component Parts

Arithmetically per capita income can be expressed as the product of several component parts:

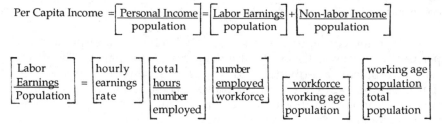

Total hours divided by the number employed is the average hours worked per year (HOURS).

The number employed divided by the workforce is the employment rate which is equal to one minus the unemployment rate (UER).

The workforce divided by the working age population is the labor force participation rate (LFPR).

The working age population divided by the total population is the working age fraction which is equal to one minus the dependency rate (DEPEND).

Thus labor income per capita can be looked upon as a function of the hourly wage rate, the number of hours worked, the rate of unemployment, the labor force participation rate, and the dependency ratio.

Finally, if economic well-being is related to per capita income, it must be *real* per capita income, income adjusted for the local cost of living. It is *real* purchasing power that allows a household to gain access to the goods and services it seeks. This adds another variable to the expression for real per capita income, local cost of living (COL).

$$PCYr = (wage)\ (hours)\ (1\text{-}UER)\ (LFPR)\ (1\text{-}DEPEND)\ (COL) + \left[\frac{(Yproperty + Ytransfer)\ COL}{Population}\right]$$

where Yproperty is property income (rent, interest, dividends) and Ytransfer is transfer payments (retirement income, social security, unemployment compensation, welfare payments, etc.).

Each of these nine variables can differ among regions with resulting differences in regional per capita incomes. What we wish to explore in this paper are the implications for local economic welfare of such differences in these variables.

5. Compensating Differences Due to Geographically Specific Characteristics

If various areas have geographically specific characteristics about which the general population has systematic preferences, the welfare of residents in those areas will be determined by the combination of income, employment, and those geographically specific qualities. If equilibrium in population movement is to be attained, overall welfare as determined by *both* the income/employment characteristics and the geographically specific qualities must be the same in all areas to the marginal migrant. If this is not the case, migration will continue, labor markets will continue to adjust, and, possibly, the geographically specific qualities will continue to be modified by the demographic and economic changes. For equilibrium to be attained, areas with particularly attractive geographic qualities will have to have somewhat unattractive employment/income characteristics. That is, there will have to be compensating differences in the employment/income characteristics of particularly attractive or particularly unattractive areas, or migration equilibrium will not be reached and population will continue to shift and, as a result, income, employment, and cost of living characteristics as well as social and natural environmental characteristics will continue to change.

Nordhaus' and Tobin's original Measure of Economic Welfare[4] included a downward adjustment from GNP associated with the increased concentration of the U.S. population in large urban areas. The conceptual basis for that adjustment was this same concept of compensating wage differentials: the likelihood that a significant part of the higher wages paid in our larger urban areas was paid simply to compensate residents for welfare-damaging features of the living conditions in densely populated urban areas.

a. Geographic Differences in Cost of Living

That local wages would adjust significantly to offset a particular local characteristic is widely accepted when it comes to local cost of living. Areas with particularly high costs of living are expected to have significantly higher money wage and income levels. In fact, one of the major explanations for the persistent differences in money wage rates between regions are the persistent cost of living differences. When these are taken into account, much of the regional variation in income and earnings disappears.[5]

In chapter 2, the ISEW was adjusted for the higher cost of living in dense urban areas by subtracting out increases in the value of residential land that gets built into the higher cost of housing. As the population shifts into densely settled urban/suburban/exurban belts such as the Boston to Washington, D.C. and the San Diego to San Francisco areas, land values and housing costs rise dramatically even though housing quality is not improved. This adjustment to the ISEW seeks to remove this element of a high cost of living from the national measure of economic welfare. However, as Professor Mishan has pointed out in his essay, this adjustment in developing the ISEW may involve double counting since the ISEW also uses the GNP deflator to remove changes in the cost of living over time. The main point and our purpose here is that an adjustment must be made to reflect cost of living or one gets misleading indicators of economic well-being. This is true at the level of the local economy too.

This is not to say that wages are expected to adjust dollar for dollar to the cost of living. The relationship between cost of living and equilibrium wage levels is more complex than that.[6] But one certainly expects and finds wages varying in a way to compensate for cost of living differentials.

This undermines any direct use of money wage or per capita income differentials to indicate relative economic health. As Krumm concluded: economic analysis provides no support for arguments that nominal regional wage differences reflect systematic differences in real wages and well-being.[7] Before interpreting nominal wage and income differences in such a way, adjustments for cost of living differences have to be made. Unfortunately, there is no reliable and systematic measure of such geographic cost of living differences. Geographic cost of living differences are not regularly and systematically measured by any public agency or research organization. As a result, we have no easy way to interpret the welfare implications of geographic differences in per capita income. What we do know is that all of the differences in local per capita incomes do *not* reflect differences in real purchasing power and therefore economic well-being.

Although differences in cost of living play an important role in explaining local wage rates and therefore local per capita income, all of the regional differences in wages cannot be explained in this way. Even when local wages are stated in real terms, adjusted for local cost of living differences, there are significant and persistent geographic differences.[8]

b. Wage Adjustments to Geographic Differences in Non-marketed Amenities

Cost of living is just one of many geographically specific characteristics that affect residents' well-being in a positive or negative manner and, as a result, call forth compensating differences in local employment and income characteristics. Other obvious candidates are climate (including temperature extremes, sunshine, humidity, and wind speed), local public services (including schools), social characteristics (including crime, poverty, and racial makeup), the quality of the natural environment (including air, water, visual, and recreational qualities), and cultural richness and diversity.

In chapter 2, the national Index of Sustainable Economic Welfare included adjustments for some of these including the costs of urbanization, air, water, and noise pollution. Similar adjustments covering a broad range of local characteristics are necessary before local per capita income is likely to be an accurate indicator of local welfare. But at the local level, because people can "vote with their feet" some of these important differences in local environmental quality may already be reflected, directly and indirectly, in other economic measures.

Empirical economic analysis over the last two decades has documented the economic value of many of these geographically specific qualities or local amenities to households.[9] In addition, empirical research has established that households have clear patterns of preference with respect to these amenities and modify their economic behavior in the pursuit of them.[10] It would be surprising, therefore, if there were not compensating adjustments in money wages related to the geographic distribution of these amenities.

Actually, the interaction between local markets and geographically specific qualities is not limited only to wage and employment characteristics. High amenity areas are also likely to have higher land values. These high land values will be reflected in higher rents. The higher rents will raise the cost of local housing and/or commuting and, as a result, the cost of locally produced goods and services. These higher costs will shift the local cost of living upward. In that sense the cost of living and local amenity values are not independent of one another.

The cost of living and local amenities will interact in another way. Climatic characteristics can influence heating and cooling costs as well as the construction cost of buildings. They may also affect clothing and automotive expenses. The point is that it is cheaper to live in areas with moderate, warm climates than in areas subject to extreme heat, cold, humidity, or wind speed.

Because of these two types of interaction between local amenities and cost of living, it is not clear that the separate effects of cost of living and amenities on compensating labor market adjustments can be determined. A particularly attractive area with respect to amenities may have high rental costs and, therefore, a higher cost of living. The higher cost of living would require offsetting higher local wages while the high amenity values would require offsetting lower local wages. The size and even sign of the effect on local wages may be indeterminate, but that would not be evidence that compensating local adjustments were nonexistent.

Since the mid-1970s economic studies have shown that local differences in the availability of amenities have a significant impact on local wage levels. I have reviewed that literature elsewhere.[11] These compensating differences in wage rates, of course, do not represent lower levels of local economic well-being. Rather, they represent the higher values derived from the local amenities.

The approach taken in these early studies was to relate local wage rates or income per capita to measures of local amenities (or dis-amenities), labor quality, and labor market conditions. The assumption was that the value of local amenities would be reflected entirely in wage differentials. More recent studies of this type have confirmed the impact of local amenities on local earnings.[12] These analyses, however, have focused almost exclusively upon the labor supply side of the local labor market. Only household decisions as "consumers" of local amenities are taken into account. The larger supply of labor attracted by local amenities is seen as putting downward pressure on wages and the full value of the amenities is assumed captured in the wage differentials that result.

This hedonic wage equation approach to estimating the value of local amenities is incomplete for two reasons. First, it ignores the labor demand or production side. Second, it ignores the possibility that inter-regional differences in rents will pick up part of the impact of local amenity differences.

Firms producing for national markets will respond to local wage differentials by adjusting their demand for labor. Higher local labor costs cannot be passed on in a competitive market. Therefore, firms will not locate in areas with higher wage levels unless there are offset-ting productivity advantages associated with that location. In addition, local amenity characteristics may affect other production costs.

High amenity areas can be expected to have higher land rental values because households compete to gain access to the amenity by purchasing living space. Producers will also have to adjust their pro-duction and location decisions to account for these higher rents which also cannot be passed on in a competitive market.

When both the production side and the interaction with land rental values are modeled along with the household location site, it be-comes clear that in general the value of the local amenities will be re-flected only partially in wages. Part of the adjustment will be through land rents.[13] Graves has gone so far as to suggest that one could simply use geographic differences in rental values to represent the aggregate of all amenity differences in a local area.[14]

This more complete analysis that recognizes adjustments on the production side as well as adjustments in rental values, suggests that geographic differences in amenities will not have as large an impact on local wages as they would if it were assumed that all of the impact was captured in wages. But since higher land rental values will increase the cost of living, this approach introduces another way that amenities can impact *real* wages, through the cost of living. *Nominal* local wage rates will not be as low as the full value of the amenity differences, but *real* local wages, when the local higher cost of living is taken into account, will. The conclusion from the earlier compensating wage differential studies remains: regional wage differentials cannot be interpreted simply as reflecting geographic differences in economic well-being; they must be looked upon as also reflecting the difference in the value of locally available amenities.[15]

This relatively complex interaction between local amenity values, land rental values, commuting costs, the cost of living, and the production advantages of a particular location suggests that the relatively simple adjustments to GNP made in chapter 2 to account for the costs of urbanization, commuting, air, water, and noise pollution can only be looked upon as crude first approximations of the type of adjustments that would also be necessary before geographic differences in per capita income could be interpreted as indicating differences in local economic welfare.

c. Compensating Differentials in Employment Characteristics

Two of the variables determining labor earnings per capita refer to employment: the unemployment rate and the labor force participation rate. One interpretation of a low labor force participation rate is that a lack of employment opportunities and low wages discourage people from entering or remaining a part of the labor force. This in turn depresses per capita income.

If households are guided in their location decisions by the pursuit of maximum economic well-being, they would take into account the employment potential and relevant wages for all family members. They would look for locational opportunities that allow them to maximize total family income (after accounting for the opportunity costs of labor force participation). If that is the case, lower wage rates for one family member may be accepted in exchange for increased employment opportunities for other family members. There is some evidence of this. Goetz and Huang found that the most important "environmental" attribute of a local area in explaining average male earnings was the ratio of female to male employment.[16] The more women employed relative to men, the lower the wage paid to men. This was interpreted by Goetz and Huang as indicating a trade off that families made, accepting lower wages for the husband in exchange for greater employment opportunities for the wife. In this situation, one would not want to interpret a lower wage rate paid to males as necessarily reflecting lower economic welfare for the household. Local per capita income, however, *would* reflect the full trade off: both the higher labor force participation rate as well as the lower male wage rate would influence the calculation of per capita income.

This suggests that regional differences in labor force participation rates should not be interpreted directly as reflecting differences in local economic well-being through their impact on per capita income. Besides there being a household decision to be made between household work/leisure and money income that will be discussed below, there may also be a trade off between wage rate and labor force participation in the location decision. If that is the case, one may not be able to manipulate labor force participation rates and wage rates independent of one another to raise per capita income. Increases in one may only come at the cost of decreases in the other. If households are in locational equilibrium given the existing mix of wage rates and employment opportunities for family members, it is not clear that per capita income can be enhanced by, for instance, boosting local wage levels. Such higher local wage levels would make the area a preferred area, given the combination of wage rates and employment opportunities, and migration to the areas would increase. The increase in the workforce and population would put downward pressure on wages and per capita incomes. The net effect on local per capita income cannot be predicted.

Unemployment rates can adjust in compensating ways too. If, from an amenity point of view, an area is not a particularly attractive one in which to live, outmigration may take place quite readily. As a result, unemployment rates may be quite low even if employment opportunities are very limited. On the other hand, areas that are attractive from an amenity point of view will attract and hold people longer as they seek ways of supporting themselves so that they can stay in the area and enjoy the local qualities. As a result, unemployment rates may be quite high no matter how rapidly jobs are created.

The unusually low unemployment rates in Massachusetts during the 1980's, for instance, were not tied to a high rate of job creation. Rather they were associated with ongoing net outmigration despite the high wage rates there. The negative amenity characteristics of Massachusetts' urban frost belt centers as well as the high cost of housing may well have been the secret behind the low unemployment rates rather than the "booming" economy. Similarly, the persistently high unemployment rates in some rural counties in the West (e.g. Western Montana) over the last decade may be tied to efforts by residents to maintain access to the amenity characteristics of the region despite the limited employment opportunities. Without that explanation, it is hard to understand the failure of the population for a decade or more to adjust to the actual employment opportunities found in these areas some of which are located less than a hundred miles from urban areas with much lower unemployment rates.

d. Conclusions on Compensating Differentials and Differences in Per Capita Income

In a national economy with mobile labor where there are geographically specific differences between areas in qualities of significant importance to households, there will be differences in money wage rates, cost of living, unemployment, and labor force participation rates which do not reflect differences in local economic well-being. Such geographic differences in average income will reflect the impact of geographically specific qualities on residents' welfare and will be compensating in nature. That is, average incomes will have to be higher in those areas where geographically specific qualities contribute the least to residents' well-being. Areas with especially attractive qualities will have lower average incomes, inferior employment opportunities, and higher costs of living *because* the area is attractive.

These compensating differences will consist in a rather complex interaction between all four of the variables. In that situation, local economic well-being cannot be measured by per capita income. Furthermore, local economic policies *cannot* eliminate the income and employment differences except by eliminating the locally specific attractive features of a local area which would not seem to be a very rational public policy.

The size of the relative impact of geographic differences in amenity qualities on, say, average money income is likely to be significant. In chapter 2, in the process of developing an Index of Sustainable Economic Welfare, several adjustments related to the geographically specific qualities discussed above were incorporated into the ISEW index. If these are put in per capita terms and the range of geographic variation is considered, one can get a feeling for the impact they can have on per capita income. Air, water, and long term environmental damage amounted almost to $300 billion or about $1200 per person in 1972 dollars. This represented 17 percent of per capita GNP on average across the entire nation. If, however, this environmental damage is unevenly distributed so that some areas face environmental damage only a quarter of the national average and other areas face damage twice the national average, the differences between areas in terms of the welfare actually experienced could be as much as 30 percent of per capita income.

Similarly, one could explore the impact on local well-being associated with the uneven geographic distribution of the costs of urbanization and commuting. In the ISEW analysis in chapter 2, these total $85 billion or $354 per person per year averaged across the entire nation (in 1972 dollars which were worth over three times what a dollar was worth in 1990). But if some areas face almost none of these costs while other areas face levels three times the national average, differences in these costs could cause as much as a 15 percent difference in local economic welfare. Suggesting that some areas face urbanization costs three times the national average is not outrageous. High land rents and long commutes *are* concentrated in a few areas in the nation. Housing costs in Boston, Manhattan, Los Angeles, and San Francisco *are* over three times housing costs in most nonmetropolitan areas and most urban areas in the interior of the country. Land rental values (the value of a house and lot less the value of the house alone) differ by a much larger factor.

Thus, just these two adjustments to the ISEW, if applied to differences in locally specific qualities could lead to almost a fifty percent difference in *measured* local economic well-being between areas with extreme differences in environmental quality and cost of living. That is, economic well-being could be over- or under-stated by as much as 50 percent. This should not be startling or taken as an exaggeration. Per capita incomes differ by as much as 100 percent between the states and by even larger amounts between the largest metropolitan areas and rural areas. Yet there is no massive population flow from the poorer of the states to the richer (e.g. from the north and south central states to New England or from most small heartland cities to metropolitan New York). In fact, the flow often has been in the opposite direction, This suggests that the general population is more cognizant of the misleading nature of per capita income statistics than are the business economists who regularly use them to guide local economic policy.

This is not to say that *all* such regional variations in these variables and the accompanying variations in per capita income are compensating in nature and unrelated to differences in local economic well-being. It is simply a serious warning that the conventional economic interpretation of regional wage and income differences as accurate measures of differences in economic welfare is far too simplistic and in conflict with both economic theory and empirical research.

6. Household Decisions and Per Capita Income

Three of the variables that determine per capita income are associated with decisions that households have to make about what pattern of behavior is best for them given their preferences and the tradeoffs the economy presents to them. These variables include the dependency ratio, the labor force participation rate, and the hours worked per year.

Consumption theory suggests that for each of these choices, households will weigh both the opportunity costs associated with each alternative and the strength of its members' preferences, and make a decision that provides the household with the greatest level of satisfaction. Each of these decisions will affect family income per person and, therefore, per capita income in the local economy, making it higher or lower. But since this impact on per capita income is the consequence of an optimizing decision by the household, we cannot label the decisions that move per capita income one way as opposed to another superior from the point of view of the households' economic well-being. Assumedly, whatever direction per capita income moves as a result of these household choices, households have chosen a path that improves their welfare as best they can. If those choices cause per capita income to be lower than it otherwise could have been, this is not a sign that households are worse off, simply a sign that households, at the margin, found the satisfactions associated with noncommercial activities superior to those associated with additional money income.

The household decisions at issue are the following:

a. The decision as to how many children to have.

b. The decision as to how the family's work efforts are to be split between home and the commercial labor market.

c. The decision as to how to divide the family's time between income earning work and leisure activities.

It should be noted that in developing the Index of Sustainable Economic Welfare in chapter 2, adjustments were considered to reflect changes over time in the amount of leisure time and the value of household work. No adjustment was ultimately made for leisure both because of the difficulty in evaluating it and because the division between work time and leisure time has not changed much over the last half century. An adjustment was made to reflect the value of economic activity that takes place within the household. In that sense, we take up here these same conceptual problems but look at them from the point of view of measuring regional differences in economic well-being. In addition, we discuss the impact of the decision to have more or less children on measures of economic welfare.

a. Family Size and the Dependency Ratio

The dependency ratio will rise and per capita income fall as households increase the number of children they choose to have. In the context of world-wide resource shortages and environmental pressures, a larger population may threaten the potential well-being of all residents. But within the household, the decision to have children cannot be looked upon solely as one that makes the household worse off simply because resources have to be diverted to support and raise the children. With an additional child, income available per family member will fall as the available resources are spread over more members, but to the parent there is the offseting satisfactions associated with having the children. It would seem grossly inappropriate within the context of household decision making to treat children as simply a gigantic cost that burdens the household.

Yet that is what is done when the per capita income of a state such as Utah with 38 percent of its population under eighteen is compared to states such as Connecticut which only has 24 percent of its population this young. This difference in the percentage of children in the population by itself would lead Utah to appear to be 20 percent "poorer" than Connecticut. It is not at all clear that that would be a legitimate economic conclusion. To accept that interpretation is to assume that families that choose to have children have made a mistake and made a choice that damaged their well-being. In that context, the boom towns surrounding large construction, oil, gas, and mining projects, populated heavily by young men with no resident families would have the highest economic well-being because there would be no dependents present. Since few, if any, would judge this to be an ideal setting in which to live, something is clearly wrong with an economic indicator that suggests that such a situation would be superior to one in which children and the elderly were present in the community.

b. The Labor Force Participation Ratio

As more family members work outside of the home for money income, per capita income rises. Straight comparisons of per capita incomes meant to tell us something about economic well-being implicitly assume that there is zero opportunity cost associated with working outside the home. The value of household work and/or family members' leisure time is assumed to be zero. This clearly is inappropriate. As more family members work outside the home, either the quality of home services declines, those home services now have to be purchased, or the amount of leisure time declines. All of these alternatives represent costs that should be offset against the additional money income that the work outside the home produces before comparisons of economic well-being are made.

As discussed in chapter 2, the services provided to families as a result of housework are quite valuable. An estimate for 1973 put that value at two-thirds of the household's after-tax money income.[17] A more recent estimate puts the value of the work of a full time homemaker with two young children at almost $18,000 per year[18] (expressed in 1987 dollars). If that homemaker were employed outside the home, the number of hours spent on household production would decline by about 25 percent.[19] This suggests both a decline in the level of household services and a major reduction in leisure time. In making welfare comparisons between areas with different labor force participation rates, the loss of welfare associated with this opportunity cost of employment outside the home would have to be taken into account. If this is not done, the difference between the 62 percent female labor force participation rate in Iowa and New Hampshire and the 48 percent rate in New York and Pennsylvania, almost a 30 percent difference, could significantly distort welfare comparisons.

That households do carefully weigh these opportunity costs of working outside the home has long been documented by economic studies. For instance, when male earnings are high, relaxing the budget constraint on households, the female labor force participation tends to be lower.[20] This rational household adjustment is likely to lower per capita income, indicating that the household and community is worse off. But it involves several offsetting changes in the determinants of per capita income which will keep per capita income from fully reflecting the improvement in household well-being: wage levels are higher, the labor force participation rate is lower, levels of expenditures on household services substitutes are likely to be lower, leisure time is greater, and the quality of household services is likely to be higher. The per capita income statistic is incapable of reflecting the overall welfare impact of these adjustments.

c. Number of Hours Worked

Although a forty hour work week continues to be typical of many jobs, the increasing importance of jobs in services and retail trade where a 30 hour or less work week is more typical has increased the range of work weeks associated with various jobs. In the early 1980s only about half of all employees were working a 38 to 42 hour work week. About a quarter were working considerably less than this and about a quarter were working much more than this. Some of those working less typically held what were considered part-time or seasonal jobs but others had "full time" jobs with work weeks well below 40 hours. Those working much more than 40 hour weeks often held more than one job or were regularly working for overtime pay.[21]

Although the hours an employee works is often looked upon as something dictated by the employer or labor market conditions, the changing structure of the labor market makes this view something of an exaggeration. As more women have entered the labor force and as the age of those enrolled in higher education has risen, many people have sought less than full time employment. The shift in employment opportunities to retail trade and services has facilitated meeting these preferences because of the greater flexibility in scheduling workers that is possible in these fields. It also seems appropriate to look at those holding more than one job as having made a choice rather than having been "forced" into working the additional hours. This is not to deny that limited employment opportunities do force significant numbers of people who would like full time employment to accept part time and seasonal employment. Even where this is the case, there usually are still valuable uses to which the nonemployment time is put.

The traditional microeconomic modeling of employment choice has the potential employee comparing the money wage associated with additional hours of work against the opportunity cost of lost leisure time and displaced productive activities outside the commercial workplace. This situation for working women with families was discussed above.   When per capita incomes are compared between locations where the number of hours worked are significantly different, as will be the case in locations with different mixes of manufacturing and service industries, the implicit assumption is made that there is no opportunity cost associated with additional hours of employment.   This would be appropriate only in the extreme situation where the people working shorter hours placed zero value on the activities in which that shorter work week allowed them to engage.   For some this may be a reasonable approximation.   For most, however, this would represent a gross distortion.

The value of time away from the job may depend upon the richness of the recreational, cultural, and social opportunities in the surrounding area.   For nonmetropolitan areas with abundant high quality recreational opportunities (fishing, hunting, hiking, etc.), for instance, reduced work hours may have a substantial value.   Put the other way, additional hours of work may have a high opportunity cost.   To the extent that reduced work hours and money income are offset by increased nonmarket activities that have substantial positive values, differences in per capita incomes associated with differences in hours worked will not accurately reflect differences in economic well-being.

d. Conclusions on the Impact of Household
Decisions on Per Capita Income

In different regions of the country, households have made different decisions about the number of children to have, the number of hours to spend on household as opposed to commercial market activities, and the number of hours to work.   These decisions were not made in a vacuum.   Local commercial market conditions, no doubt, had a significant impact on these decisions and some of them can be seen as more or less "forced" upon households by limited local income and employment opportunities.   But that does not mean that the full dollar value of the resulting differences in per capita income accurately reflects differences in economic welfare.   The additional time available for leisure and household activities is not a total waste with zero dollar value.   Nor are children and retired adults merely a negative drain on the economy: their lives and activities are certainly valuable.

These different household decisions can have a major impact on per capita income.   The workforce as a percentage of the adult population is about 70 percent in New Hampshire, Nevada, and Vermont but only 45 percent in West Virginia.   Even in industrialized states such as

New York, Pennsylvania, and Michigan only about 57 percent of the adult population is in the workforce. At the extremes this could lead to a 50 percent difference in per capita income. For less extreme comparisons the difference can be easily 25 percent. If differences in dependents per employed worker were also considered, another significant source of regional difference (as much as a 20 percent difference) in per capita income would emerge. A similar point could be made about areas dominated by manufacturing as opposed to those dominated by services where hours worked per week are 20 percent lower. Clearly these different household decisions can have an impact on per capita income that is not closely associated with real differences in economic well-being.

7. Conclusion

The array of problems associated with interpreting differences in local per capita incomes as quantitative indicators of differences in local economic welfare is quite large. Use of per capita income statistics as indicators of local economic health ignores the way labor and land markets function to compensate for locally specific characteristics and contradicts the judgments embodied in important household choices. For most of these problems there is no regularly published data available to try to correct the per capita income index so that it would be a more accurate indicator of local economic well-being.

If per capita income is not an accurate indicator of how well various areas' economies are doing and cannot be used to accurately diagnose economic ill health, then it certainly cannot be used to suggest appropriate local economic policies to improve local economic health. Policies based on this potentially faulty diagnosis are clearly suspect.

This is not to say that we cannot identify local economic problems and develop policies to cope with them. It simply means that there is no summary statistic that will accurately provide an overall measure of local economic well-being. Economic health has too many dimensions to be conveniently summarized in a single quantitative index. Elsewhere I have discussed such a broader-based approach to evaluating local economic health and promoting real local economic development.[22] Such an approach has to focus squarely upon the fact that it is primarily qualities not quantities of things that are both the primary inputs and primary outputs of economic activity. In addition, the significant role of noncommercial goods, services, and resources in determining economic well-being has to be recognized. In that context, it is not surprising that a single, commercially-oriented, quantitative index such as per capita income cannot adequately measure local economic health.

If, despite the conceptual and data problems outlined above, one wanted to try to adjust a particular local area's per capita income statistic for known differences in locally specific qualities so that at least some crude correction to that commonly used economic index could be made, this paper has outlined the type of adjustments one would want to try to make. Most of those adjustments would dramatically narrow the apparent geographic differences in economic well-being and remove the primary social justification offered for most local economic booster activities aimed at the quantitative expansion of the local economy.

Here, in conclusion, is a partial list of the more important adjustments that would have to be made.

a. *Cost of Living*: Although no government agency gathers data on geographic differences in cost of living, several private organizations try to do this for various urban areas. The federal government *does* gather data that allow adjustment for the largest determinant of local costs of living: housing costs.

b. *Natural Amenities*: Economists over the last two decades have begun to quantify the value of various qualities associated with the natural environment: air and water quality, recreational resources, visual beauty, climate, etc. These values could be used to make crude adjustments.

c. *Social Amenities*: Economists have also begun to quantify the value of lower crime rates, congestion, noise pollution, and the value of higher quality neighborhoods, schools, and other public institutions. Some adjustment can be made for these aspects of local quality.

d. *Differences in the Mix of Market and Nonmarket Activities*: Data is readily available on geographic differences in the number of children per household, the number of retired persons, labor force participation, and hours worked per week. These data would allow some crude adjustments that both respected the value of nonmarket activities and recognized the fact that limited economic opportunities can force employment decisions upon people that they would not otherwise make.

Although crude adjustments could be made to improve the accuracy of the comparisons of the economic health of various geographic areas based upon per capita income, this approach locks the analysis into the search for a single quantitative measure of well-being. In evaluating the well-being of our communities, we should be moving in the opposite direction: a broader, multi-dimensional definition of what we seek from the local economy and how well we are doing in these multi-faceted pursuits. The narrow focus upon a commercial, market-based, quantitative measure was an analytical mistake to begin with. It is important to begin describing and analyzing economic activity within our communities in richer detail so that the role played by noncommercial activities and resources is more fully recognized. Until that is done, some of the primary determinants of our community's well-being will continue to be ignored while we continue the pursuit of self-defeating and self-destructive local economic policies.

Chapter 7

IS A WELFARE INDEX POSSIBLE?

E. J. Mishan
Economist and Author

I. Introductory Remarks

The endeavor to construct an index that more closely reflects changes in society's welfare than an index of movements in Gross National Product (GNP) or in Net National Income (NNI) is a laudable one. It is also seemingly feasible inasmuch as indices that are more representative of changes in welfare than either of the above can be devised. It transpires, nonetheless, that the more we exert ourselves in pursuit of an index that is widely acceptable, as being one that reflects changes in actual welfare, the greater the difficulties become, a fact readily acknowledged by those intrepid enough to make the attempt.

The difficulties may be arranged within three broad categories: (1) those of gathering the requisite data which, however, can be expected to diminish over time; (2) those of processing the information gathered and of refining or revamping the data as to accord better with our ideas of welfare; and (3) those difficulties which inhere in the very conception of social welfare.

There will occasionally be some overlap between the first two categories. In the main, however, I shall be directing my remarks, first, to some of the problems falling within the second category and, in addition, to those within the third category. The latter are of two kinds. On the one hand, there is the question of expenditures that may or may not be treated as consumption during the year. On the other hand, and more basically, we have occasionally to depart from the normative economist's standard assumption which equates expressed choice with welfare. Indeed, we have continually to reconsider the connection between choice and welfare. In particular, three levels of potential disjunction merit attention:

(1) The common fact that many important choices made by a person at some moment of time come to be regretted soon afterward. We may reasonably conjecture that the more rapid the pace of technical change, and the wider the range of options available, the higher the proportion of ultimate regrets.

(2) In general, the sorts of goods produced and also the methods of production necessarily affect society's "lifestyle." As such they shape the behavior, the character, and the values of that society and, inevitably therefore, people's capacity for enjoyment. Certainly there can be no presumption in already affluent communities that an increase in the area of choice increases human welfare.

(3) The more potent and the more far-reaching are the consequences on citizens' welfare the less tangible and the less measurable are they likely to be. And, incidentally, wherever they can be detected they appear to be on balance inimical.

The remaining paragraphs of this section consist of brief remarks on the transition from changes in GNP to changes in net consumption, the latter being regarded as a necessary first stage in deriving an index of changes in welfare.

As commonly understood, GNP is an aggregate of the expenditures both on finished goods and on total (or gross) investment. Since the latter, gross investment, includes not only new additions to the country's capital stock but also what is called "replacement investment," expenditure on this "replacement investment" appears twice in the calculation: once in the estimate of gross investment and again as an estimate of the amortization costs of capital (put aside by firms specifically to replace plant and equipment as they become obsolete) which amortization costs are entered into the prices of, and therefore into the aggregate expenditure on the finished goods. Net National Product (NNP) results from removing this double-counted item, being equal then to GNP less the estimate for replacement investment. This NNP figure is then equal to the aggregate of finished consumer goods plus net investment--that is, the investment that augments the existing capital stock. By use of appropriate definitions, the calculation for

NNP is exactly equal to NNI or the aggregate of incomes paid out during the year.

All the above aggregates are initially estimated in money terms; the corresponding 'real' aggregates as conventionally understood emerge simply from the use of a base-date price-index as a 'deflator.'

Economist are, however, much more concerned with changes over time of these 'real' aggregates than with the aggregates themselves--which is a source of comfort inasmuch as the errors in computing changes are much smaller than errors in computing aggregates, bearing in mind that, in any case, the focus is on proportional changes, not absolute ones. For this reason, economists attempting to measure changes in aggregate or per capita 'real' income feel justified in using proportional changes in GNP, or per capita GNP, as a proxy.

Yet if we are concerned not so much with proportional changes in per capita 'real' income but rather with proportional changes in per capita welfare over time, as was the explicit objective of such pioneers in this field as Nordhous and Tobin, and is of course the objective also of the ISEW Report, we have first to essay a more searching calculation for per capita *net* consumption prior to the yet more exacting and elusive task of devising an index of welfare. Thus it is at the point of undertaking the calculation of net consumption--that is, net of all incidental goods and 'bads' that escape the price mechanism--that we cross the Rubicon, there to discover, as we press on, how tortuous and impenetrable is the welfare territory we seek to conquer.

Let us step back then and begin with the conventional estimate of aggregate 'real' consumption, defined as equal to aggregate 'real' income less net 'real' investment. This figure for aggregate 'real' expenditure on consumption or finished goods has then to be corrected for the consumption of public goods and 'bads'--the 'bads' including additional effluent, pollution, environmental disamenity, etc. during the year. Further corrections to this resulting figure have then to be made, since some expenditures on what passes for finished goods are more accurately perceived to be expenditures on intermediate goods: as additional input-costs of maintaining a given level of finished goods or a given level of welfare. It may be argued that these expenditures on intermediate goods, or input costs, include all or part of those on defense, education, on transport, on medicine, on the provision of legal services, on advisory agencies, on bureaucratic information, on crime prevention, items which I touch upon later.

The treatment of defense is instructive in this connection. It may be convincingly argued that, in the existing circumstances, society clearly indicates--through the political process--that it prefers to spend the sums budgeted on external defense rather than using the same resources to produce any other assortment of goods. Looked at in this way, the resulting expenditure on external defense is properly regarded as a good in the over-all pattern of resource allocation that conforms with society's expressed preferences. Nonetheless, this economic justification for it is wholly consistent with the judgment of fact that the enormous sum being spent on defense confers no greater sense of security than that enjoyed in earlier years when a fraction of that sum was spent.

Once we make this judgment of fact, which countenances the subtraction from aggregate 'real' consumption of the increase in military expenditure compared with some earlier year, we are making a move toward the calculation of net consumption and, in fact, in this case doing so by reference to people's welfare.

II. The Question of Distribution

All efforts to adjust the welfare index to accommodate changes in distribution, intragenerational or intergenerational, must be regarded with misgivings. They are either arbitrary or politically biased and are, therefore, invariably a focus of attack.

Among the attempts to generate distributional weights within an intrageneration context is the adoption of some convenient elasticity of the marginal utility of real income such as (minus) unity. Among the politically-determined methods is the derivation of 'util' weights by reference to the priorities of decision-makers. This may be derived indirectly as, for example, comparing the marginal income tax levied on different income groups. Alternatively, the weights may be derived directly by putting questions to decision-makers (as recommended by the authors of the UNIDO Manual).

Neither method can be taken seriously as an acceptable method for converting 'real' consumption in dollars to real utility, or welfare. With respect to the former method, the choice of some convenient though arbitrary elasticity, there is less justification, in any case, for the presumption that--within a high income society--the marginal significance of money is inversely related with income among the bulk of the population. As for the latter method, it is too closely related to prevailing political sentiment: thus the weights derived vary over time with changes in popular feeling and with changes in budgetary policies.

The above reservations against the introduction of distributional factors into the calculation are reinforced by considerations bearing on their importance or, indeed, their relevance. The year-by-year changes in the distribution of income, or rather of net consumption, are not likely to be large. Only the adoption of a very sensitive system of distributional weights would make a noticeable difference over time between a weighted and an unweighted index. Be that as it may, the growing incidence of the so-called Jones' Effect in high consumption societies (i.e. the relative income hypothesis originally proposed by Dusenberry) makes it harder to vindicate the traditional economists' concern with distribution. For the significance of the Jones' Effect is that what is coming to matter to people today is not so much their absolute living standards, their basic needs or even their physical comforts, but their position in the income and wealth hierarchy. The income differentials are therefore more indicative of psychic wants than physical wants. To be blunt about it, the income comparisons are invidious, and more likely to invoke envy and resentment. As such the economist's traditional concern with income distribution--other than what little is necessary to remedy any residual hardcore destitution--is unwarranted in already affluent countries. The moral obligation to redistribute income is far from being a compelling one in these circumstances.[1]

I should therefore favor the removal of all dollar weights in the computation of a per capita welfare index even if only to avoid unnecessary controversy or accusations of arbitrarily 'doctoring' the figures. In deference to a lingering concern with the distributional issue, however, it may be prudent to complement the per capita welfare index ('undoctored') with an index of distribution.

Exception may also be taken to proposed adjustments to be made in the welfare index in an endeavor to promote intergenerational equity. A minor criticism of the formula proposed by a World Bank economist--based on using discounted present value of an expected stream of net profits from mining to calculate an equivalent stream of returns in perpetuity--is that it depends itself upon some chosen rate of discount. And the use of any rate of discount will down-weight the interests of a future generations as compared with the present or earlier ones. Since the use of a discount rate in projects involving different generations has been shown to be economically erroneous,[2] the formula proposed has to be rejected as, indeed, must any formula involving a discount rate.

A more basic criticism of the position taken in the ISEW Report is that it appears to veer from what *is* to what *ought* to be. Ideally perhaps, the net profits or royalties from the depletion of an irreplaceable asset should be wholly invested as they accrue so that present generation receive no more benefit from their being mined than will future generations. Yet as we know, what ought to be done is not being done; and it is unlikely that it ever will be in the absence of legal compulsion.

To be sure, if we were concerned instead with the measurement of income itself rather than consumption a case could be made out for concern with the depletion of capital for that purpose--at least, if we follow Hicks and define net income during the year as the amount that could be consumed so as to leave unchanged the stock of capital.

Clearly this definition can produce a different figure from that emerging from defining net income as the sum of factor payments made during the year since during that period there could be destruction of capital or windfall gains. Thus if there were a destruction by man or by nature of either man-made or natural capital during the year, income on the Hicksian definition will be that much smaller than income as the sum of factor payments. For those concerned with the sustainability of future income, the Hicksian definition with its regard to the maintenance of the stock of capital will be the more appropriate.

The ISEW Report however is not directly interested in measuring income, actual or sustainable, but in net consumption which is to serve as an indicator of welfare. The issue in this connection therefore is whether we are to measure what is actually consumed during the year, as being an index of welfare actually experienced during the year, or whether we try and measure what we think we ought to consume during the year if per capita net consumption is to remain constant over the future.

This commendable concern with intergeneration equity does pose unresolvable difficulties, and however arbitrarily dealt with it is sure to meet with objections. The ISEW proposal for a depletion tax (proceeds of which could be invested for the benefit of future generations) accords with the views of a number of environmental economists, including Talbot Page. Were it introduced as a policy measure, it would of course tend to slow down the consumption of irre-placeable resources, which is all to the good. But it could not be de-pended upon to contribute to intergeneration equity. For one thing, we cannot determine what the future returns would be to the investment of the proceeds of the depletion tax, though we may reasonably hope they would be positive. Far more important, however, if intergenera-tion equity is translated into a constant per capita net consumption over time, the hope of achieving this desideratum would require that we have fairly reliable estimates of what future per capita real income would be (in the absence of our interventions, if any), to say nothing of estimates of future generations' propensities to consume, to invest, to destroy, or to multiply their numbers.

The fact is that we really do not know if per capita income or per capita net consumption will be increasing or decreasing over the next one or two decades. So much depends *inter alia* on success in control-ling effluent, pollution, resource depletion, and on the scale of illegal immigration, on crime abatement, and on conflict avoidance. Thus we have no idea whether the objective of a constant per capita net con-sumption over the future would require that currently net consump-tion be increased above actual net consumption, or decreased, and by how much. By the same logic, neither can we know whether the ISEW measure of sustainable net consumption should be calculated to be above or below the year's actual net consumption.

Clearly we can avoid this difficulty, and avoid arbitrary assump-tions in the endeavor to resolve the unresolvable, by restricting our-selves to measuring actual net consumption in each year over the past up to the current year. If then society were, for example, so improvi-dent as to consume within a single year about a half of its natural re-sources, actual net consumption in that year would be impressive, though leaner years would follow. While we can all agree that no re-sponsible society should behave that way, should it ever do so we have no excuse for not recording the fact.

In conclusion, the interest rightly taken by economists in the material welfare of future generations can be more usefully directed into computing an annual measure or index both of the nation's man-made capital and its natural capital. At all events the construction of a supplementary capital index to accompany the per capita index of wel-fare would be a far less controversial resolution of the intergeneration issue than the method proposed in the ISEW Report.

III. The Treatment of Leisure

As a rule, economists tend to speak not so much of measuring social welfare but, more circumspectly, of measuring the contribution that economic activity makes--or could make when guided by economic maxims--to social welfare. For it has to be recognized that noneconomic factors such as climate, political events, community mores, and "Acts of God," also directly affect people's wellbeing. Nonetheless, such noneconomic factors themselves will often influence economic activity if only in attempts to modify their initial impact on society's welfare. The measurement of economic activity may, therefore, be regarded as providing in familiar circumstances at least a rough index of changes in welfare.

Thus, one of the more critical questions we have to face in the construction of a welfare index is whether we should confine ourselves to economic activity alone, say to the measure of net consumption, so deliberately ignoring "leisure" under the tacit assumption that, in some sense, its value does not change much over time, or whether instead leisure should be explicitly valued.[3] Whichever alternative we adopt we shall be uncomfortably aware that varying amounts of "leisure" time are necessarily involved in the consumption of the range of finished goods.

In adopting the latter alternative, we are conscious first that there are difficulties in defining leisure in such a way as to make it an unambiguous component of welfare. A proportion of the work for which people are paid generally yields them positive satisfaction, a proportion that can be substantial for artists and professional men. Yet having decided to cut the Gordian knot by adopting the device of measuring changes in welfare by changes in net consumption, we are exempted from bringing these incidental satisfactions into the calculus. Again, the fact that some of the tasks we undertake in our leisure time are also tedious or in some part distasteful need not exercise us. Inasmuch as the choice of allocating our leisure time between different activities is our own, it is not unreasonable to treat the whole of our leisure time also as a good--a nonmarket good--provided always that it is voluntary.

To be sure, the intensity of the satisfaction or the dissatisfaction that accompanies our leisure or our work may vary over time, and vary substantially. But these variations will be difficult to detect, and yet more difficult to evaluate. Since this elusive factor has perforce to be omitted from the calculation, the accuracy of our index will depend, *inter alia*, upon the level of satisfaction or dissatisfaction remaining constant over time, or at least not changing so radically as to vitiate our measure of welfare.

It should be recognized that even if leisure, or hours of employment, were to remain virtually unchanged over time, there would still be a strong case for including leisure, or "the consumption of leisure," in the welfare index. For as compared with the changes in a welfare index based on net consumption alone, once a value is imputed to leisure the movements in the resulting welfare index will differ from the former according to the relative weights in the latter of leisure and net consumption. Thus a net increase of x per cent in per capita consumption of market (and public) goods can no longer be assumed to increase per capita net welfare by x per cent. With the introduction of a value for leisure, an x per cent rise in per capita net consumption will, *cet. par.*, result in a per capita increase of welfare that is below x per cent--the higher the weight of leisure, the further below x per cent. Insofar, then, as it reduces the role of net consumption alone as a generator of welfare, the inclusion of leisure restores perspective.

According to conventional economic accounting, an hour's leisure to a particular person is to be valued as about equal to an hour's earnings; at least, on the fiction that he is permitted to choose the number of hours he works. Even with this fiction, however, the equivalence is valid only at the margin. The *average* value of his hours of leisure will therefore be greater than an hour's earnings.

Whether to make allowance for the excess of average over marginal value of leisure, and if so by how much, are matters of empirical judgment or, rather, of shrewd guesswork. All we can safely say is that, in the event, the adoption of actual earnings per hour as a proxy for the value of an hour's leisure will result in a conservative estimate of the contribution of leisure to the welfare index.

To the question that arises next, whether the leisure of women or nonwhites should be valued at less than the value of leisure for white males, since hourly earnings of each of the former are below those of the latter, the answer would seem to be in the affirmative--assuming, as indicated above, that at given rates of pay people are allowed to choose their hours of employment. To the extent that this assumption is at variance with the facts, the use of these different hourly earnings to measure the value of the leisure of women and nonwhites may be less reliable. Even so, if the sort of constraint on hours worked as between the three broad groups are comparable, we may refrain from engaging in somewhat arbitrary refinements.

Granted, then, that the relation between the marginal and the average values of leisure is about the same for the three groups, there can be no objection to estimating an over-all average value for leisure in some base year by weighting the average value of leisure for each group according to its aggregate leisure as a proportion of total aggregate leisure for the three groups combined.

Consideration must now be given to the proportion of the 24-hour day, or the seven-day week, that has to be marked out for division between hours of work and the remaining hours of leisure and non-market activities. It is common for economists to adopt an average of a 16-hour day as the norm in calculating the remaining hours of leisure, its being supposed that about eight hours out of the 24-hour day are reserved for sleep.

This assumption of a 16-hour day to be divided between work and leisure is not easy to justify. Accepting the conventional notion of an (eventually) increasing marginal valuation curve for leisure, the standard construct shows that of the individual, when given the choice, working successive hours until the marginal value of leisure is about equal to the hourly rate of pay. Hours of leisure beyond this point, then, all have successively higher valuations--including the hours set aside for sleep. Since there is no economically justifiable reason why the priority that the individual places on the hours of sleep, necessary to his survival, be dismissed simply because he is not awake and bustling about, I propose that the full 24-hour day be regarded as the relevant period for the division between work and leisure. If, therefore, a person elects to work seven hours during a working day, his leisure hours will number seventeen.

Allowing that there is agreement to value an hour's leisure as equal to or greater than the relevant wage rate, we have now to turn to the problem arising from the tendency of real wages to grow over time and, as an apparent corollary, the real value of leisure also. But does it make sense to increase the real value of leisure over time simply because the marginal productivity of labor is increasing? According to Nordhaus and Tobin we can suppose either that the real worth of an hour's leisure continues unchanged irrespective of the movement in real wages, or else that, over time, leisure also rises in value in virtue of the opportunities provided by innovations and the accumulation of (leisure) goods.

The latter supposition depends upon the belief that more goods-- or at least more laborsaving appliances and more recreational goods-- tend to enhance the value of the individual's leisure time. Although one can conceive of circumstances for which initially the belief is valid, it hardly requires a philosopher to surmise that the enjoyment of leisure is not always positively related to the number of things that can be crammed within a given interval of time; that, indeed, the current trend toward packing more goods into our lives, or more "consumption activities" into the limited time at our disposal, is hardly a recipe for enhancing the quality of life. It is at least as likely that once the stage of material abundance associated with what we call " the affluent society" has been reached or surpassed, leisure becomes less enjoyable.[4] Of the two alternative suppositions, my strong preference is for adopting the former; that is, taking the value of leisure as remaining unchanged over time.

Accepting this view, the perceived rise in the nominal or money value of leisure (equating it, that is, to the money wage rate) will be entered, according to its weight, into the over-all price index that is used to deflate the aggregate money value of the consumption of both (market) goods and leisure.[5]

Finally, the importance of leisure in the resulting index of welfare, depending as it does on its weight in the index relative to the consumption of (market) goods, must vary with the base year chosen for its initial valuation. For the assumption of an unchanged real value of leisure will act over time to 'drag down' the overall rise in the index of welfare (or, alternatively, to slow down the over-all decline in the welfare index). Hence, the farther back the base year chosen, the lower, cet. par. will be the aggregate real value of leisure and, therefore, the less drag on the movement of the over-all welfare index.

IV. The Value of Household Services

As has been frequently noted, of the multifarious tasks undertaken in the home, chiefly by women, some are far more satisfying than others. Moreover, in human terms, some are more valuable as, for example, looking after the children or creating a comfortable and cheerful home ambience. There is, nonetheless, no warrant for treat-

ing the services provided by this sector differently from the goods produced in the industrial sector. In this latter and dominant sector, we
may recall, we have chosen to disregard any positive utility derived
from the different occupations--conventionally regarded as rents in allocation analysis--restricting our measure of welfare to the value of
goods consumed. Regardless, therefore, of whether a person classifies
his activity, or any part of it, as "work" or "leisure," or "pain" or "pleasure," consistency requires that we continue to restrict our measurement of welfare to the valuation of all goods (which includes services)
consumed by the community however generated. Provided, then,
there is a market rate for each of the significant activities undertaken in
the home,[6] and a breakdown of the average week into each of these activities, a value can be attributed to the services produced in the home.

True, information about the composition of housework--or,
rather, the services it produces--may be difficult to obtain. But if we assume that the quality of the housework does not change much over
time, the rise in the money value of household services (which, as
mentioned, tends to follow the rise in money wages) will enter as a
matter of course into the overall price index used to 'deflate' the aggregate money value of consumption to its 'real' value. As in the case of
leisure, therefore, the more recent is the base year that is adopted, the
greater will be the weight of household services in the welfare index.

If, on the other hand, we assume instead that at least some
household services do improve over time, we may be able to translate
the improvement into a quantitative increase, the unit cost of the service in question rising less than the movement in money wages.
Should this increase in productivity of the household service result in
no increase in its consumption, there will be an increase in leisure
which has to be valued accordingly.

At this point, a *caveat* against double counting must be invoked.
We are *not* to include the market value of any labor-saving device that
increases household productivity in the consumption aggregate during
the year of its purchase. In the circumstances, the contribution of the
said device is properly valued as the annual increment of productivity-
-that is, the value of the additional service, or of the additional leisure,
it confers each year--that is spread over the lifetime of the labor-saving
appliance in question.

We may conclude that there is no warrant for separating household services from other services contributed to aggregate consump-

tion. In principle, therefore, the same method of valuation may be extended to all services enjoyed by the community. Unfortunately, once we reflect on the implications of extending the coverage in this way--extending it, that is, to all the services we occasionally offer to others or provide as a matter of routine--we tend to lose confidence in the index of net consumption as also an index of welfare. The misgivings that arise from this and from other considerations, however, will be given more airing toward the end of this essay.

V. Additional Observations on Capital and the Environment

This penultimate section consists of a number of shorter observations, some of them at variance with the arguments put forward by the authors of the [ISEW] Report, others being in the nature of suggested modifications of their methods of calculation.

1. **The capital value of finite resources**. In calculating an index of capital resources, depletion over time poses no special problems. The rise in nominal or money value of the stock of any natural resource resulting from its growing scarcity does not obscure the diminution of the stock year by year provided we continue to use the same base-year resource price. Nor does the rise in the price of any product or service that is associated with the rise in the 'real' value of a natural asset require special consideration, even when the asset in question is land--whether used for agricultural production or for urban sites.

Hence there is no warrant for a separate calculation of the rise in landlords' rents in response to growing urban densities, nor any either for treating these higher real rents as a form of external social cost which has to be subtracted from aggregate consumption along with other social costs such as noise or pollution. This rise in urban rents (relative to average wages) does, of course, entail a distribution effect in favor of landlords. But if we are restricting ourselves to net per capita consumption, the distributional effects do not concern us. The essential point to bear in mind is that the part of the rise in price of any consumer good that is attributable to a rise in the price of an asset[7] is properly reflected in the price index used to deflate the money value of net consumption in any reference year. No further correction is called for.

2. **Human capital**. Annual expenditure on higher education is today mostly expenditure on vocational training irrespective of how it is financed. As I have indicated already, it is best conceived as the an-

nual investment necessary to maintain the stock of human capital that is required to operate the modern economy. The real value of this stock of human capital will expand with the growth of the economy so that, using the customary dichotomy, the expenditure per annum on human capital can be divided into the amount invested in order to replace removals from the stock of human capital and the investment in human capital that augments the stock. As with industrial capital, the quality of human capital will also change over time as to meet requirements for more sophisticated methods of production. But whatever the sums spent on the variety and quality of human capital during the year, they are effectively inputs into the production of goods. As such they enter into the cost of finished products and services. In order to avoid double counting, all such spending on vocational education should be subtracted from aggregate consumption.

Now if we were to construct an index of the total stock of capital, natural and man-made, there would be no good reason for excluding human capital. The belief that it is of prime importance is not likely to be challenged by orthodox opinion. Many countries that are poorly endowed with natural resources--such as Japan, Holland, Switzerland, Denmark--are among those enjoying the highest living standards. And the so-called German miracle, which by 1960 made West Germany the country with the highest living standards in Europe, bears eloquent testimony to the overriding importance of human capital--a term which comprehends both technical skills and those ingrained habits of enterprise and industry.

Although its inclusion would obviously increase the value of aggregate capital stock, the difference its inclusion would make to the movement over time compared with an index of the non-human capital stock alone may not be very much. The greater the divergence over time between the indices respectively of human capital and non-human capital, the more influence on the over-all index will be exerted by human capital.

3. **Domestic capital goods**. The distinction made between those consumption goods that are classified as domestic, or consumer, capital goods and those that are classified as consumer services is one that turns on the time period chosen. Taking the period as equal to a year, as is the common practice, it follows that if the finished good is one that is not entirely consumed within the year then neither should the whole of its value be entered as consumption in that year: only the portion that is used up during the year should be entered.

This much is evident in the case of private houses, automobiles, private yachts and planes, and will be readily extended to furniture, to domestic appliances, to television sets, refrigerators, washing machines, vacuum cleaners, hair primpers, vibrators, clocks, and many other implements and gadgets. Bearing in mind that every product, down to the ordinary pencil, can be conceived to be an item of capital inasmuch as it is a source of a stream of services released at different times over the future, the decision whether to include the value of the item in the year it is purchased or whether, instead, to include only the value of the services used during that year follows from the above principle.

Yet before putting ourselves to the trouble of detailed calculations, we ought to have some idea whether converting the expenditures in a given year on a large number of domestic capital items into the annual values of the services they give rise to over the future would alter significantly the year-to-year aggregate value of net consumption. My guess is that we could omit such refinement and enter into the year of purchase the whole of the value of quite a range of domestic capital items without noticeably changing the movement of the welfare index. This would be an even safer guess if we were to represent changes over time by, say, a five- or ten-year moving average.

4. **Public Spending on the Environment.** Were government spending to vary with aggregate expenditure on a per capita basis, there would be a straightforward case for omitting all government spending from the index. But in fact, largely in response to the demands of modern wars and the welfare state, government spending has been growing apace as a proportion of NNI. There has then to be a case for ignoring all government expenditures in estimates of net consumption, or for ignoring them save for particular items.

It can plausibly be contended that the bulk of the spending of modern government does not contribute much to social welfare, most of it being transfer payments (including pensions), external and internal defense, and payments for agencies and new infrastructure necessary to cope with the increasing complexity and hazard of a rapidly changing "high tech" society.

The government, nonetheless, can also make substantial contributions to environmental preservation and to reductions of effluent and pollution. Insofar as, say, pollution diminishes as a result of legislation, the costs are borne directly by industry and are passed on to the consumer in the form of higher market prices.   In this case no provision need be made for the improvement since, on the one hand, the measurement of pollution in those years will be that much the less--less, therefore, to be subtracted from the figure of aggregate consumption.   On the other hand the costs of the operation are taken care of since the price deflator will indicate the reduction in the real output of finished goods consequent upon the use of resources necessary to deal with the pollution.   No change in the methods proposed by ISEW is necessary.

If, instead, the government itself incurs expenditures in reducing pollution or in cleaning up lakes and rivers, the case is no different. Such improvements will again take the form of a reduction in those years of the measured amounts of pollution and effluent remaining, as in the preceding case.   The opportunity costs of the operation will again take the same form as a reduction in the finished output of the private sector (resulting as it does from taxation, implying a reduction in spending power on private goods).   If we follow the ISEW method, and therefore ignore the additional spending of government, it again "all comes out in the wash."

Only in the event that the government directly produces public goods, say the creating of national parks and reforestation programs (where such public goods are not included along with reductions in pollution damage) must the government expenditures be entered into the calculation.   In this case then, the consequent reduction in private consumption, via taxes, has to be explicitly augmented by the value of the public goods created.

5. **Environmental Damage**. The basic concept by reference to which we are to evaluate environmental damage, among other 'bads' suffered by society during the year, is worth reconsidering.

In general, what is sought is a money measure of a net change in welfare, whether that change be for the better or for the worse.   This measure is in fact provided by the Hicksian Compensating Variation, CV. For the individual it can be defined as a transfer of money to or from the person which, following the (proposed) change in welfare, restores his original level of welfare. If therefore the change were a beneficial one--say a fall in the price of a good x or the provision of a public park--the CV would be the most the individual affected would be willing to pay for the beneficial change. *Per contra*, if the change to him were unwelcome--say a rise in the prices of goods y and z, or exposure to some new environmental disamenity--the CV would be the minimal sum that would exactly compensate him for the misfortune in question.

Since the CV is implicit in our measurment of the value of private goods, being in fact what people are willing to pay for them (using their prices as a proxy[8]), consistency in the use of CV requires that all 'bads' produced during the year--environmental damage and other disamenities--be calculated as the minimim sums that would reconcile people to bear with them.

As I have pointed out in a number of places,[9] the frequent resort of economists to propose the measurement of a 'bad' by what people are willing to pay for its removal is inappropriate: it is *not* equal to the CV. In the circumstances, such a sum is in fact equal to a quite different measure called the Equivalent Variation, EV, by Hicks.[10] And an estimate of the EV, or willingness to pay in order to avoid suffering the particular 'bad' in question can crucially understate the value of the cost or loss to society as properly measured by the CV.

A simple example will illustrate. Imagine the establishment of a vast chemical plant within a designated area in the near future. The inhabitants believe that the side effects of the operations could expose them to a high risk of a slow and painful death. The very most they are able to offer the corporation to site the plant elsewhere, the EV in fact, is equal to $100 million. It transpires, however, that the corporation will not site the plant elsewhere for less than $180 million.

Now suppose the courts lay it down that it is the corporation which has fully to compensate all the inhabitants of the area before siting permission can be granted. Are we to assume that an offer by the corporation of the $100 million will just suffice to reconcile the inhabitants to siting the plant within their area? Far from it. After all, their maximum offer of $100 million is determined, *inter alia*, by their income and wealth. Had they been twice as wealthy they would have offered more. No matter how much they dread the idea of such a chemical plant in their midst, the $100 million is the most they can dredge up, given their budget constraints.

No inconsistency is therefore involved if they now refuse an offer of $500 million from the corporation. Indeed, in the circumstances the CV could be infinitely high: no sum of money would be large enough to reconcile them to the siting of the chemical plant in their area.[11]

6. **Travel costs**. Since commuting to work is best regarded as a regrettable necessity, the least that has to be done is to subtract these travel expenses from the net consumption of finished goods. It would be in order to subtract some amount also for the loss of the time that is spent in commuting. After all, if corporations themselves arranged to pay all travel expenses of their personnel (including amounts necessary to compensate them for additional time and discomforts endured), paying them instead a net-of-travel wage or salary, then as travel costs rose over time so also would the costs of finished goods. The implication is not so clearly perceived when expenditures on travel enter the national accounts as items of consumption.

A good deal of so-called leisure travel, however, may also qualify as a regrettable cost since the expenses are incurred not for the joys of the journey itself but for the anticipated pleasure of being within a particular area. Thus any reduction in time or money on travel would not feature as a reduction but as a gain in welfare.

Again, tourist travel today is chiefly air travel, and it is rare to meet any one who actually relishes the actual air journey, to say nothing of the time spent in the airport. Although it is not amiss for some purposes to treat the vacation along with the travel as an undecomposable package for which the consumer is willing to pay, since we are concerned with the change of welfare over time it makes sense to separate the amount and type of travel from the actual vacation sought. This enables us to focus on the particular elements of "diswelfare" in the package that are likely to grow over the future, namely, the increasing loss of enjoyment in consequence of the increased queuing and waiting in airports along with other discomforts and anxieties.

Similar remarks are applicable to motorized leisure travel wherever the main purpose of driving is not the joys of the journey but simply to transfer one's person to the location chosen.

7. **Advertising**. In view of the annoyance caused by the ubiquity of billboards, of the nuisance inflicted on the public by an unending stream of "junk mail," of an incalculable number of misleading advertisements, and of massive advertising expenditure on tobacco, liquor, and fast cars, having the net effect of undermining the health of the population and increasing the risk of painful death, there can be no

convincing presumption that, on balance, the alleged good effects of advertising--those of information and entertainment--exceed the bad ones.[12]

There is, therefore, a strong case for removing advertising expenditures in general, though particularly for commercial advertising, from aggregate consumption.

8. **Crime**. It is not enough to subtract from aggregate consumption any increased expenditures on internal defense above those incurred in the base year. Such expenditures include, or ought to include, those on police, on security agents and private detectives, on more elaborate locks, on defense weapons and security systems, and on insurance premiums. Yet such vastly increased outlays fall short of the additional costs of crime for the simple reason that they have signally failed to maintain the sense and level of security that prevailed during the years immediately following World War II. Since then, crime has burgeoned at an alarming rate, especially crimes of violence, in all Western countries--a development that may plausibly be treated as one of the untoward externalities arising from postwar economic growth.[13]

The subtraction to be made for the social loss resulting from the increased incidence of violent crime goes far beyond the restricted calculation familiar to economists--that of the opportunity cost to society of the human and other resources that are diverted into crime. The appropriate concept in this as in many other cases is that of the compensating variation. In this instance it is the minimum sum the community would accept to reconcile it to the growth of crime dating from the base year.

Such a sum would certainly be difficult to estimate. Yet at least a "guesstimate", or range of guesstimates, should be made of so critical a component of welfare. Its omission must surely result in an overestimate of the rise in per capita welfare, or in an underestimate of its decline.

It is far from impossible that the erosion of mutual trust between people, its replacement by lurking suspicion and the feeling of vulnerability, the spread of "no-go areas," the unease at being alone in the streets after dark, and the anxieties suffered by parents--all of which are direct consequences of increased incidence and threat of violence--are more than enough to offset all the material gains made over the last four decades.

VI. Epilogue

This is about as far as I wish to go while remaining within the bounds of generally accepted economic principles. One can say more only by pushing on beyond the limits of the tangible and the in-principle-measurable, or else by extending economic principles to the more intimate aspects of our lives. Although a venture into this more speculative realm of enquiry cannot be shirked, we must be prepared to find ourselves being increasingly assailed by skepticism and disillusion. The warning may be taken seriously if my pessimistic reflection is illustrated by reference to considerations that so far--out of necessity or out of prudence--have been omitted from the grand computation.

Let us turn first to the treatment of household services which are still, for the most part, performed by women even when allowance is made for household maintenance and repairs done by either party in the home. Although it is admittedly distasteful, it is not impossible to evaluate also the sexual services rendered to each partner by a cohabiting couple whether married or not. By adopting the market prices of such services, quite a sizable chunk could be added to the service sector of the economy, and therefore to our figure for aggregate net consumption.

To be sure, the services of a harlot may be less satisfactory, or at least less valued by a person than services when provided gratis, and as a matter of course, between the cohabiting couple. Ideally conceived, the sexual act should also be an act of love and affirmation--in virtue of which the resolute (though perhaps insensitive) economist may be prepared to put a higher value than the going market rate on the sexual act whenever it is performed by mutual consent and without negotiation.

This is discomfort enough, yet we cannot stop there. For surely the value of any freely proffered personal service may be evaluated, in the first instance, by reference to the market price of a surrogate service. Again, however, a value so attributed could be a gross underestimate. For the worth of the service to the recipient depends, or should depend, upon the spirit in which it is offered and the spirit in which it is accepted. In general, the personal services that we receive as a free offering from others, arising as they do from a sense of responsibility, of duty, or of charity, or else from esteem, affection, tenderness, or love, may well be regarded as being of incalculable value.

There is nothing to stop us either from extending the same argument to the entertainment and affection we enjoy when receiving or providing hospitality: extending it also to the games we play with friends, to the comfort and counsel they occasionally offer us, and even to the various forms of accommodation and assistance forthcoming in times of need. For all such voluntary and friendly services there are, indeed, substitutes of some kind, from television programs to family-counseling and other agencies. In all cases, however, the market surrogate is only formally compatible since it cannot provide also the disinterested sympathy of the friend or relation; it cannot generate the flow of feeling that comes with services gladly given and received.

Insistence on elements of formalism that would require such services to be valued "at the margin" does not much alter the above conclusion. The freely-gifted personal service cannot be increased by the recipient "subject to his budget constraint" in order to reach a value equal to zero. The provision of freely-gifted personal services is restricted by time and by many circumstances, also by the character and endowment of both donor and recipient. Such personal services therefore continue to be valued highly on the scale of welfare as may be inferred by the risks taken, and by the time, trouble, and expenditure, invested today by many people, old and young, in endeavors to discover another human being who is willing to show love, tenderness, understanding, consideration, and sympathy.

Allowing that some value could be imputed to the provision of all personal services freely provided between people, the weight of such services in the over-all welfare aggregate would serve to reduce significantly the impact on it of market and public goods. Moreover, insofar as such freely-gifted personal services will decline over time,[14] their inclusion will impart a downward trend to the resulting per capita index.

Secondly, the economist's presumption that welfare rises with more goods per capita, or with "an expansion in the area of choice," is questionable. For one thing, the continuing flow of a proliferation of new goods, and new brands and models of a vast range of modern appliances, makes it virtually impossible to find time to gather the information necessary to assess their suitability. Bewilderment tends to exceed pleasure in those time-absorbing shopping excursions, and the outcome is as likely as not to be regretted. Homes are increasingly cluttered with electronic gadgetry, with unread books and journals, with clothes that are never worn. The attempt to consume a growing plethora of goods, to avail oneself of more entertainment and travel opportunities, presses ever harder against the constraint of time. Try as one might only a few morsels can be ingested of each day's tantalizing abundance.

Again, nearly all labor-saving innovations along with the trend toward self-service act over time to reduce our direct communication with, and dependence upon, others in different walks of life, so augmenting the forces making for mutual estrangement in the modern city. Thus innovations that are prized as reducing the costs of goods eventually contribute to a decline in human welfare.

Again, even the more obvious and blatant externalities, whose costs can seemingly be measured, tend to be underestimated. The subtractions made for the pollution and disamenity resulting from automobile travel fall short of the destruction wrought. The unceasing clamor, the sense of suffocation and danger suffered by pedestrians, the hideousness of traffic-inspired architecture, the unwieldy growth of metropolitan areas, the desolation of the suburbs, and interminable spread of ribbon building, all of which in the last four decades have all but submerged the distinctive architectural features of once-famous cities of the world--these dismal developments are indeed difficult to evaluate, which is no good reason for ignoring them.

On a more general level, the very spread of technical progress itself along with the promotion of international competition--factors lauded by free-market economists--is productive of anxiety. Both as consumers and producers, we are pressed closer to the edge of obsolescence. As consumers, for instance, the electronic all-sorts we purchase are superseded today almost before we start using them. More importantly, however, it is as workers that we feel more vulnerable. Occupational skills that may have taken us years to master have become increasingly prone to "overnight" obsolescence in a "high tech" economy geared to ruthless innovation. Continued economic progress in already affluent societies has adverse effects on well-being that are no less burdensome for being intangible.

The more we begin to reflect about the incidental but far-reaching consequences of rapid industrial progress upon the many intimate aspects of human welfare, the more we become prey to searching doubts about the possibility of constructing a welfare index. For in the process of adapting our lives to cope with rapid scientific and technological change, so much is happening simultaneously to our routines, to our tastes, to our manners, to our conduct, to our self-regard, to our character and our values, and therefore, inevitably also to our capacity to enjoy life, that any index of the changes in the amounts of goods available to consumers would seem quite incidental to trends in the over-all experience of welfare.

I have to confess, then, that I find it hard to avoid feeling oppressed by an enervating sense of the futility of such an exercise: as if one were engaged in a desperate but foredoomed attempt to extend the dimensions of an already crumbling edifice.

Finally, and to top up the portion of pessimism being served, let me remind economists that a large portion of what passes as final output bears comparison in concept with the treatment of education as an annual input into the system necessary to maintain the stock of human capital from which flows the stream of labor services. Into the same category can be placed a part of additional government expenditures; for example those costs of extending the administrative infrastructure necessary to monitor and control the dynamic economy. Thus agencies set up to monitor the introduction of new chemicals in industry and agriculture, and to keep tabs on scores of thousands of new products and by-products of economic enterprise, do not of themselves add a little to welfare--at least not in comparison with an earlier age that was exempt from the new risks. Such agencies come into being in response to public demand and in order to allay anxieties--in a bid, therefore, to maintain the level of welfare.

Taken over a historical period many of the services currently being offered by the private sector are also of this character and, therefore, their consumption--however valued by the market--cannot rightfully claim a place in the grand computation. In this connection we may include the services provided by banks, by labor unions, by employment agencies, by welfare counselors, by travel offices, by lawyers and accountants, by marriage and computer-dating bureaus, by race-relations organizations, by post-abortion "hot-lines," and so on and on. Such services and many more that are springing up were just not needed in the earlier economy of small towns and villages. They come into being and flourish as populations become more mobile and more alienated, as urban areas expand to unmanageable metropolitan dimensions, and as, in response to material abundance, the resultant mode of living becomes increasingly complex, frenzied, and wearing. They are better regarded as "regrettables" rather than as sources of additional gratification.

Similar remarks are relevant to the services of clinics and centers established in order to deal with a variety of nervous and psychological disorders arising from the stress and the tensions associated with modern lifestyles.

Where so much of the nation's effort and ingenuity is channeled into producing specialized services and sophisticated equipment which, in the last resort, cater to basic biological and psychological needs--needs which were more simply met in the smaller close-knit communities of pre-industrial civilizations--it is hard to call a halt to the train of instances that come to mind of new services and opportunities that turn out, on reflection, to be more like contributions to a higher cost of living than to a higher standard of living.

Chapter 8

POLICY CHECKING AND POLICY MAKING

Jan Tinbergen, Emer. Professor
Erasmus University, Rotterdam

I. Introduction

The present essay has been written at the request of the editors of this volume and should be a critical evaluation of the work done by the Study Group on what they call the Index of Sustainable Economic Welfare. The Index's nearest objective is to offer better information on sustainable economic welfare than gross national product, which is the first concept developed to express in a single figure a nation's economic performance and that nation's means to enjoy well-being. A unique survey of figures over long periods and for many countries was published more than two decades ago by Kuznets.[1] A critical evaluation must start with the identification of the fundamental objective of the construction of indices of the type mentioned. Clearly that objective is to attain, with the aid of an appropriate social order and an appropriate socioeconomic policy, the optimal level of sustainable economic welfare over a period of time. In this definition of the objective or aim several of the elements mentioned must be specified with more precision. This will be an important part of the comments offered in this essay.

By the social order of a nation or a group of nations we understand the set of institutions that together characterize the nation or the group of nations considered. Institutions may be abstract or concrete. An example of an abstract institution is a market. An example of a

concrete institution is a ministry, a factory or a school. Institutions operate on the basis of a charter or a set of rules that regulate its activities.
The order as a whole was created by the nation's policy makers and is
changed from time to time. In the framework of the social order the
policy makers of the nation or the group of nations decide on the nation's (or the group of nations') social policy. Thus, around 1850 the developed nations had a capitalist order, where a large number of decisions made were market decisions of individuals and firms. These exerted demand for and supply of large numbers of goods and services.
The nations considered are called market economies. Around 1950 the
Soviet Union and a number of other nations had another order, called
centrally planned economies. In these economies a large number of
decisions were made by government agencies, in contrast with the capitalist nations, where government institutions played a very modest
role. In 1850 a large number of underdeveloped nations had a feudal
order and were colonies of developed countries. Between 1947 and
1970 most colonies became independent nations, initially still feudal,
with a beginning of capitalist elements.

A socioeconomic policy is characterized by a number of *aims* and
a number of *means*, applied in order to attain the aims. The aims may
be formulated in a very general way, such as *maximum welfare* of the
population under the restrictions imposed by nature, logic or other
forces. The aims may also be specified more concretely, for instance full
employment, balance of payments equilibrium, public finance equilibrium and a reasonable income distribution. Ideally this specification
should be the result of an elaboration of the welfare maximum under
the restrictions admitted. Such an elaboration may be obtained with
the aid of the method of 'Lagrange multipliers.'

Means are phenomena of which the character or size, or both,
can be determined by policy makers. Examples are tax systems, systems
of social security or other institutions. The policy of F.D. Roosevelt's
'New Deal' introduced a new social security system. The policy of the
Marshall Plan made available to the allied nations financial help for
their reconstruction of war damage. Both had a qualitative element, a
change in structure, as well as quantitative elements, the sizes of the
new flows of payments. Quantitative elements of aims will be called
'targets' and those of means will be called *'instruments.'* A purely
quantitative policy (which does not introduce new structures) usually
is a *short-run* policy, and can be described by targets and instruments. It
can be shown that the number of instruments must be equal to the
number of targets.

The operation of an economy can be described by a number of structural variables and coefficients, occurring in a system of equations. All these entities together are often called a *model*, since the description practically always is a simplification of reality.

So far we discussed the concepts needed for an evaluation of the society of one nation or a group of nations. For today's problems it is necessary to consider the *global* society: the interrelations between the world's nations have become so important that the appropriate policies and orders must take into account the welfare of all citizens of our planet. Among the reasons why the interrelations have been strengthened are some recent developments, of which one is the *pollution of the environment*. Especially the pollution of the atmosphere and of the oceans has increased rapidly as the consequence of population growth, the increase in the number of cars and the development of various types of chemical industries. In the past there have been interrelations, such as trade and transport, but large countries were engaged in foreign trade as a low percentage of their total national income only, and, as a first approximation, could neglect the impact of foreign trade.

Another phenomenon that more recently has become so important that it forces the scientist to take it into account, is the *destructive power of weapons*. That power is such that Professor H. Alfven proposed no longer to call them weapons--which suggests that they add to security--but *'annihilators'* which is a better characterization of their nature.

Not only should our welfare concept be extended to all relevant *space* (the whole globe), there are good reasons also that they extend it in *time* and to cover the entire future. The adjective 'sustainable' in the definition of the phenomenon to be measured indicates this extension. The necessity to do so will become clear if our analysis shows how difficult it will be to identify and to implement a policy to safeguard the welfare of *all future generations*. In all probability this is the greatest difficulty we must face and the aspect where the largest gap between desirable--or even necessary--and actual human attitudes exists.

The central phenomenon of our analysis, welfare, may also be called happiness and is usually thought to be based on existing preferences of the individuals involved. A possible alternative is 'corrected' welfare which means that artificial components, such as the impact of advertising or some forms of propaganda, would be eliminated. This 'correction' might be made by a group of 'wise' men or women, supposed to be able to make a distinction between 'imagined' and 'true' preferences. Such 'corrections' are of doubtful value and had better be avoided. They introduce elements of arbitrariness which are hard to defend. Most individuals are confronted with opinions of wiser people and absorb parts of these opinions. If interviewed about their own preferences they will use the elements of such opinions they actually understood and adhered to and that seems the most appropriate way to deal with the welfare concept.

The evaluation of the Study Group will consist of three parts. The most fundamental question concerns the *welfare concept* to be used. The present author will defend the widest conceivable interpretation of welfare, of which economic welfare is only a *part*. Other components are happiness derived from family life, friendship and even economic welfare also includes such elements as satisfaction--or dissatisfaction--from *production*, especially work. Finally, welfare has an equity component. This part of the evaluation will be discussed in Section II.

A second part of our evaluation is based on the statement that calculation of the Index essentially is an act of *checking the policies* so far implemented. But is it all that must be checked? This part will be dealt with in Section III.

The third question to be faced by our analysis is whether the activity of the Study Group, the calculation of the Index, is the *only* activity needed in order to implement an optimal socioeconomic policy in the framework of an optimal socioeconomic order. To the author of this essay it seems that *other activities* will also be needed. The Index may be a check of the policies actually implemented. But an index cannot express the sustainability of the welfare measured. Sustainability can be evaluated only by knowledge of the policies chosen and carried out. If the check results in a rejection of these policies we should not stop our activities, but at least indicate *what other policies should be adopted*. This subject will be dealt with in Section IV.

This program for the evaluation of the Study Group's work constitutes a generalization into various directions of that work. Since in many respects that work consists of a generalization of previous attempts to understand and measure in the best way humanity's welfare the program announced confirms, in several ways, my sympathy and approval of the Group's approach. It illustrates, in a remarkable way, what possibilities exist to integrate theological or ethical analysis with economical analysis in its widest sense.

II. Narrower and Wider Welfare Concepts

Human welfare is a concept of central importance to economists and economic policy makers. Economic science, however, is not the only science dealing with human welfare: happiness depends on more than the economic aspects of human life, as set out in Section I. Interesting illustrations can be derived from a sociological inquiry by Levy and Guttman.[2] These authors collected figures by surveying, on two occasions (spring and summer 1973), more than 1800 inhabitants of Israeli towns. The aspects of happiness they selected for measurement were 21, of which I drop one ('mood'), because I think it is too vague. The 20 others are shown in the following table.

Aspects of Happiness Chosen by Levy and Guttman

satisfied with social group	ethnic relations
success in acquiring friends	country success in ethnic integration
health condition	security situation of Israel
sufficient income	general situation of Israel
able to save	government handling economic problems
satisfied with work	government handling security problems
safe to walk at night	health ministry handling health problems
employer-worker relations	satisfied with medical services
satisfied with economic situation	government handling current problems

In addition, welfare also depends on income distribution. Large income differences express, among other characteristics, less equity than smaller income differences. Ideally these other characteristics (e.g. larger schooling differences) should be corrected for, and this remains a problem to be solved. As a first, crude indication, however, an index of income distribution may be a factor of the Index, with a negative influence.

In order to deal with some other highly topical problems of mankind at least two additional aspects must be added: security and natural environment. Security may even be decomposed into internal and external security, where internal security refers to the threats by people of one's own nation and external security to the threat of war.

With regard to the purely economic aspect of welfare a distinction must be made between welfare experienced as a consumer (and derived from the consumption of the goods and services bought with one's income) and welfare experienced as a student and a producer. A student may feel happy because the subjects taught interest him or her or unhappy because they do not interest him or her, or they are not understood. A producer may feel satisfaction from his or her creative activity or bored if that activity is simple and monotonous. In two brief notes I tried to make this point and to contribute to the measurement of these components of welfare.[3]

III. Additional Checking Needed

As set out in Section I, more checks may be needed than only the level of welfare attained so far. For the design of the best socioeconomic policy from now on it may be necessary to know some of the restrictions we are subject to. An important restriction is the total known reserves of all resources we think we need for future welfare: energy resources such as coal, oil, natural gas, metal ore resources, arable land reserves and so on. We must also know what future development of technology we may assume in order to judge what possibilities exist to maintain or, hopefully, raise the level of welfare attainable for later generations. We must also know what the probable increase in population of the earth is, since too quick an increase in population may imply that not enough resources will be available for future generations. There is a non-negligible possibility that we are not sufficiently cautious in this respect: very few people are aware of what we may leave our offspring with. The subject of the sustainability of welfare is grossly neglected.

Discounting of future welfare is not correct if we want to express the aim of an equitable distribution among future and present generations.

Also neglected, but not to that extent, is the necessity to redistribute today's world income. World income distribution is very unequal and Summers *et. al* has shown that no reduction of that inequality has taken place between 1950 and 1980.[4] In addition it is improbable that so far, after 1980, inequality has been reduced. This implies an ever increasing propensity of the Third World population to migrate to the prosperous parts of the world: North America and Europe. The flow of, partly 'illegal' immigration is increasing notwithstanding the fence between the USA and Mexico and other devices to reduce it. Unless a substantial increase in development assistance is organized in order to create employment in their home countries the flow of immigrants will flood the prosperous regions of the world and contribute to social unrest, cultural conflicts and political instability. What is needed amounts to at least two percent of the prosperous nations' GNP instead of the 0.7 percent so far considered as a norm (and fulfilled only for one half, 0.35 percent).

Our conclusion cannot be other than that a vast amount of additional testing is needed if we want to contribute essentially to a really sustained future level of welfare for the world and for our own nations.

IV. Policy Making Needed

As set out in Section I, we need more than testing our current level of welfare. If sustained welfare is what we aim at we must participate in the process of policy making. With a high likelihood that present policies are insufficient to produce sustained welfare our duty is to participate in the choice of another policy, especially in the choice of the means.

The most important means are the set needed to maintain peace. In my opinion *disarmament* is crucial, combined with a reorganization and strengthening of the United Nations. Participation in the discussions about this reorganization and strengthening constitutes an important task to all of those responsible for or interested in future generations and should be studied considerably more intensively by political parties and hence especially by the leading politicians. But also spiritual leaders and teachers and their organizations should participate in such discussions. A very modest and elementary attempt to sketch some of the questions to be investigated may be found in a booklet I wrote for the Nuclear Age Peace Foundation.[5]

A second category of policy means which requires reconsideration is all that is known as *development co-operation*. Among them Official Development Assistance (ODA) is crucial. So far the amount suggested by most experts (of the Pearson and of the Brandt Commission, for instance) was 0.7 percent of GNP. The actual amount made available is only half of this, 0.35 percent. A reconsideration of the question led me to the proposition that 2 percent, so six times the amount made available, is necessary. Only such an amount provides the developing countries with a perspective that their incomes will be substantially improved. The criterion I propose is that within 30 years their income in relation to the incomes of the industrialized countries should be doubled. Financing such an amount could be done by a substantial reduction in military expenditures.

A third category of policy means required are the means aiming at the maintenance of our level of welfare for *future generations*. In order to maintain that level forever we need continued technological progress, so the quantity of consumer goods needed can be obtained from the processing of regularly diminishing quantities of natural resources. We also need a population policy in order to keep constant total population--or at least a much lower rate of growth than today's, especially in developing countries. Many developed and some developing nations are on their way to such a policy. But a lot more family planning is desirable and there is a frightening unawareness of this desirability or, rather, necessity.

The fourth category of means of socioeconomic policy is the choice, by each nation, of its preferred *social order*. Essentially this must be the nation's own choice. The choice is one among many different sorts of order, but to begin with a choice between market economies and centrally planned economies often has been suggested to be the main choice. Closer study shows, however, that these purely capitalist and purely communist orders do not exist anymore. Pure capitalism did not even exist in 1850, when Karl Marx lived and introduced these concepts. And ever since reforms have raised the *role of government*, in order to eliminate the sharpest edges such as children's work, dangerous work, night work or too long working days. In communist countries, the first of which was created in Russia in 1917, production for the market existed already quite some time before Mikhail Gorbachev introduced more democracy and production for the market. It was important for agriculture, in particular for protein and vitamin rich food (dairy products, vegetables and fruit). So the real choice is what sort and degree of mixed economy is chosen. There is not, however, only a one dimensional set of choices; the space of possibilities shows more dimensions, as may be illustrated by the example of Japan. Its system certainly is close to a market economy, but its income distribution is less unequal than American, and industrial democracy is stronger.

V. Conclusions

As may have become clear the present author is very sympathetic to the work done by the Study Group on the Index of Sustainable Economic Welfare. He interprets that work to be based on a feeling of responsibility for not only today's welfare but also for that of future generations: this is expressed by the word 'sustainable.' If this interpretation is correct, this responsibility implies that the work to be done does not stop with checking the effects of past policies. The index, however enriched, can only indicate welfare at the period of observation. It cannot indicate the sustainability of that welfare. Our responsibility also implies the indication of present and future policies, and the attitudes of the present population needed to attain the aims of a sustained welfare and an optimal distribution of world welfare in the frame of the social order chosen. It is necessary to take world welfare as the criterion and not national welfare or welfare of a limited group of nations only, because the interdependence of nations is so strong that neglect of the welfare of other countries leads to a neglect of sectors or areas of our own nation. Not only the best policies must be chosen, but in some important problems the best policies can only be implemented if people's attitudes reflect an understanding of mankind's needs and their consequences.

Understanding of the need for a clean environment has improved and international decision making on environmental policies will soon be possible. Understanding for the need of a better world income distribution is less clear and on this issue attitudes have to be corrected in order to avoid more immigration from poor countries by providing more development assistance. Understanding for the need of future generations is least developed and here much remains to be done. An example of what is still not understood is the necessity to limit the number of children per family to not much more than two as an average.

Chapter 9

ECONOMIC MEASURES AND PUBLIC POLICY

Richard D. Lamm
Former Governor of Colorado

I.

One of the main obligations of any generation (and clearly of public policy) is to ascertain and define the new set of challenges with which it is faced. Every generation must come to grips with its own new realities, and these realities are constantly changing. Time is a kaleidoscope and every month, every year, every decade a new pattern emerges on that public policy kaleidoscope. It is absolutely imperative that we recognize and react to that new pattern of reality. Public policy is not static. It is ever-evolving, ever changing, and we must take great care not to repeat the mistake of von Clausewitz's generals and always fight the last war.

Every generation must as a matter of highest priority meet the challenge of history and correctly recognize and react to the new challenges of its time. This is not always easy. Barabara Tuchman has noted that:

> Policy is formed by preconceptions and by long implanted biases. When information is relayed to policy makers, they respond in terms of what is already inside their heads and consequently make policy less to fit the facts than to fit the baggage that has accumulated since childhood. [1]

We continue to look at the new world in old ways. We try desperately to change new realities to fit our old prejudices.

II.

That said, one must approach this process of issue identification with large quantities of humility. Public policy, like beauty, too often lies in the eye of the beholder. Every generation throughout history has had multiple messiahs who have preached their own brand of salvation and bent the facts to fit their preconceptions. Too many people have answers to questions which are clearly the wrong questions. Looking back on history, the correct identification of the major challenges of one's time often looks easier than it was in fact. Everything is clear in retrospect. It is clear beyond doubt, looking back on it from over fifty years, that Churchill better assessed the Hitlerian threat than did Chamberlain. Looking back from this distance, so many of the dynamics and subtleties become blurred and we thus underestimate and underrate the difficulty of persuading a society on the nature of a new reality. England in the 1930's was full of bright and able people, educated at the finest schools and who had generally been correct in all of their geopolitical decisions up to 1932. Yet these brilliantly educated, very world-wise and smart people too often felt Hitler was merely "an understandable expression of German nationalism" and/or was a needed bulwark against the threats of Communism. Churchill--almost alone--assessed the extent and nature of Hitler's plan for Europe.[2] But the fact that he had such a difficult time persuading other people should show us the immense difficulty in raising new issues in society. As Kenneth Boulding has said, the difficulty with public policy is all of our experiences are in the past yet all all our decisions deal with the future.[3] It is and always has been terribly difficult to get society to recognize new threats. There is an immense amount of self denial in the human character. The status quo by definition is very functional to large numbers of people. To change that status quo in any measurable way will always take immense amounts of effort and will always be met by an army of skeptics, guarding the citadel of status quo.

III.

But we also know from the thoughtful study of history that most utopians and most doomsayers have been wrong. Will and Ariel Durant, after a lifetime of studying history, observed "that 99 out of every 100 new ideas that come at a society are bad ideas."[4] It has been very stabilizing to societies and to nations to give a heavy burden of proof to those arguing for dramatic change. History shows, as a group, they are usually wrong. Most prophets, alas, have been false prophets.

IV.

"We grow or we die."

Sign in Chamber of Commerce Office

V.

That said, I would suggest that the major challenge of our time is to adjust to a new world of limits. I believe that evidence is overwhelming that both population and resource consumption are on a collision course with our existing social, political and economic institutions. We live, I fear, in an unsustainable society. The relentless geometry of population growth and resource consumption cannot continue. The earth is sending us messages that we ignore to our great peril. If, as Huxley observed, "all truths begin as heresy," one of the great truths that our world is going to have to learn (and learn soon) is that neither population growth nor economic growth as now defined can continue very far into the future. Infinite human wants and the relentless geometric growth of population are fast running into the finiteness of our globe.

VI.

"If an enormous source of low-cost energy is discovered, it is easy to predict what the immediate consequence would be. Our political and economic leaders would collectively breathe a great sigh of relief and would then discard all notions of energy limits. They would rejoice over the advent of a period of uninhibited growth in global rates of energy consumption.

"In order to estimate the consequences of likely rates of growth of global energy consumption, we must remember that essentially all of the energy released by human activity winds up ultimately as heat in the environment. First we need some data. The solar power incident on the earth can be calculated by multiplying the solar constant (1.35×10^3 W/m^2) by the projected area of the earth (pRe^2). This gives 1.7×10^{17} watts of which 34% is reflected back into space, leaving 1.1×10^{17} watts of solar power entering the earth's atmosphere. Romer shows that the rate of energy use by humans is 8×10^{12} watts. A simple quotient shows that human activities put into the earth's atmosphere about 10^{-4} of the power the sun puts into the earth's atmosphere. The simple arithmetic of growth shows that one would gain a factor of 10^4 in 14 doubling times. At a growth rate of 3% per year the doubling time is 23 years and 14 doubling times would take about 300 years. The arithmetic would suggest that at modest growth rate, in 300 years human activities would put about as much thermal power into the earth's atmosphere as the sun puts in! The absurdity of this situation is obvious. Independent of the 'greenhouse effect,' global warming from this direct heating would likely render the earth uninhabitable long before the passage of 14 doubling times."[5]

Albert A. Bartlett

VII.

We thus must ask ourselves: Can our existing political institutions reform the status quo and adapt to the new realities that a finite globe is imposing on us? Can they adjust and accommodate the multiple challenges that are inherent in this new world of public policy? One stands in awe at the magnitude of the problem. If humankind has to control its numbers and its voracious consumption of resources we will have to change the existing order of our world more than it has ever been changed. There is simply no precedent for the scope and magnitude of the change that will be required.

The first challenge that our world faces is to get some sort of consensus that massive change is necessary. This may be the singularly most difficult aspect of this problem. The ancient Greeks used to say, "To know all to ask is to know half." Our society is understandably skeptical of the current requests for massive change in our existing way of life. Malthus and his intellectual cousins have, to date, been false prophets. The philosopher Schopenhauer once said, "Every man confuses the limits of his mind for the limits of the world." Humankind has been amazingly successful in pushing back the limits of our globe. The prevailing ethic in almost all of the industrialized world is simply *not* one of adapting to limits. Man has been an ingenious animal and a very adaptable animal. Any person that has pondered history recognizes that we all are guessing about the future. History is full of examples where one course of action looked necessary but some intervening event canceled out what looked like the clear course of action. The future is a multilateral equation and one part of the equation can change dramatically and affect the whole answer. "History has many cunning passages," T.S. Elliot observed, and in those "cunning passages" often lie answers that we never dreamed of at a particular point in history. "Nature is full of things," observed one author, "patiently waiting for our wits to sharpen." Barrier after barrier, limit after limit, has fallen when confronted with human ingenuity. Mankind has generally been successful by following the "golden mean," and discounting both utopians and doomsayers. Public policy must take all claims of dramatic change with a certain level of skepticism. New epochs are terribly dislocating. They bring much turmoil and destruction with them. No sane person changes an existing order, except on the basis of overwhelming evidence. It is a terribly heavy burden to be a change agent in our society, especially the kind of revolutionary changes that will clearly be necessary if the world has to adapt to a new world of limits. One does not impose a new order on the basis of incomplete evidence. Those that advocate massive change should have a massive burden of proof on them that their interpretation of the facts is correct.

Change happens best in societies when it is incremental. Mankind digests change a step at a time, and massive change imposed too fast is profoundly destabilizing.

I am thus caught in a cruel dilemma. I recognize that society's survival has required it to be skeptical of just the kind and degree of dramatic change that alone can save our society. We have, for very logical and practical reasons, immunized ourselves against the very cure that can save.

VIII.

"We are entering a climacteric of civilization in which no one can have more without someone having less."

Henry Kissinger[6]

IX.

I believe it is very doubtful that our existing political and economic institutions can handle the transition into the new environmentally benign world that will be required of us by this new world of limits. Up to now, there is little evidence that democracy can call upon people for sacrifice or discipline. Democracy seems to be a marvelous energizing and heretofore successful way of organizing a society. It will be the ultimate of ironies just at the moment when democracy is proving its strength in a bi-polar world that it will be found lacking to deal with the new reality of a finite world.

Unless we can find some environmentally benign type of economic growth, we shall be faced with the unenviable task of allocating scarcity. A society which has developed prosperity through the unlimited use of natural resources will have to develop new distributional schemes that will test the resilience of our institutions. It will require degrees of social control that are likely unacceptable to a democracy. In a democracy, politics is the management of expectations, and we face a growing gap between expectations and reality.

The ancient Greek philosophers warned us that democracy would eventually be unsustainable. Aristotle and Plato felt that in the long run democracy was unsustainable. Cicero and Seneca thought democracy an unworkable and inferior system. No less than a founding father of our system, John Adams, observed:

> Democracy never lasts long. It soon wastes, exhausts and murders itself. There was never a democracy yet that did not commit suicide.[7]

This clearly has not proved to be the case. Economic growth has essentially rescued democracy. We have been able to avoid the factionalization that the Greek philosophers warned about because economic growth raised up all segments of society. Every generation could be promised and generally delivered a better and richer standard of living. Democracy was very effective in distributing the spoils of a virgin continent and it was even successful in regenerating old societies into the new world of wealth. But to be successful it required new spoils almost every year to distribute. An economically growing society soothes over many inherent tensions. The vast majority of the people see that stability and the existing order gives a higher standard of living to virtually everyone within the society. But democracy does not appear to be good in calling upon people for discipline and sacrifice and belt tightening. Though it is true that this has been done in times of war, I do not believe we can take solace from the war analogy. If the greenhouse effect and the population explosion prove to be anywhere near as serious as threats as they now appear, it will be virtually generations that will be faced simultaneously with massive economic and social transformations. We will not be able to offer people a growing pie or even a "light at the end of the tunnel" because the process of restoring balance between the species and the carrying capacity of the world will be so long term and so massive in scope. It will require us to change our whole life styles, our values and our attitudes. It will require a massive change in directions, in virtually everything that we've built up. The 19th century saw incredible energy released when humankind learned they were not victims of the status quo and could change the conditions of the economy and the environment. Man no longer had to bow before the inevitability of nature, and humankind became itself a change agent beyond its wildest dreams.

But if the environmental threat is as serious as its proponents say, we clearly live in a hinge of history, where that existing world is unsustainable, and the new world will require traits and institutions in many ways the opposite of what the old world required. It will be far more traumatizing than the discovery of a new world by Galileo's telescope.

We are seeing in Russia, Poland, the Balkans that societies that do not promise people a better life on a more immediate basis are inherently unstable societies.

New worlds always come with much pain and conflict. Arnold Toynbee, writing shortly before his death, observed:

Now that the terms of trade are turning against the 'developed' countries in favor of the 'developing' countries, how will the peoples of the 'developed' countries react?

They are going to find themselves in a permanent state of siege, in which the material conditions of life will be at least as austere as they were during the two World Wars. The wartime austerity was temporary; the future austerity will be perennial and it will then become progressively more severe. What then?

When the peoples of the 'developed' countries are forced, by events, to recognize the inexorability of the new facts, their first impulse will be to fight back. And since they will be powerless to assault either 'natives' or nature, they will assault one another. Within each of the beleaguered 'developed' countries there will be a bitter struggle for the control of their diminished resources.

This struggle will merely worsen a bad situation: It will somehow have to be stopped. If left unchecked, it would lead to anarchy and to a drastic reduction of the size of the population by civil war, famine and pestilence, the historic reducers of populations that have outgrown their means of subsistence. Consequently, in all 'developed' countries, a new way of life--a severely regimented way-- will have to be imposed by ruthless authoritarian governments.[8]

In another article Toynbee expanded on this theme:

Man is a social animal; mankind cannot survive in anarchy; and if democracy fails to provide stability it will assuredly be replaced by some socially stabilizing regime, however uncongenial this alternative regime may be. A community that has purchased freedom at the cost of losing stability will find itself constrained to re-purchase stability at the price of sacrificing its freedom. This happened in the Greco-Roman world; it could happen in our world too if we were to continue to fail to make democratic institutions work. Freedom is expendable; stability is indispensable.[9]

Ultimately, the laws of nature will take precedence over the laws (and institutions) of man and social stability will take precedence over political freedom. It is comforting to have them not in conflict, but when they do conflict, the outcome is predictable.

Democracy has served me well; it has served us well. Its alternatives are draconian and unacceptable to me personally. We should and will fight mightily to solve our problems with democratic means. The challenge of the future will be to see if we can adapt an institution that has historically run on growth to an institution that can manage the type of change and sacrifice that time the new world will require.

X.

If we have any hope in a democracy to educate the public on the rapid change that lies in our future, we must be sure that they understand better where they are at present.

Democracy has survived some pretty tough times and has, over a short period of time, called upon people to sacrifice, but only after it has been adequately explained to the people the reason and the need for sacrifice. This requires us to better measure where we are today and where we are likely to be tomorrow. Our sense of urgency thus depends heavily on the accuracy of our yardsticks.

No society can ever see itself objectively in a stream of time. There is an "uncertainty principle" in public policy just as in physics. Historian Arnold Toynbee describes it this way:

> The position of our western society in our age cannot become known with any certainty of knowledge 'til the voyage comes to an end; and so long as the ship is under way, the crew will have no notion whether she is going to founder in mid-ocean through springing a leak, or be sent to the bottom by colliding with another vessel, or run ashore on the rocks, or glide smoothly into a port of which the crew will never have heard before they wake up one fine day to find their ship at rest in dock there. A sailor at sea cannot tell for which, if for any, of these ends the ship is heading as he watches her making headway during the brief period of his own spell of duty. To plot out her course and to write up her log from start to finish is a task that can be performed only by observers who are able to wait until the voyage is over.[10]

Toynbee's metaphor may be correct in a cosmic sense but it does not adequately explain that ships have instruments that help gauge where they are at a particular time and where they should be tomorrow. A ship captain's most important task is to anticipate the future journey and to find measurements telling him/her accurately where he is heading, what are the obstacles, and what will be the weather. The captain thus needs both a compass and a barometer; a compass to tell him where the ship currently is and, of equal importance, a barometer to better gauge what is coming.

The 21st century will require us to better understand our public policy geography; to know where we are in a particular time but also to better know where we are going. Similarly the GNP measurement of our economic welfare is inadequate. It gives us an assessment of an economy at a particular point in time but it may not measure the most important variables. It does not and cannot tell us how we are adjusting to the new environmental realities humankind is faced with.

If one looks at Miami, Florida on any particular day statistics show clearly that the average person in Miami is born Cuban and dies Jewish. A snapshot has thus not given us accurate information because it has ignored the true dynamic. We must find better yardsticks to gauge the full dynamic of a world where infinite demands are running into finite resources. There probably isn't any perfect yardstick, because just as the ship captain needs more than one instrument, so also does society need more than one instrument to gauge where they are at in a particular time. It would appear that some debate must take place on what measure should go into a new index of sustainable economic welfare. The principal authors of this book have suggested the need to include three values: the significance of household production, the importance of reducing income equality (relative to the current situation), and the value of sustaining productive resources for use by future generations.

This might not be the complete answer but it is certainly the right question. When a new threat arises we need new methods to measure that threat.

Paul Blumberg observes," When an object is falling from a great height, one can focus either on its altitude or on its rate of descent."[11] When an economy that depends on massive amounts of natural resources moves into a time of resource and environmental constraints, it must measure not only its altitude but also its rate of descent.

XI.

"The problems of the future will differ fundamentally from former problems that we have dealt with successfully. In the past human energy focused on solving the problems of the world as we found it. The future's critical problems will be those of the world as we have made it."

Peter Schwartz[12]

XII.

Recognizing thus that we are all guessing and that "he who has a crystal ball usually eats ground glass," one can put forth the most likely scenario:

A.   That our environmental/population problems will not be solved without a crisis; that democracy is a crisis-activated system; and that it is impossible for any leader to ask for the kind of sacrifice and discipline that will be necessary to transform our society into one consistent with the limits of the environment;

B.   That when that crisis takes place there is considerable question whether it can be solved by democratic means. Restoring balance with the limits of the globe is not just another issue in a long string of issues that democracy has had to adjust, but an issue that goes right to the core of our institutions, our mores, and the myths that we live by. There is little historical evidence that an over-indulged society will voluntarily make the kind of steps that will most likely be necessary to bring our society within the limits of our world. The epoch of the infinite will not easily give way to the epoch of the finite. A society whose dominant institutions, cultures and mores were built to protect man against nature will find it difficult to use the same framework to protect nature against man;

C.   I sense we live in a time like 1914 where dramatic and traumatic events lie just over the horizon and neither our experience nor our imagination is large enough to perceive what is about to happen;

D. The only chance I can see to adapt to this new world by democratic means is by a change in our culture, in our values, in our attitudes. The solutions must start in our hearts and habits rather than in the political system or a technological breakthrough. The solutions are more theological than political; more in our hearts than in our heads. But to engage in time we must find better ways of measuring what our industrial society is doing to our natural world: we are living on the upper end of some gigantic geometric curves. Just as 'no tree can grow to the sky,' no species can forever multiply and no resource can be geometrically consumed. We must learn to come to grips with the finiteness of our planet, and nothing in our human history can give us guidance to the magnitude of this transformation.

Chapter 10

THE INDEX OF SUSTAINABLE ECONOMIC WELFARE: A CASE STUDY OF THE FEDERAL REPUBLIC OF GERMANY*

Dr. Hans Diefenbacher, Economist
Protestant Institute for Interdisciplinary Research, Heidelberg

I. Introduction

For more than fifteen years, there has been an ongoing discussion in the Federal Republic of Germany (FRG) on the value of the Gross National Product (GNP) as a measure of economic and social welfare.[1] Already in 1976, Ursula Wehner related the concept of ecological and social costs of production to the national income accounting system;[2] some years later, Utz Peter Reich and Carsten Stahmer analyzed the suitability of a national welfare measure in regard to its ability to include indicators for environmental quality.[3] In 1985, Adolf Theobald suggested replacing the GNP by an "ecological national product" that would combine new indicators for the quality of life.[4] His concept, however, was not elaborated upon; quite to the contrary, the book reads as an appeal to the public to participate in the design of new measurement systems. As one of the most recent books, in 1988 Frank Beckenbach and Michaele Schreyer published a volume that contains investigations of problems of recording and measuring different social costs of productions, e.g. air pollution, passenger-car traffic, health costs and so on.[5]

*This essay was written before German reunification. It deals with what was West Germany.

One of the first publications of an empirical analysis in this field that attracted great attention was an attempt to develop a new method of an ecologically oriented bookkeeping.[6] Criticism of the national accounting system is widespread but theoretically oriented. Only recently has it led to some experiments to calculate ecological and other damages that are not included in the GNP or--even worse--contribute to its growth. Lutz Wicke tried to add up the negative external effects of using the environment in production and consumption. His estimation of the total cost of pollution exceeds 100 Billion DM, that is, roughly, twice the military budget of the FRG.[7] A few months ago, Christian Leipert published an analysis of ecological and social costs that evolve as a consequence of economic growth. Leipert's attempt is to calculate the percentage of "defensive expenditures" within the GNP--expenditures that do not really contribute to economic welfare, but need to be spent in order to compensate for negative developments accompanying economic growth. According to Leipert's results, defensive expenditures as a percentage of GNP increased from 7% to 11.6% in the period from 1970 to 1988.[8]

However, the calculations both of Wicke and Leipert--as well as those publications that don't go beyond theoretical critiques--do not include most of the long-term consequences of production and consumption. Hence, these approaches to create a different national accounting system do not adequately incorporate the aspect of sustainability. This was one of the most important reasons for the attempt to compute a time series of the Index of Sustainable Economic Welfare (ISEW) for the FRG that is presented here.

Other questions that emerged after reading the ISEW index for the U.S. are of a more methodological nature. Are the data that are necessary for the computation of the ISEW actually accessible, or would it be impossible to apply the calculation procedure to another country? Which data are available not only allows one to draw conclusions about their degree of availability and understanding, but at the same time, can serve as an indicator of which problems a society considers it important enough to collect data.[9] The question of the availability of data leads to problems on an even more general level: Does the relative weight of the different variables vary from country to country? And if this is the case--are these variations an expression of differences of the development of these countries or an expression of different utility functions of its inhabitants? What, finally, are the conditions for international comparisons of welfare measures?

This paper will not pretend to answer all these questions. However, by presenting one specific case study it can demonstrate the difficulties of such international comparisons and work out some of the strengths and weaknesses of the ISEW a bit more clearly. The next section develops the computation of the ISEW for the FRG. The calculation follows the same procedures as for the U.S. as far as possible. The following pages explain the nature of and the reason for those divergences that were unavoidable. Section 3 of this paper is a short conclusion about the results of the West German case study, and section 4 summarizes some outcomes and methodological problems of the comparison between the ISEW time series for the U.S. and the ISEW time series for the FRG. Finally, section 5 gives some suggestions on how the calculations of ISEW could be further used; this section, again, takes up a discussion about improvements of national income accounting within the FRG.

2. The Calculation of an ISEW Time Series for the Federal Republic of Germany

As pointed out above, the calculation of the ISEW time series for the FRG as closely as possible follows the methods that have been applied in the computation of the time series for the U.S. Table B.10.1 gives the total calculation tableau of the ISEW/FRG from 1950 to 1987; it is set up like the corresponding table for the U.S. (See table A.1 on pages 80-83.) The following explanations do not contain a complete set of instructions for the computation of the ISEW; only the unavoidable alterations are listed.

Two common problems must be dealt with in many of the FRG calculations of time series variables; therefore, they should be discussed at the beginning. The first problem touches most of the time series that go past the year 1960. In this year, the counties of Saarland and West-Berlin were integrated into the statistical accounts of the FRG. Between 1945 and 1959, those two areas are not included in the statistical figures. For the period of 1950 to 1959, the figures from official sources must be increased by the proportional difference that exists in 1960 between the data with and the data without Saarland and West-Berlin.[10] In the average, this means that the official figures in the period of 1950 to 1959 are augmented by slightly more than 6%.

The second problem comes from an annoying habit of the central statistical office of the FRG. In time series data adjusted for price the office frequently changes reference years. For example, the statistical yearbooks[11] give the deflated values of GNP for the period examined here--in succession--in prices of the years 1954, 1962, 1970, 1976 and 1980. And at the same time, the office not only adds the new data to its time series, but also corrects numerical values of prior years. These rectifications of data lead to inaccuracies when connecting time series that are based on different reference years. Therefore, statistical figures are taken, wherever possible, from the two volumes of "long" time series the central statistical office published.[12] In the 1973 volume, the period from 1960 to 1970 is given in prices of 1962, and in the 1988 volume, the same years are given in prices of 1980. The two time series are connected by using the arithmetical average for those years from 1960 to 1970, where numerical figures on the basis of two different reference years are given. From 1962 to 1980, this procedure leads to an average total inflation of 219.99%; the margin of fluctuation goes from 203% to 235%. For an interim result, all numerical figures are given in prices of 1980. For a better comparability to the ISEW of the U.S., the times series finally are standardized to prices of the year 1972.

COLUMN B: PERSONAL CONSUMPTION

The statistical figures for the period from 1950 to 1959 are increased by 6.9% in order to include Saarland and West-Berlin.[13]

COLUMN C: DISTRIBUTIONAL INEQUALITY

The officially published statistics in the FRG do not allow the calculation of a time series for household income quintiles with satisfactory exactness as is the case with the ISEW for the U.S. For the FRG, a quintile distribution of household incomes can be obtained only for some specific years, and not from official sources. The so-called "welfare survey" gives a quintile income distribution for the year 1980,[14] as well as the cross-section data of the "socioeconomic panel" of the universities of Mannheim and Frankfurt for the years 1984 and 1985.[15] Calculating the quintile distribution of household income given in these surveys into the ISEW index of distributional inequality would result in an index-value of 2.17 for the year of 1980, 2.62 for 1984, and 2.56 for 1985, respectively.[16] These index-values are about one third lower than the index-values for the U.S.--a fact that could be interpreted as indicating that the household incomes in the FRG are more equally distributed than in the U.S.

Remarkable as this finding is, it would be of no consequence to the calculation of the ISEW time series, because the only aspect of distributional inequality that is taken into account is the *relative* change of the income distribution in relation to the reference year of 1951. An *absolute* measure of distributional equality is not a part of the ISEW. The differences between the index levels of the FRG and the U.S. would not necessarily lead to a different weight for the personal consumption figures in the two countries--as already mentioned, only the relative change compared to the reference year of 1951 is important.

The findings of the "socioeconomic panel" suggest that there are huge and even growing income differences *within* social groups that would not be adequately accounted for by a computation of quintiles.[17] But these differences seem to be a particularly important aspect of income inequality.

The role of income inequality taken here as a substitute for the quintiles cannot represent these structural changes either.   But although the wage ratio is an imperfect expression of *functional* income distribution, it is quite an important factor in determining *personal* income distribution.   The index that is calculated here on the basis of the wage ratio presumably is no worse an indicator of the relative changes of personal income distribution than the index used in the ISEW of the U.S.

The calculation of this substitute index is shown in table B.10.2. Column B gives the national revenue, column C the gross income from wages and salaries.[18] Column D is the actual wage ratio (column C as a percent of column B).   But this actual wage ratio must be corrected because the amount of self-employed labor as percentage of the total labor force is changing.   Column E shows the percentage of wage earners.[19] Column F is the adjusted wage ratio: column D standardized with column E to a "constant" percentage of self-employed labor, with the year 1960 of column E as the basis of standardization.[20] This adjusted wage ratio, finally, is related to the year 1951, like the ISEW index for the U.S.   The result is given in column G (transferred to column C in table B.10.1).

This index of income inequality is moving in an opposite direction to the ISEW index: the *higher* the index value, the *more equal* the income is distributed.   Therefore, weighted personal consumption is obtained by *multiplying* personal consumption (column B) with the index (column C).

COLUMN E: HOUSEHOLD LABOR (+)

For the FRG as well as for the U.S., there are only estimates for the size of household production available, and these only for some years and not as time series.[21] It is interesting that these estimates as a percentage of the corresponding GNP are decreasing over time, with only one exception.[22] The range of the estimates generally is between 25% and 50% of the GNP, again with one exception.[23] It is not easy to compare these estimates because they differ methodologically in defining household labor, in separating working hours from leisure time and in "pricing" the household products. On the other hand, the results are thoroughly comparable to studies from other countries.[24]

Taking these ranges of the available estimates of the size of household production and calculating an average percentage in relation to the GNP, it can be assumed that the value of household production declined from 42% of the GNP in 1950 to 35% of the GNP in 1987. This certainly is a rather drastic difference with the ISEW for the U.S. where--according to the assumptions made--the value of household production decreased from 58% of the GNP in 1950 to a mere 28% of the GNP in 1986. Other results of computations of the size of household production in the U.S. would indicate, however, that the assumptions for the FRG could be plausible as well for that of the U.S.[25]

COLUMN F AND COLUMN I: SERVICES OF (+) AND EXPENDITURES ON (-) CONSUMER DURABLES

For consumer durables, the statistical data base is much worse for the FRG than for the U.S. The publications of the central statistical office evaluate consecutive expenses of selected private households. But these income and expenditure samples have been surveyed only since 1963, and only every five years. The statistical yearbooks for the FRG give the results of these surveys for three different categories of households: two-person, low-income households of retired people and welfare beneficiaries; four-person, medium-income households of workers and employees; four-person, high-income households of employees and government officials.[26] But neither the data on the selected households with consumer durables nor these expenditure surveys allow the computation of the aggregations necessary for a comparable ISEW variable.

To a certain extent, the calculations of Peren solve the problem.[27] Peren analyzes macroeconomic consumption functions, thereby presenting a time series of consumption expenditures of private households. But his computations comprise only the years from 1968 to 1981. By taking this time series it is, however, possible to construct an analogy to the data of the official statistics to estimate the year by year expenditures for consumer durables between 1950 and 1987.

Another serious problem comes up with estimating the annual services of consumer durables. Since there is no data on the stock of consumer durables available, it is necessary to assume an average economic use of these products and calculate the value in use according to these assumptions. Here, the assumption of the ISEW calculation for the U.S. is adopted, although an average useful life of ten years seems to be rather long. Between 1970 and 1982 for example, the average useful life of passenger cars was between 9.1 and 9.7 years, and the average "life span" of washing machines, electric driers or electric stoves today is between seven and eight years.

However, we cannot apply this method for the years between 1950 and 1960. There are no data at all for the period from 1940 to 1948 that would be suitable to estimate the stock value of consumer durables. Certainly the average period of economic use of consumer durables in the years after World War II was considerably longer. The estimate for the stock of consumer durables in the year 1949 comes from the expenditure surveys presented in the statistical yearbooks of the fifties and from some statements on the stock of several different items. It has to be noticed that the expenditures for consumer durables in the fifties and the eighties, as a percentage of the weighted personal consumption, is much lower in the FRG than in the U.S.

COLUMN G: SERVICES OF STREETS AND HIGHWAYS (+)

The official statistics of the FRG do not report any stock values of streets and highways. As a substitute, the public expenditures for transport and communication are listed.[28] Only 50% of these expenditures are taken to increase the welfare of the population. This deduction is made to cover the commuting costs as well as the public expenditures for communication.

COLUMN H: PUBLIC EXPENDITURES ON HEALTH AND EDUCA-
TION (CONSUMPTION) (+)

To be as close to the ISEW-construction for the U.S., the following public expenditures for education are included here: 50% of the expenditures for universities that were reduced by the expenditures for
university hospitals, and 75% of the expenditures for adult evening
classes and general adult education (occupational retraining, vocational
training and so on).[29] For those years for which these data are not
available an equivalent percentage of the total budget for education is
listed.

According to the calculations of the ISEW for the U.S., the public
health expenditures must be reduced by the level of expenditures for
the year 1950. In the FRG, the 1950 expenditures are especially low. On
the other hand, it can not be thought appropriate for these years to include parts of the expenditures for relief payments and pensions to war
victims. These payments and pensions certainly were of a compensating nature and not welfare increasing, although they included health
expenditures. But all in all, the growth of public health expenditures
might be a little overestimated because the level of the year 1950 was so
low.

COLUMN J: DEFENSIVE PRIVATE EXPENDITURES FOR HEALTH
AND EDUCATION (-)

This variable must be related to a different data base because the
social insurance system of the FRG is rather different from the system
of the U.S. Attendance at public schools and universities is free; at public schools, there are even free instructional materials. The percentage
of defensive expenditures in the area of advanced vocational training
is so small and so insufficient in the official statistics that it will be neglected here.

The situation of defensive private health expenditures is totally
different. The part of the population without health insurance can be
neglected as well--it has been constantly under 0.5%.[30] The basis for the
calculation of the defensive private health expenditures, therefore, is
the total of the gross contributions to private health insurance funds
plus the gross income of compulsory health insurance plans.[31] The latter are included at the 50% level, because social security payroll taxes
should not be considered here. As the calculations for the ISEW in the

U.S. suggests, 50% of the growth of these expenditures, compared to the expenditure level of 1950 are considered to be defensive.

COLUMN K: EXPENDITURES ON NATIONAL ADVERTISING (-)

The figures of advertising expenditures are derived from compilations of the umbrella organization of the West German advertising industry.[32] Again, there is a problem of connecting two time series that are calculated on the basis of different computation methods; the problem--and its solution--is only of technical interest. However, we adopt the concept of Xenophon Zolotas,[33] who subtracts half of the cost of advertising, on the assumption that only half of it gives valuable information services to consumers. For the FRG, this procedure seems to be more reasonable than the differentiation between country-wide and regional or local advertising campaigns.

COLUMN L: COST OF COMMUTING (-)

The cost of commuting for the period between 1960 and 1987 can be taken from the calculations of Christian Leipert.[34] For the years of 1950 to 1959, an annual increase of 200 million DM (in current prices) is assumed. In those years between 1960 and 1987 for which Leipert does not give figures, the numerical values of the variables are simply interpolated--a procedure the author presumably would be satisfied with.

The method Leipert uses to get to his results is not the same as applied in the ISEW calculation for the U.S. First of all, the total expenditure of private households for transport is added up and divided into expenditures for passenger cars and public transport. Next, Leipert takes data from empirical traffic research to determine the share of the total traffic volume that has to be assigned to commuting. The combination of these results, then, allows calculation of commuting costs.

COLUMN M: COST OF URBANIZATION (-)

This is, again, one of those variables that can not be directly transferred from the ISEW for the U.S. to the ISEW for the FRG. The air-raids of World War II destroyed in some cities up to 80% of the housing, and in the year 1960, a total of 16% of the population were expatriates from the countries of eastern Europe.[35] These factors together led to an extreme shortage of housing in the fifties that makes it impossible to compute an estimate of costs of urbanization comparable to the U.S. In addition to that it must be taken into account that due to legal restrictions a sizable part of the rented flats and houses are subject to rent control.

For all these reasons, no assessment of urbanization costs will be considered before the year 1965. For the period between 1965 and 1987, again the cost estimates of Christian Leipert are simply used.[36] Leipert computes extra expenditures of private households for building and for rental payments that are compensatory for increasing urbanization. The calculation has to overcome many difficulties arising from the lack of appropriate data. For a more technical description of the computational methods see Leipert's publication.[37]

COLUMN N: COST OF AUTO ACCIDENTS (-)

The cost of auto accidents is derived from Leipert and from answers to questions by the government to an interpellation of the parliamentary group of the ecological party.[38] Only material damages, no personal injuries are taken into account.

PRELIMINARY REMARK TO COLUMN O - COLUMN U

As in the ISEW calculation for the U.S., in the FRG it is an especially difficult task to compute a time series for ecological damages and for the long-term consequences of economic activities. Most important are three categories of problems:

- There is no "safe" theory as a basis for the decisions about which type of damages, which sort of long-term consequences of economic activities to include and which not. The decision rule applied here is very simple: only those items are included where there can be no doubt at all that they have led or will lead to increased costs or to the infringement of welfare.

- Sometimes there is no "safe" method for the valuation of damages. How to valuate reduced water quality, or the reduction of value for the use of a specific site for recreation? With some problems, there are fully developed valuation methods, whereas with others, only indirect methods like the "willing-ness-to-pay-analysis" exist--methods that are very difficult to apply and that give rather vague results only.

- For some problems, the available data are so fragmentary that it is at best possible to assess the order of magnitude of such costs. The unavailability of data is even more critical during the decades of the sixties and the fifties.

Any figure presented in column O to column U can be questioned. Any figure gives the impression of a numerical exactness that can never really be obtained. To make these problems a little more tolerable, all these calculations are made with assumptions that lead to "conservative" estimates: what is presented is the *lower limit* of costs. This may lead to an underestimation of ecological and long-term damages of economic activities--but it can not be disputed that the problems are at least of that size.

The figures of the times series of environmental costs (column O to column S, i.e. water, air and noise pollution and loss of wetlands and farmlands) use the cost estimates of Lutz Wicke for the year 1985.[39] The estimates for water and noise pollution are combined with the assumptions of "pollution growth rates" made in the ISEW calculation for the U.S. The cost estimate for air pollution is related to an index that combines the emissions of the four main pollutants NO_x, SO_2, CO, and dust. The loss of wetlands and farmlands, finally, is combined into one time series "loss of soil and reduction of soil quality."

COLUMN O: COSTS OF WATER POLLUTION (-)

The figures of this variable contain assessments of costs[40] for:

- pollution of rivers and lakes:
  - diminished fresh-water fishing;
  - costs of drinking water conditioning;
  - decreasing recreational value;
  - decreasing aesthetic pleasure of people living near rivers and lakes;

- sea pollution:
  - oil tanker accidents;
  - sea birds dying of oil pollution and garbage;

- cleaning of beaches;
- diminished tourism;

- ground-water poisoning:
  - nitrates;
  - chlorinated hydrocarbons and other toxic chemicals.

COLUMN P: COSTS OF AIR POLLUTION (-)

As already said above, the estimate of costs of air pollution made by Wicke for the year 1985 are transformed into a time series by using a combined index of NO_x, SO_2, CO and dust emissions.[41] This index is given in table B.10.3. The cost estimate is developed mainly with a willingness-to-pay analysis and contains assessments for health problems, material damages, damages to the vegetation including the "Waldsterben" (death of forests).

COLUMN Q: COSTS OF NOISE POLLUTION (-)

Sixty percent of the population of the FRG considers noise to be an environmental pollutant of great importance.[42] The cost assessment for noise pollution comprises diminutions in the value of houses and property due to street noise, noise abatement measures like noise barriers and detuners, decreasing labor productivity due to noise problems at the workplace and, finally, workmen's compensation benefits.

COLUMN R AND S: LOSS OF WETLANDS AND FARMLANDS (-)

It is assumed that, during the period from 1950 to 1987, the cost of the reduction of soil quality and of the losses of top soil increased from 1.1% to 3% of the GNP. At first glance, this might seem too high, but it must be brought to mind that many different types of costs must be considered here; however, the cost of soil deterioration is--as compared to water or air pollution--only partially understood. The cost estimates that Lutz Wicke and Christian Leipert carried out or referred to are only fragmentary.[43] The costs for cleaning up old trash dumps can be better calculated than health costs due to the consumption of food that was grown on contaminated soil. And very little is known about the long-term damages of heavy metals, pesticides and fungicides and their synergistic effects with other chemicals in the soil.

COLUMN T: DEPLETION OF NONRENEWABLE RESOURCES (-)

As in the ISEW for the U.S., the total value of mining production each year is given here.[44]

COLUMN U: LONG TERM ENVIRONMENTAL DAMAGE (-)

Also here, the method of calculation is adopted from the ISEW for the U.S. According to the statistical data that is available for the FRG, we calculate the tax or rent to be 10 DM for one ton of coal equivalent. Because it is not possible to calculate total energy consumption between 1900 and 1945 for the area of the FRG,[45] we assume that the accumulated non-interest-bearing account in the year 1949 to be 15% of the GNP for this year.

COLUMN V: NET CAPITAL GROWTH (+/-)

This is one of the rare variables where the calculation procedure of the ISEW for the U.S. can be used without any alteration.[46] The different steps of the computation are shown in table B.10.4.

COLUMN W: CHANGE IN NET INTERNATIONAL POSITION (+/-)

For this variable, the balance of international capital transactions is used.[47]

COLUMNS X, Y, Z AND AA give the results of the computation as compared to the GNP, and the ISEW per capita as compared to the GNP per capita.

3. The Results of the Case Study of the FRG

Table B.10.5 shows the ISEW for the FRG as compared with the GNP; table B.10.6 gives the same time series per capita. There are three characteristics of these graphs that are evident immediately:

- First of all, the graphs of the ISEW and of the ISEW per capita look very similar. There is no great difference that can be ascribed to the change in the population figures.

- Second: In the period between 1950 and 1980, the graphs of the ISEW and of the GNP roughly moved in the same direction, but with a different slope; the ISEW is not as steep as the GNP. This changed drastically after 1980, where we find an ongoing growth of the GNP, but a rather sharp decline of the ISEW.

- Third: The amplitudes of the ISEW are greater than that of the GNP graph. This indicates that the ISEW is more sensitive to the changes of the business cycle than the GNP. This is especially visible in the "economic dip" of 1967/68 and the oil crisis of the year 1973; the response of the ISEW takes place with a time lag that is a little longer than the speed of response of the GNP.

What are the changes for the different variables as compared to the ISEW as a whole--and, of course, compared to the GNP? The first columns of table B.10.7 give some interesting answers to that question. This table shows the growth rates of the different variables between 1950 and 1986.[48] Within these 36 years, the real GNP increased 4.82-fold, whereas the ISEW in 1986 is 3.09 times higher than for 1950. It is not possible to give a growth rate for the costs of urbanization because these costs are considered only after the year 1964. And it would be senseless to include the net capital growth and the change of the net international position in this table; the ups and downs of these two variables are shown graphically in tables B.10.8 and B.10.9, respectively. The comparison of the ISEW--and the GNP-growth rates with the change in the different variables give some additional insights:

- *Below* the growth rate of the ISEW are only a few variables: water, air, and noise pollution and the cost assessment for the depletion of non-renewable resources. This might be more an indication of the cautiousness of the assumptions that have led to rather low cost estimations.

- *Between* the growth rates of the ISEW and the GNP are--among others--some variables whose quantitative importance (see below) is quite high: the services of household labor and the cost assessment for long term environmental damages. To a certain extent, these items neutralize each other.

- *Above* the growth rate of the GNP are all the "traffic variables"--services of streets and highways, cost of commuting and auto accidents. This seems to be an appropriate reflection of the above average increase of private motorization and traffic density in the FRG--a consequence that the growth of mobility was brought on mainly by the expansion of individual traffic. The above average expenditures on and services of consumer durables are an expression of the increasing use of equipment by private households.

- *Far above* the GNP growth rate are the growth rates of the health variables (costs and expenditures), the advertising expenditures, and the costs associated with the loss and pollution of our top soil. Although the "cost explosion" in the health sector is a very popular political issue in the FRG in 1990, these exorbitant growth rates seem to be the result of the very low standards in the early fifties, whereas the expenditures on advertising can be explained as a result of the copying of American business practices that had previously been unknown.

It is more difficult to explain the cost increases expressed by the soil variable, even more if compared with the rather low increase of the other environmental costs. But even here there is a rather plausible explanation. The environmental problems of air and water pollution were discovered early and have been the focus of clean-up efforts over the past fifteen years. Although economic growth has eaten up some of the success of these efforts, rather large improvements have been made. The degradation of the soil in its many different facets--erosion, biocides used in agriculture, over-fertilization, deposition of SO_2, trash dumps, garbage incinerators and so on--was the last environmental issue that people fully became aware of. Clearly, it is the environmental problem with the most long-term consequences.

What is the relative importance of the different variables *within* the ISEW? The first columns of table B.10.10 show the variables as a percentage of GNP, both for the years 1950 and 1986. Most important is the services of household labor, and the difference in magnitude between this variable and the environmental variables. It shows the problems of interpretation of such a time series. A rather minor change in the method of calculation could be as influential for the ISEW as the doubling or even trebling of the cost assessment for auto accidents, water or noise pollution. On the other hand, in any serious attempt to correct the GNP, in regard to its social, environmental and long-term aspects, it is not possible to avoid this area of human productivity.

Another very influential factor is the cost assessment for long term environmental damages. It was said above that the assumptions on the amount of the "rent" or "tax" that is "collected" is decisive for the influence this variable will have within the ISEW. If energy consumption were "taxed" at a higher rate, this item could well turn into a factor as important as household labor--or even larger. The tax assumed here--10 DM for 1 ton of coal equivalent, that is 0.01 DM for 1 kg coal or, approximately, 0.7 liter of gasoline--is still rather low (at least compared with those suggestions for pricing energy that are made in order to increase the attractiveness of energy saving devices).

Finally--what is the reason for the peak of the ISEW in 1980 and the rather sharp decline in the years after that maximum? The interplay of many and quite different factors can explain this development:

- The peak in 1980 can be ascribed to an extraordinarily high value of net capital growth in this year. After 1980, in six out of seven years the figure of net capital growth is even *negative*.

- After 1980, the change in the net international position is negative as well, reaching an order of magnitude as never before.

- In the eighties, personal consumption is growing very slowly; it is declining in fact from 1981 to 1982 and from 1985 to 1986. In any of these years, personal consumption is a steadily declining percentage of GNP.

- The index of distributional inequality is in 1980 nearly the same as in 1950. But since 1980, the income distribution has become more and more unequal; in fact, the distribution in the last 37 years has never been more unequal than in 1987 (see table B.10.2).

- Finally, the cumulative negative effects of soil degradation and of long term environmental damage have become more and more painfully noticeable.

4. ISEW-U.S. and ISEW-FRG: Results and Methods Compared

The first columns in table B.10.7 and table B.10.10 show the development of the different variables in the ISEW of the U.S. A comparison of the ISEW and GNP of both countries shows that the overall development of both time series is very similar. However, a variable by variable comparison shows many differences that need to be analyzed in detail. For the time being, we can only name the most important of them.

The GNP and the ISEW in the U.S. are growing more slowly than in the FRG. This and the trend of many cost variables indicate that the level of development in the U.S. in 1950 was much higher than in the FRG, but that the FRG caught up a good portion of this difference in the last 37 years--benefits and problems. Just one example: In the FRG, the services of streets and highways increased three times as much as in the U.S., but the cost of auto accidents two and a half times and the cost of commuting nearly twice as much.

The biggest difference within one single variable occurs with the services of household labor. In the U.S., its value in the year 1986 is 1.59 times the 1950 value; in the FRG, its value increased 4.82 times in the same period. Correspondingly, the share of household labor as a percentage of the GNP declined in the U.S. from 58.2% to 28.3%, and in the FRG from 42.0% to 35.0%. However, the computation for the FRG was made on the basis of an assumption that necessarily led to these relations to the GNP, whereas the U.S. calculations were independent from the value of the GNP. This is a methodological difference that requires more and detailed analysis of the concept of household labor.

5. How to Proceed

The computational work on the case study of the ISEW for the FRG was started out of curiosity. Two questions were of interest. Would it be possible to calculate this index for another country? What would be the determining factors for the results?

This paper shows that it is possible to come to a time series that is quite similar to the ISEW for the U.S., although some serious changes of method had to be made. The availability of data is just not as good in the FRG. What should be done is to test the influence of these changes more thoroughly than was done here. This could be undertaken either by trying to evaluate more of the missing data for the

FRG--or by testing the U.S. results by applying the "West German methods" into the original calculation.

Of course, there are additional items that could--or even should!--be considered as costs in the index. It could be possible, for instance, to subtract expenditures for pornography and for alcohol abuse. More rewarding maybe would be to make an attempt to distinguish between the services of and expenditures on armaments and of other military budgets. The citizens of a state require public security--but not tanks or rockets, guns or soldiers; expenditures for these are only a limited part of the means which should be applied in order to attain the desired degree of public security--a successful disarmament process would be more efficient and less costly at the same time.[49] And finally, there is no cost assessment for the harmful effects of unemployment. The variable of distributional inequality alone can not account for its detrimental effects.

These amendments to a "next version" of the ISEW--yet to come--is its greatest advantage. It is a sign of hope that the parliament of the FRG and of the county of Schleswig-Holstein recently started discussions on the measurement of welfare in the national accounting system. They started partly as a result of public hearings. The central statistical office is also working to develop concepts to measure social and environmental aspects of the economic process.[50] The formulation of the ISEW can help make us realize that we need a public debate before we find the new concept of welfare that we urgently need. New concepts have to replace the idea of unlimited growth that lie behind the conventional GNP.

Table B.10.1

Index of Sustainable Economic Welfare, FRG 1950-87

Year A	Personal con- sumption B	Distrbu- tion in- equality C	Weighted personal consumption (B/C) D	Services of house- hold labor E	Services of consumer durables F	Services of streets and highways G
1950	146.90	103.75	152.41	95.48	14.02	0.96
1951	154.18	100.02	154.21	104.97	14.34	1.50
1952	163.31	94.24	153.91	113.81	14.47	1.77
1953	179.13	96.28	172.46	122.59	16.38	1.96
1954	191.21	96.65	184.81	131.11	17.74	2.41
1955	209.89	91.75	192.57	146.16	18.68	2.77
1956	226.51	92.28	209.02	156.09	20.48	3.09
1957	239.35	90.43	216.44	164.19	21.43	3.38
1958	249.28	92.61	230.86	169.52	23.09	3.92
1959	262.52	88.98	233.59	181.05	23.59	4.45
1960	281.34	85.26	239.87	198.97	24.47	4.91
1961	294.24	90.38	265.95	206.69	27.39	5.35
1962	308.04	92.71	285.59	215.43	29.70	6.68
1963	316.11	94.03	297.25	220.31	31.21	7.15
1964	330.39	91.12	301.05	233.63	31.91	7.62
1965	351.72	92.02	323.66	244.99	34.63	7.72
1966	363.52	94.39	343.14	251.04	37.06	8.00
1967	368.49	93.97	346.28	249.64	37.57	8.26
1968	383.65	88.49	339.48	262.76	37.04	8.93
1969	405.15	89.35	362.00	281.11	42.97	9.36
1970	419.69	93.90	394.08	293.82	49.97	9.67
1971	431.27	96.93	418.03	301.13	54.59	10.45
1972	452.10	96.14	434.66	312.20	58.24	10.40
1973	465.66	98.03	456.51	325.21	58.43	10.17
1974	468.67	103.36	484.43	324.19	56.19	10.10
1975	484.97	103.50	501.96	317.88	59.53	9.80
1976	505.42	98.60	498.33	333.91	63.59	9.23
1977	526.59	98.78	520.16	341.01	68.45	9.42
1978	538.68	96.18	518.08	350.34	70.20	9.95
1979	557.76	95.46	532.41	362.32	70.97	10.90
1980	570.03	100.05	570.32	365.76	69.07	10.62
1981	578.65	102.14	591.04	363.88	64.95	9.94
1982	573.27	100.96	578.75	358.49	65.40	8.97
1983	583.08	95.50	556.83	363.37	64.59	8.24
1984	595.13	91.83	546.52	373.31	68.32	8.21
1985	602.36	90.34	544.17	378.52	69.65	8.28
1986	601.40	87.92	528.76	385.23	69.27	8.20
1987	613.27	87.65	537.56	389.92	72.03	8.00

Table B.10.1 continued

Year A	Public expenditures on health & education H	Expenditures on consumer durables I	Defensive private expenditures on health & education J	Expenditures on national advertising K	Costs of commuting L	Costs of urbanization M	Costs of auto accidents N
1950	0.43	30.00	0.00	0.44	4.37	0.00	2.03
1951	0.88	31.40	0.30	0.59	4.34	0.00	2.24
1952	0.98	32.83	0.48	1.05	4.51	0.00	2.44
1953	1.27	34.28	0.73	1.36	4.91	0.00	2.64
1954	1.45	35.92	0.95	1.59	5.29	0.00	2.85
1955	1.72	37.69	1.23	1.79	5.55	0.00	3.05
1956	2.10	39.55	1.45	2.10	5.74	0.00	3.25
1957	2.33	41.60	1.93	2.59	5.92	0.00	3.53
1958	2.60	43.74	1.58	2.81	6.06	0.00	3.73
1959	2.85	46.05	3.29	3.19	6.31	0.00	3.93
1960	3.23	48.41	3.57	3.59	6.71	0.00	4.25
1961	3.68	50.75	4.06	4.16	7.81	0.00	4.88
1962	4.17	52.28	4.67	4.47	8.87	0.00	5.56
1963	4.78	53.77	4.92	4.80	9.92	0.00	6.24
1964	5.82	55.19	5.23	5.24	10.89	0.00	6.44
1965	6.01	56.79	5.88	5.71	11.47	0.82	6.85
1966	6.24	58.45	6.76	6.13	12.69	1.59	7.12
1967	6.58	60.07	7.26	6.27	14.08	2.35	7.46
1968	7.14	61.47	7.85	6.63	15.05	2.93	7.80
1969	7.59	63.40	8.61	6.61	15.67	3.31	8.14
1970	8.61	65.95	8.82	6.26	15.93	3.61	8.96
1971	10.19	68.68	9.71	6.00	16.85	3.88	9.63
1972	11.33	71.76	10.65	5.90	18.00	4.19	10.31
1973	12.02	74.63	12.09	5.73	18.80	4.42	9.49
1974	13.58	77.13	13.01	5.53	19.32	5.01	8.81
1975	14.21	78.89	14.59	5.47	21.21	4.99	8.63
1976	14.47	82.55	16.23	6.08	21.59	5.37	8.81
1977	14.25	85.64	16.55	6.63	22.35	5.80	9.49
1978	14.99	88.91	16.66	7.17	23.65	6.30	10.17
1979	15.76	91.71	17.14	7.60	24.16	6.62	10.85
1980	16.77	93.62	17.65	7.73	24.75	6.87	11.57
1981	16.83	94.66	18.73	8.28	24.77	6.99	11.19
1982	16.49	95.38	19.08	8.43	24.98	7.26	11.53
1983	16.31	96.00	18.97	8.77	25.40	7.28	11.39
1984	16.21	96.31	19.10	9.19	26.09	7.56	11.53
1985	16.58	97.32	19.70	9.40	26.57	8.10	11.78
1986	16.88	97.90	20.07	9.62	26.90	8.15	13.04
1987	16.95	98.74	20.52	9.87	28.40	8.38	13.04

Table B.10.1 continued

Year A	Costs of water pollution O	Costs of air pollution P	Costs of noise pollution Q	Soil degradation R/S	Depletion of nonrenewable resources T	Environmental damage long term U	Net capital growth V
1950	6.73	19.95	9.25	2.61	12.16	35.45	0.00
1951	6.94	22.06	9.53	3.01	12.56	36.95	-6.78
1952	7.15	23.30	9.83	3.42	14.48	38.53	-6.64
1953	7.37	22.90	10.13	3.85	15.47	40.09	8.08
1954	7.60	24.62	10.45	4.29	16.43	41.76	9.59
1955	7.83	27.01	10.77	4.98	17.50	43.60	18.56
1956	8.08	28.75	11.11	5.54	18.76	45.55	30.69
1957	8.33	28.88	11.45	6.06	19.46	47.51	31.03
1958	8.59	28.08	11.80	6.49	17.80	49.42	32.25
1959	8.85	28.57	12.17	7.19	17.27	51.36	42.32
1960	9.13	31.15	12.54	8.19	18.62	53.47	72.90
1961	9.41	31.77	12.93	8.80	17.20	55.63	25.09
1962	9.70	34.06	13.33	9.49	16.73	57.94	66.21
1963	10.00	36.66	13.75	10.03	17.06	60.43	56.69
1964	10.31	37.86	14.17	10.98	15.59	63.00	49.33
1965	10.62	38.97	14.60	11.89	14.47	65.65	53.46
1966	10.95	39.27	15.06	12.56	13.33	68.31	56.69
1967	11.29	39.47	15.53	12.87	12.35	70.98	71.64
1968	11.64	39.67	16.01	13.96	12.20	73.87	14.59
1969	12.01	40.45	16.50	15.37	12.34	77.02	29.72
1970	12.37	41.34	17.01	16.53	13.28	80.38	53.51
1971	12.76	40.75	17.53	17.42	13.80	83.78	70.70
1972	12.76	40.35	18.08	18.56	15.23	87.32	83.98
1973	12.76	39.67	18.26	19.87	16.92	91.11	39.32
1974	12.76	38.88	18.45	20.34	18.44	94.77	56.36
1975	12.76	38.29	18.63	20.47	18.23	98.24	58.31
1976	12.76	37.80	18.88	22.06	19.27	101.95	18.41
1977	12.76	37.60	19.01	23.11	19.27	105.67	51.73
1978	12.76	37.41	19.21	24.34	19.21	109.56	40.40
1979	12.76	37.21	19.40	25.80	19.18	113.64	57.48
1980	12.76	36.92	19.60	26.68	19.67	117.54	109.00
1981	12.76	35.44	19.80	27.19	20.90	121.28	-38.14
1982	12.76	33.97	20.00	27.43	20.52	124.90	-4.70
1983	12.76	33.48	20.19	28.45	19.45	128.55	-13.72
1984	12.76	32.99	20.40	29.91	21.02	132.31	9.49
1985	12.76	31.91	20.61	31.03	20.83	136.16	-6.57
1986	12.76	31.12	20.81	32.29	18.96	140.03	-19.27
1987	12.76	30.44	21.02	33.42	17.80	143.91	-3.37

Table B.10.1 continued

Year A	Change in net international position W	Index of Sustainable Economic Welfare ISEW (sum) X	ISEW (per capita) Y	GNP (sum) Z	GNP (per capita) AA
1950	1.38	175.99	3,531.95	227.33	4,562.13
1951	-1.06	174.39	3,462.44	251.06	4,984.72
1952	0.02	179.11	3,532.65	273.43	5,393.07
1953	-1.32	215.79	4,216.94	295.87	5,781.87
1954	-1.34	232.87	4,500.54	317.90	6,143.91
1955	-1.18	258.85	4,952.39	356.01	6,811.31
1956	-0.29	291.98	5,519.74	381.97	7,220.94
1957	-2.87	301.55	5,638.68	403.67	7,548.31
1958	-4.58	321.33	5,924.81	418.72	7,720.47
1959	-10.63	336.47	6,134.41	449.30	8,191.52
1960	3.72	398.93	7,196.57	496.08	8,949.13
1961	-7.83	368.45	6,557.80	517.77	9,215.49
1962	-0.90	437.90	7,704.54	542.25	9,540.39
1963	0.90	438.95	7,648.62	557.16	9,708.53
1964	-1.88	442.32	7,630.05	593.71	10,241.43
1965	4.83	479.30	8,176.48	625.57	10,671.81
1966	0.00	496.40	8,392.48	644.15	10,890.44
1967	-15.44	493.67	8,327.00	643.67	10,857.08
1968	-7.81	446.20	7,499.21	680.83	11,442.46
1969	-22.87	475.30	7,912.75	731.95	12,185.49
1970	19.01	573.24	9,451.39	768.83	12,676.26
1971	9.20	603.40	9,845.95	791.88	12,921.46
1972	10.32	635.74	10,308.44	825.10	13,378.84
1973	10.08	619.60	9,997.45	863.81	13,937.86
1974	-25.26	626.34	10,093.47	865.44	13,946.56
1975	-10.41	645.90	10,446.55	852.90	13,794.45
1976	-0.86	615.72	10,006.66	900.49	14,634.76
1977	1.21	669.27	10,900.18	924.36	15,054.66
1978	4.60	661.08	10,779.64	954.53	15,564.53
1979	6.70	700.54	11,417.03	992.29	16,171.87
1980	-0.27	781.33	12,690.97	1,006.93	16,355.36
1981	3.75	653.93	10,601.60	1,007.00	16,325.70
1982	-1.97	657.00	10,659.02	997.31	16,180.06
1983	-11.15	616.47	10,036.49	1,016.22	16,544.65
1984	-22.23	614.80	10,049.78	1,049.58	17,156.99
1985	-32.01	583.95	9,569.14	1,069.92	17,532.74
1986	-45.08	543.65	8,902.61	1,094.73	17,927.03
1987	-24.28	583.31	9,531.37	1,114.05	18,203.80

Table B.10.2
Index of Income Inequality

Year a	National income b	Income from employed labor c	Wage ratio (c/b) d	% of employed labor e	Adjusted wage ratio f	Index of distributnl inequality g
1950	81.59	47.88	58.68	68.5	66.14	103.75
1951	98.89	58.05	58.70	69.8	64.92	100.02
1952	112.10	64.73	57.74	70.7	63.05	94.24
1953	120.80	71.48	59.17	71.7	63.71	96.28
1954	129.94	78.11	60.11	72.7	63.83	96.65
1955	149.51	89.08	59.58	73.9	62.24	91.75
1956	166.00	99.85	60.15	74.4	62.41	92.28
1957	181.65	109.52	60.29	75.3	61.81	90.43
1958	194.36	118.84	61.14	75.5	62.52	92.61
1959	210.49	127.28	60.47	76.1	61.34	88.98
1960	240.11	144.39	60.13	77.2	60.13	85.26
1961	260.75	162.81	62.44	78.0	61.80	90.38
1962	282.11	180.13	63.85	78.8	62.55	92.71
1963	297.80	193.15	64.86	79.5	62.98	94.03
1964	327.25	211.17	64.53	80.3	62.04	91.12
1965	358.45	234.13	65.32	80.9	62.33	92.02
1966	379.78	252.06	66.37	81.2	63.10	94.39
1967	380.74	251.84	66.14	81.1	62.96	93.97
1968	418.09	270.38	64.67	81.6	61.18	88.49
1969	462.94	304.07	65.68	82.5	61.46	89.35
1970	530.40	360.64	67.99	83.4	62.94	93.90
1971	588.19	409.11	69.55	84.0	63.92	96.93
1972	645.34	450.26	69.77	84.6	63.67	96.14
1973	721.89	510.93	70.78	85.0	64.28	98.03
1974	772.96	563.12	72.85	85.2	66.01	103.36
1975	803.57	587.20	72.07	85.4	66.06	103.50
1976	882.15	631.29	71.56	85.7	64.46	98.60
1977	938.33	676.03	72.05	86.2	64.52	98.78
1978	1,010.24	721.64	71.43	86.6	63.68	96.18
1979	1,087.92	777.85	71.50	87.0	63.44	95.46
1980	1,148.60	844.41	73.52	87.4	64.94	100.05
1981	1,187.25	882.95	74.37	87.5	65.62	102.14
1982	1,223.52	902.52	73.76	87.3	65.23	100.96
1983	1,286.24	920.91	71.60	87.1	63.46	95.50
1984	1,357.93	954.00	70.25	87.1	62.27	91.83
1985	1,420.03	991.00	69.79	87.2	61.78	90.34
1986	1,509.42	1,041.20	68.98	87.3	61.00	87.92
1987	1,568.30	1.081.51	68.96	87.4	60.91	87.65

Table B.10.3
Index of Emission of Pollutants

Year	Emission of Pollutants (index)
1950	203.22
1951	224.67
1952	237.31
1953	233.21
1954	250.77
1955	275.08
1956	292.78
1957	294.11
1958	286.03
1959	290.99
1960	317.25
1961	323.54
1962	346.93
1963	373.39
1964	385.62
1965	396.88
1966	400.00
1967	402.00
1968	404.00
1969	412.00
1970	421.00
1971	415.00
1972	411.00
1973	404.00
1974	396.00
1975	390.00
1976	385.00
1977	383.00
1978	381.00
1979	379.00
1980	376.00
1981	361.00
1982	346.00
1983	341.00
1984	336.00
1985	325.00
1986	317.00
1987	310.00

Table B.10.4
Computation of Net Capital Growth

Year a	Tangible assets b	Growth of labor force (in %) c	Increase of tangible assets d	Requirement of tangible assets for increased labor e	Net capital growth f
1950	231.91				0.00
1951	229.16	1.74	-2.75	4.03	-6.78
1952	226.04	1.54	-3.13	3.52	-6.64
1953	238.13	1.77	12.09	4.01	8.08
1954	253.30	2.35	15.17	5.58	9.59
1955	277.78	2.33	24.47	5.91	18.56
1956	313.58	1.84	35.81	5.12	30.69
1957	349.88	1.68	36.30	5.26	31.03
1958	385.05	0.83	35.17	2.92	32.25
1959	428.20	0.22	43.15	0.84	42.32
1960	529.64	6.67	101.44	28.54	72.90
1961	559.80	0.96	30.16	5.07	25.09
1962	627.53	0.27	67.73	1.53	66.21
1963	686.21	0.32	58.68	1.99	56.69
1964	735.34	-0.03	49.13	-0.20	49.33
1965	791.86	0.42	56.52	3.06	53.46
1966	845.56	-0.38	53.70	-2.99	56.69
1967	900.78	-1.94	55.22	-16.42	71.64
1968	911.34	-0.45	10.56	-4.02	14.59
1969	949.52	0.93	38.18	8.46	29.72
1970	1,013.12	1.06	63.60	10.09	53.51
1971	1,090.81	0.69	77.69	6.99	70.70
1972	1,174.30	-0.04	83.49	-0.48	83.98
1973	1,222.54	0.76	48.24	8.92	39.32
1974	1,276.73	-0.18	54.20	-2.16	56.36
1975	1,322.68	-0.97	45.94	-12.37	58.31
1976	1,329.63	-0.87	6.95	-11.46	18.41
1977	1,377.67	-0.28	48.04	-3.69	51.73
1978	1,424.03	0.43	46.36	5.96	40.40
1979	1,493.83	0.87	69.80	12.32	57.48
1980	1,619.15	1.09	125.31	16.31	109.00
1981	1,592.85	0.73	-26.30	11.84	-38.14
1982	1,595.47	0.46	2.62	7.32	-4.70
1983	1,584.46	0.17	-11.00	2.72	-13.72
1984	1,596.25	0.14	11.79	2.30	9.49
1985	1,602.10	0.78	5.85	12.42	-6.57
1986	1,593.19	0.65	-8.91	10.36	-19.27
1987	1,600.73	0.69	7.55	10.92	-3.37

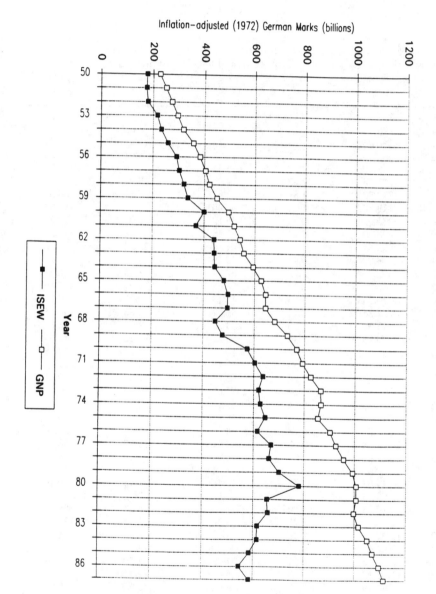

Inflation-adjusted (1972) German Marks (billions)

Table B.10.5
ISEW and GNP - Germany

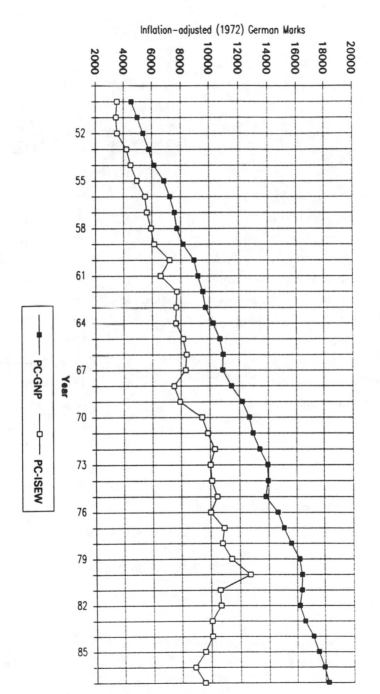

Inflation−adjusted (1972) German Marks

Table B. 10.6

Per capita ISEW and GNP - Germany

Year

PC-GNP

PC-ISEW

Table B.10.7
Growth Rates of ISEW Variables

	USA 1950	USA 1986	FRG 1950	FRG 1986
GNP	1:	3.26	1:	4.82
Services of household labor	1:	1.59	1:	4.03
Services consumer durables	1:	5.96	1:	4.94
Services of streets and highways	1:	2.89	1:	8.33
Public expenditures on health & education	1:	31.73	1:	39.26
Expenditures on consumer durables	1:	4.98	1:	5.14
Private expenditures on health & education	1:	15.79	1:	66.90
Expenditures on advertising	1:	3.03	1:	22.43
Cost of commuting	1:	3.72	1:	6.16
Cost of urbanization	1:	8.88	------------	
Cost of auto accidents	1:	2.43	1:	6.42
Cost of water pollution	1:	1.70	1:	1.90
Cost of air pollution	1:	0.89	1:	1.53
Cost of noise pollution	1:	2.30	1:	2.27
Cost of soil degradation	1:	3.13	1:	12.80
Depletion of non renewable resources	1:	3.03	1:	1.56
Long term environmental damage	1:	3.08	1:	4.06
ISEW	1:	2.17	1:	3.09

Billions of (1972) German Marks

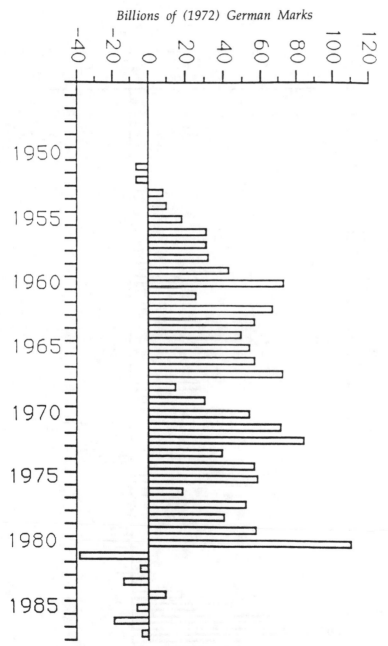

Table B.10.8. Net Capital Growth

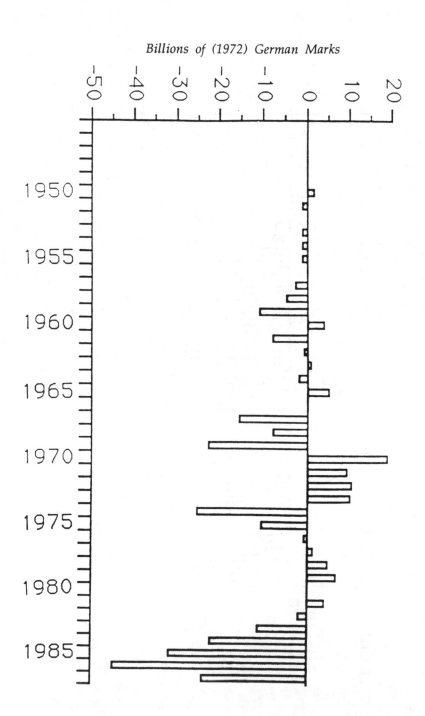

Billions of (1972) German Marks

Table B.10.9 Change in Net International Position

Table B.10.10
ISEW Variables in % of GNP

	USA		FRG	
	1950	1986	1950	1986
Services of household labor	58.2	28.3	42.0	35.0
Services consumer durables	2.5	4.5	13.2	9.0
Services of streets and highways	1.2	1.1	0.4	0.7
Public expenditures on health & education	0.2	1.9	0.2	1.5
Expenditures on consumer durables	7.9	12.1	6.2	6.5
Private expenditures on health & education	0.5	2.5	0.1	1.8
Expenditures on advertising	1.2	1.2	0.1	0.9
Cost of commuting	1.6	1.9	1.9	2.6
Cost of urbanization	1.1	2.9	----	0.8
Cost of auto accidents	2.2	1.7	0.9	1.2
Cost of water pollution	1.6	0.8	3.0	1.2
Cost of air pollution	4.7	1.2	8.7	2.7
Cost of noise pollution	0.4	0.2	4.0	1.9
Cost of soil degradation	3.2	3.1	1.1	3.1
Depletion of non renewable resources	3.8	3.5	5.3	1.7
Long term environmental damage	15.7	14.8	15.6	13.1
ISEW	70.8	47.1	77.4	53.3

Part C

REVISING THE INDEX

Chapter 11

RESPONSE TO THE CRITICS AND REVISION OF THE ISEW

In this concluding chapter, we describe the revisions we have made (or not made) in the ISEW in response to our critics. At the end of this chapter we present revised estimates of the ISEW and its components.

Is A Welfare Measure Possible?: The Question of Values

Several respondents have been critical of the entire enterprise involved in constructing a composite measure of economic welfare. Since no set of objective criteria can be developed for this purpose, they suggest that measuring welfare is a pointless exercise. Eisner has chided us for substituting our own values for those provided by choices made in the market. Should our society then accept the information provided by national income accounts as the most reliable knowledge we have of economic welfare? Or should we conclude that the well-being of society is unknowable because some element of judgment is involved in measuring welfare?

In fact, we have begun the ISEW with one element of the existing national accounts, consumption expenditures, notwithstanding the critique by Mishan that higher consumption levels may not contribute to welfare and the analysis by Power that regional variations in the relation between income and welfare may be considerable. Furthermore, Eisner himself acknowledges the need to impute a number of values that are not directly observable because they are not recorded as market transactions. Thus the real issue is not whether to impute unrecorded values, but which values should be included and on what basis. Carson and Young apparently accept the need to measure values not included in national income accounts, but they recommend that those values be relegated to satellite accounts. That method, however, ignores the importance of recording the relationship between market and non-market accounts.

We fully support the idea of including satellite accounts to provide statistics on social conditions such as literacy, nutrition, drug addiction, crime, or family violence, which cannot be measured in monetary terms. Such accounts pose no problem. Yet, to the extent that aspects of welfare can be expressed in the common denominator of money, we believe they should be included in a composite indicator, rather than being relegated to satellite accounts. It is important to combine the benefits and costs of production in a single account, so that the net effects can be discerned. As long as GNP is treated by economists as the "central framework" around which satellites revolve, political leaders and the media will continue to view the GNP as a measure of welfare. The need for an alternative *composite* indicator of well-being, with prestige and publicity equal to GNP, will persist even if the United States adopts the United Nations System of National Accounts.

Unlike GNP, which covertly advances its values, the ISEW introduces values explicitly, so they can be examined. First, we have included an index of income distribution. Even though the value of more even distribution cannot be derived from observing the market, there is a general social consensus, visible in the political process and the graduated income tax, that seeks to protect the poor against destitution and that seeks to limit the gains of the rich. Whereas the particular methodology we have applied in deriving our distribution index is somewhat arbitrary, the need for some such index in a sustainable welfare measure is grounded in public values. Second, we have chosen methods of valuing natural resources at levels higher than the market because we have refused to accept the simple logic of discounting future benefits and costs. One might still fit this within the logic of the market by imagining future generations participating in current markets vicariously. Nevertheless, we recognize that we are imputing values based on *our* concern for the future, and that this valuation may not be universally shared.

Moreover, we have chosen to include some imputed values in the ISEW and not others. For example, we excluded production within the so-called "underground economy," composed of barter transactions and unreported income. We did so for practical rather than theoretical reasons: estimates of the size of the underground economy vary from 5% to 40% of the measured economy, and estimates of changes over time are equally diverse. Without a conceptual basis by which to determine which estimates seemed most plausible, we chose to leave out this component until further research provides reliable data. Nevertheless, since we included other components based on arbitrary estimates, we accept the fact that the decision to exclude the underground economy was in part a value judgment.

There can be no doubt that the way in which an index of welfare is constructed reflects certain values. This is true not only of the ISEW, but of any other measure of welfare, including GNP when it is used for that purpose. Despite all claims that GNP is not a measure of welfare and that it was not intended for that purpose, *in practice* it functions that way in the political arena.

Ironically, when Carson and Young raise this issue, they provide evidence that directly contradicts their claim that economists do not refer to GNP per capita as a welfare measure. They quote from a World Bank booklet, *The Development Data Book*, which is aimed at nonspecialists: "GNP per capita helps measure the material standards and *well-being of a country . . .*" (our emphasis). The rest of the quote notes that GNP is not concerned with distributional equity or personal fulfillment, but the plain meaning is that higher per capita GNP means being better off economically. This sort of normative usage of GNP is the central dogma of the economic faith, and it is precisely what we are complaining about. Carson and Young point out that economists are careful in their technical work to distinguish between income accounts and welfare measures. (Indeed, the very need to assert the distinction shows the power of GNP in the popular imagination.) Yet they seem purposefully oblivious of the fact that reporters, government officials, and economists refer to GNP or GDP as a welfare measure on a daily basis.

Policies are debated in terms of what is "good for the economy," where "the economy" means GNP. Growth of GNP is the primary justification for trade policies that hurt some sectors of the economy and help others. This argument only makes sense if one operates on the implicit assumption that the general welfare is served by growth of GNP. International comparisons based on per capita GNP also regard it as a measure of well-being. When the GNP is used, explicitly or implicitly, for purposes of measuring well-being or national prestige, it is just as value-laden as any other index. The fact that the GNP is composed of preferences revealed in the market should not grant it a privileged political position, especially when preferences to avoid damaging the environment, for example, have not been allowed expression through market transactions.

Perhaps economists should not be held entirely accountable for the havoc wreaked by the misuse of their invention after it has left the laboratory. However, they should not be allowed to absolve themselves of responsibility for the use of GNP as a welfare measure until they have developed a more satisfying alternative that can gain widespread acceptance.

We do not object to the use of the GNP for the limited purposes for which it was originally intended: to help policy-makers in determining how to achieve full employment of economic resources. We do, however, object when per capita GNP surreptitiously becomes the sole measure of welfare of a society. This is inappropriate in the United States, but it is a far more serious problem in the Third World. In many countries, economic development policies have been justified in terms of how they will promote growth of GNP, disregarding the distributional and ecological repercussions of those policies. Policies driving people off their land are defended on the grounds of increasing production for the export market rather than for subsistence. Policies that deplete resources, ravage the environment, and destroy human health are supported as necessary for increases in output. Enormous amounts of human suffering, both present and future, are caused as a result of a faulty accounting system that includes only the benefits of increasing output but none of the costs.

On the other hand, we are not proposing that GNP be abandoned, for it serves other purposes than the estimation of economic welfare. The point is rather that when the GNP functions politically as a welfare measure, it should not be allowed to masquerade as a measure that is somehow more objective than alternative ways of determining well-being. Any welfare index involves choices based on values, and those value-decisions are inescapable. The question for public policy then becomes not which index is the most objective but which most plausibly includes a range of widely shared values.

Comments on and Revision of Individual Columns

We are deeply indebted to the respondents who challenged many elements of the ISEW. We have modified our initial procedures in a number of ways to accomodate their criticisms. Nevertheless, in some cases we have not changed our calculations because we do not entirely agree with our critics.

In the discussion that follows, reference to columns is based on table A.1 of the original ISEW which follows chapter 2. The columns of the revised ISEW at the end of this chapter are labeled somewhat differently because of the removal of two columns from the original and the addition of two new columns.

Column B

The response by Thomas Power raises the important issue about whether personal consumption (which is closely associated with personal income) can be used as the starting point of a welfare measure. The problem is that income in one part of the country is not directly comparable to income elsewhere. Regional income differences reflect differences in the cost of living and in the amenities attached to alternative locations. Firms do not have to bid as much in the labor market to attract workers to areas that have attractive living conditions. Thus high amenities mean low wages. Yet at the same time, the high housing demand in those areas will lead to high rents; workers will not move there unless wages are adequate to pay the higher rents. Thus, even though nominal wages may be higher in high amenity areas, real wages, net of the higher cost of living, will tend to be depressed relative to low amenity areas. For rather similar reasons, as Power explains, regional differences in employment rates persist over time due to differences in amenity levels and cost of living, *not* to the failure of certain areas to adapt and develop. The problem that Power thus implicitly points to in any national index of well-being is the misleading character of aggregating diverse relationships between income and welfare. In other words, if it takes twice as much income to achieve the same level of well-being in Connecticut as in Mississippi, then it is inappropriate to lump income (or consumption expenditures) from these two states together in one index. This may indicate that the ideal way to construct a welfare index would be by estimating welfare in a number of regions and summing these values. Or perhaps, regional income differences could be weighted in some way to give an adjusted level of income (or consumption expenditures) as the starting point of an ISEW. Power does not spell out these implications in his paper, but he certainly points in the direction of a fundamental reorientation in thinking about the relationship between income and welfare.

Another problem, alluded to by Mishan, is the fact that perceived well-being appears to vary more with relative income than with absolute income and that increased consumption adds little to happiness. To the extent that increasing income and consumption is a function of status competition and addictive behavior, then it does not reflect growing satisfaction. Thus, a one percent increase in personal consumption expenditures may add much less than a one percent increase in well-being. If we assumed that a 10% increase in consumption adds only 7.5% to well-being (i.e., a marginal income utility of .75) and column B were adjusted accordingly, per capita ISEW would have declined from around $2240 in 1951 to about $2100 in 1990. We have not chosen to follow this line of reasoning. Nevertheless, this demonstrates that, since column B is the largest component of the ISEW, our results are very sensitive to the assumption that well-being increases at the same rate as consumption.

Columns C and D

Several respondents are critical of our method of incorporating income distribution in the Index of Sustainable Economic Welfare. They point out that a rationale for our particular methodology is lacking. Carson and Young are critical of the arbitrary character of the method of calculating distributional inequality. Eisner suggests that the distributional index should be applied to the ISEW as a whole rather than to personal consumption alone. Mishan proposes that distributional issues should not be combined with categories dealing with aggregate quantities. Diefenbacher is critical of our use of an index of distribution that cannot be used in international comparisons because it reveals only changes over time (i.e., not an absolute, but a relative measure of income inequality) and because similar data are not available in other countries.

Starting with the last concern first, we are cognizant of the problems involved in designing an index so that it can be used in other countries. We expect that analysts who seek to duplicate the ISEW elsewhere will have to contrive other types of estimates based on available data, as Diefenbacher has done for Germany. (In the case of income distribution, he used the ratio of wage income to total income as a proxy.) As a result, the statistics developed in various countries will not be entirely comparable. Yet all international economic comparisons are approximations because categories differ between nations.

Mishan raises the question of whether a single index number should be used that combines categories that are not precisely comparable. This is the most fundamental issue regarding the inclusion of distributional data in the ISEW because it poses the obvious question of how to combine two sets of numbers derived from different scales. Yet until output and distribution are brought together into one composite indicator, they do not allow us to consider the trade-offs that are being made as one index rises and another falls. For example, without a common scale, if output increases by 3% and the measure of distribution worsens by 4%, we have no method of balancing those conflicting trends. In an effort to right that imbalance, the ISEW brings them together.

We have not adopted Eisner's proposal that the index of income inequality should be applied to column X (the sum of the columns) rather than personal consumption alone. There is no reason to believe that the effects of income distribution have any bearing on the distribution of the effects of pollution, accidents, resource depletion, or most of the columns in the ISEW other than personal consumption. Perhaps a case could be made that the adjustment should also apply to expenditures and services from consumer durables (columns F and I in table A.1). However, since income distribution primarily affects the capacity of individual households to make market purchases, we have continued to apply it only to those purchases (column B) and not to the imputations in later columns.

We have, nevertheless, considered a number of possible ways to measure income distribution. Gottfried recommends that we carry out a sensitivity analysis of our assumptions, and Carson and Young have proposed an alternative measure. We will therefore describe several options, discuss the sensitivity of our results to the various options, and explain our rationale for choosing one of them.

Harmonic mean. This method, which we used in our original index, emphasizes the variations in the relationship between the highest quintile and other quintiles. The share of the highest quintile is divided by the share of each quintile. The sum of those five ratios is divided by five. As Carson and Young point out, this amounts to the ratio of the highest quintile to the harmonic mean of the five quintiles. This formulation is indeed arbitrary because the harmonic mean of income distribution has no precise connection to well-being. However, since all other measures are also arbitrary, this one is useful as a basis for comparison.

Top quintile option. The index proposed by Carson and Young (though they suggest it only as an indication of the arbitrariness of all choices) is the share of the highest income quintile divided by the average of all five quintiles. Since the sum of the shares of the five quintiles is one hundred percent, by definition, this method amounts to comparing the share of the highest quintile across time. This is not so much an index of income distribution as an index of envy.

Low quintile option. The reverse of the top-quintile procedure is to calculate only variations in the share of the lowest income quintile. That is equivalent to dividing each quintile by the lowest quintile, adding the results, dividing by 5, and normalizing the outcome. The rationale for this method is that improvements in the lot of the poorest segment of society are the most significant because the marginal utility of added income can be presumed to be greatest for them than for others. An index that gives special weight to the plight of the poorest members of society also fits well with the theory of justice propounded by John Rawls in the book by that name.[1] Rawls argues that in making a choice about living in a socially or economically stratified society in which we do not know our position in that society, we would tend to choose social rules that would protect the interests of its poorest or weakest members.

Weighted ratios of shares. Another method would be to assign arbitrary weights to the ratio of the quintile shares. The rationale for weighting the ratios in this way would be based on the concept of the diminishing marginal utility of income: the value of an additonal dollar of income is not as great for the rich as for the poor. Since our index measures inequality rather than equality, we weighted the highest quintile most heavily and the lowest quintile the least. We calclated a normalized index based on the expression $(b + 2c + 3d + 4e + 5f)/b$, where b is the lowest quintile and f the highest. (In addition to 1, 2, 3, 4, 5, we also tested weights of various magnitudes including 1, 10, 20, 30, 60. The results were almost completely insensitive to these differing weights so we used the set 1, 2, 3, 4, 5 in our comparison.)

The Gini coefficient. The usual measure of distributional equality is the Gini coefficient, the difference between actual distribution and equal distribution. It gives equal weight to all income levels by calculating the square root of the sum of the squared differences of each quintile from a 20% share.

To compare these alternatives with the original method, we calculated the average per capita ISEW for five-year blocks for each method.

Average for:	Harmonic mean PC-ISEW	Top Quintle PC-ISEW	Low Quintle PC-ISEW	Weighted ratio PC-ISEW	Gini Coeffcnt PC-ISEW
1951-55	2864.7	2915.3	2809.0	2806.5	2898.7
56-60	2992.5	2992.5	2929.4	2934.4	2986.4
61-65	2992.9	2999.3	2986.2	2983.7	2984.8
66-70	3304.6	3138.6	3398.4	3422.0	3180.1
71-75	3304.1	3174.8	3460.1	3467.5	3192.6
76-80	3343.3	3302.8	3465.3	3455.5	3286.7
81-85	3035.2	3226.3	3114.2	3079.8	3137.1
86-90	2993.6	3322.7	3206.0	3114.2	3196.1

We also calculated the variation for each method by dividing the lowest value year for the distributional index (not the respective PC-ISEWs) between 1950 and 1990 by the highest year:

Variation in:	Harmonic mean	Top Quintle	Low Quintle	Weighted ratio	Gini Coeffcnt
	.794	.906	.804	.790	.868

Of the new alternatives, the top quintule method flattens out the rise and fall of per capita ISEW the most, while the weighted ratio method manifests the greatest variation. This amounts to a mere 15% difference in the high-low variation of these two methods. The growth of PC-ISEW from 1950-1990 is nearly the same for the top-quintile method (25.8%) and the weighted method (27.2%). The growth of per capita ISEW in the absence of any index of distributional inequality is approximately 33%. Thus, the distributional index affects the ISEW but this weighting does not dominate it.

Our preferred method, the index based on the lowest quintile, was the median in terms of its variation between low and high years. That was not, however, the basis of our decision. Our intent was to develop an index that gives disproportionate weight to the condition of the poorest members of society. They are the people for whom many government programs were initiated. Concern for the well-being of the poor is the basis for state and federal transfer payments and in-kind assistance (such as food stamps). The weighted index also emphasizes the lowest quintile, but it requires an arbitrary system of assigning values to the relation between the shares of income by each quintile.

It should be clear, however, that the choice of methods is not especially significant, especially since the overall growth rate of per capita ISEW between 1950 and 1990 is not much affected by the choice. As noted above it accounts for the difference between 26% and 33% growth in per capita ISEW. By comparison, the growth of per capita consumption during the same period is approximately 125%.

We would also like to emphasize that the income distribution figures we used only approximately reflect disposable income differences because they measure pre-tax income and because they do not include all transfer payments. (They do, however, include Social Security payments, unemployment compensation, and certain cash grants to the poor such as AFDC and SSI.) The Census Bureau recently began calculating distribution of after-tax income, net of all transfer payments.[2] However, since that time series did not go back to 1950, we chose to use the pre-tax series that did. In any case, the annual changes in the after-tax, after-benefits series closely match the changes in the series we used. Nevertheless, the after-tax, after-benefits series does reveal some significant results. In 1990, for example, the lowest quintile of households received 3.9 percent of pre-tax income.[3] After adding capital gains and employer provided health insurance payments and subtracting government cash transfers to the poor, the lowest quintile received only 1.1 percent of income. Subtracting federal and state income taxes, which fall more heavily on the rich than the poor, raises the lowest quintile's share to 1.4 percent. The "graduated" income tax has little effect on the distribution of disposable income. However, when all forms of transfer payments are added (including the value of Medicare and Medicaid), the lowest quintile's share rises to 5.1 percent. Thus, cash and non-cash transfer payments are much more effective at redistribution of income than the income tax. Yet, if we consider that the lowest quintile would receive only 1.1 percent of income in the absence of transfer payments, that indicates efforts to achieve some semblance of equality by means of employment policies, minimum wage laws, and investment incentives have failed.

Column E

Diefenbacher has raised the issue of the sensitivity of our results to our assumptions in the case of the services of household labor. He notes that a major difference between the U.S. and the German versions of the ISEW is the rate of growth of household services. In the U.S., they are estimated to have grown by a factor of 1.59 between 1950 and 1986, whereas in Germany this column increased by a factor of 4.03. The difference is based largely on differences in the methodologies

used rather than actual economic differences between the two countries. Which methodology is correct? If Diefenbacher's assumption is
correct that the value of housework keeps pace with growth of GNP to
some extent, then the U.S. ISEW would increase at a rate approximately comparable to the growth of GNP. (If column E of table A.1 had increased by a factor of 4 during the same period, then the value of
housework would have equaled over $1.2 trillion in 1986, leading to a
calculated growth of ISEW of almost 300%. Note that personal consumption in 1986 was approximately $1.15 trillion.)

The growth in this sector suggested by Diefenbacher's figures appears grossly exaggerated. Given the general shift away from the
household economy to the market economy (i.e., purchase rather than
production of services such as child care and meal preparation), the
movement of increasing numbers of women into market employment, and the growth of the number of single person households (with
fewer housework and child care demands), the slow growth of this sector of the economy seems entirely plausible. In fact, our estimate for
the U.S. (which is based on Eisner's calculations) indicates that the
growth of this component of the ISEW has precisely kept pace with
population growth. This makes intuitive sense if one assumes the
amount of household services produced per person have remained
constant over time.

To make sense of Diefenbacher's assumption that the real value
of housework has increased by a factor of more than four would require some explanation as to how the quality or quantity of household
production per person has dramatically increased. Even if the time of
those performing the work were now more valued in the market-place
(a problematic assumption given the long-term stagnation in real wage
rates), that should not affect the estimate of the value of housework.
We are attempting to measure outputs, not inputs. When an executive
earning $100 per hour changes a child's diapers or cooks a meal at
home, the services rendered are no more valuable (and perhaps less so)
than when the equivalent task is performed by someone whose market
wage is $5 per hour.

Nevertheless, it should be understood that alternative assumptions about the effects of technology on the productivity of the household are possible and that our final results are sensitive to those assumptions. If Diefenbacher's methodology is appropriate for this component of the ISEW, then the growth of column E swamps all other
components, and sustainable welfare has been growing steadily
throughout the period of our study.

Columns F and G

With regard to services from capital, both from consumer durables and from streets and highways, we have been influenced by the criticism of Eisner and Carson and Young and revised our estimates upwards. In the case of consumer durables, we have chosen to multiply the net stock of consumer durables by 22.5% (rather than 10% as before) in each year. We assume that this would account for the combination of interest (the implicit annual payment for the services of capital) and depreciation. (Actual depreciation averaged around 15% but varied year to year. Since interest rates also varied year to year by an unknown amount, we simplified the procedure by choosing a single value for the combination of depreciation and interest.) The results of using this figure also seemed conceptually appropriate. According to our revised estimate, the services from consumer durables exceeded expenditures in only a few recession years. Why should this be the case? In a no-growth economy, expenditures would equal services (because they would simply replace worn-out goods). In a growing economy, expenditures should slightly exceed services, and in a declining economy services would slightly exceed expenditures. This has served as a rough guideline by which to check our estimate.

In the case of services from streets and highways, we have changed our estimate from 5% of gross stock to 7.5% of net stock. (We might add here that our figures for 1985 to 1990 are extrapolations from earlier years rather than actual measurements.) The value of services is much lower than for consumer durables because depreciation accounts for only about 2.5% of net stock of highways, compared to about 15% for consumer durables. Adding the same implied interest rate of 7.5% that we used in calculating the value of services from consumer durables, we arrive at 10% of net stock as the gross value of services of streets and highways. However, since we have assumed as we did in the original calculations that one-fourth of all vehicle miles are for commuting and thus do not represent a service but a defensive expenditure, we multiplied that 10% by three-fourths. The net value of services, then, is equal to 7.5% of net stock.

Eisner and Young and Carson also propose that we include other forms of government capital besides highways and streets, but they do not specify what they have in mind. There are few other forms of government capital the services of which are consumed directly by citizens. The main exceptions are government-owned enterprises such as sewage treatment facilities, water supply systems, airports, and other fee-for-service, publicly-owned businesses. However, the services of these activities are already included in the estimate of personal consumption.

Columnns H and J

There seems to be some confusion among our respondents about the exact meaning of columns H and J in table A.1. The intent is to include only those parts of health and education expenditures that can be construed as functioning as consumption, NOT investment in human capital. Thus we assume that some portion of expenditures on health make people feel better and contribute directly to their happiness or well-being. In the case of education, we assume that one half of the reason for attending post-secondary institutions is purely for the sake of learning rather than increasing one's lifetime earning potential. We explicitly omitted educational expenditures that could be regarded as purely for the purpose of increasing human capital. (See comments below on column V.)

We have, nevertheless, modified our procedure in light of Eisner's criticism of using 1950 as an arbitrary base year from which to measure changes in medical expenditures. As a result, we have simply subtracted one-half of all medical expenditures in each year on the assumption that they are defensive expenditures.

Column K

We have omitted advertising expenditures entirely in the revised ISEW. Eisner, Carson, and Young correctly point out that advertising is an intermediate expenditure rather than a final expenditure and thus would not show up in personal consumption or even the gross national product.

Column L

With respect to commuting costs, we acknowledge the validity of the point that Eisner makes regarding the use of annual services of automobiles rather than expenditures on them. We have not, however, altered our estimates since the services of consumer durables, including cars, tend to approximate expenditures for those goods, ranging from 80% to slightly over 100% of them.

Column M

As a result of Mishan's comments, we have removed the column entitled "Cost of Urbanization." In fact, it was misnamed in the original ISEW. It should have been entitled "Defensive Cost of Population Growth" because it was intended to refer to the rise in the cost of land for housing that results from both population growth and increasing housing density. For example, the cost of a house in some areas might have increased by a factor of five in fifteen years, mainly due to higher land values, or by a factor of two or three in constant dollars. We originally assumed that the increase in the real cost of housing services treated higher land prices as a factor of production that had become more valuable. We stand corrected. The housing services deflator does treat higher land values as inflationary rather than as contributing to output of services. Thus the 350% increase in expenditures for housing expenditures represents a real increase in the quantity and quality of housing structures.

An alternative method of estimating urban disamenities would be to follow Nordhaus and Tobin in their approach. They estimated wage differentials among cities in relation to size and density of population on the assumption that higher wages would be necessary to attract workers to areas with disamenities. Unfortunately, as Power explains in his essay in this volume, this approach is also misleading. Wage differentials reflect not only differences in amenity levels but also cost of living differentials. Thus only wage differentials *net* of differential living costs provide a true measure of variations in amenities and disamenities among urban areas and in relation to rural areas. Determining this is not in principle impossible, but it is well beyond the scope of this study.

Columns O, P, and Q

Both Eisner and Gottfried have recommended that we estimate the loss of services from the stock of air, water, and quietness (or whatever is lost by virtue of noise pollution). At a minimum, this would involve using data on ambient standards rather than emissions of pollutants. Since noise pollution exists only as long as it is being emitted, this distinction is not appropriate for it. For water pollution, the distinction between ambient standards and emissions makes sense for lakes, but not for rivers, since the latter are polluted only when there are discharges. Thus, it is not clear what would be required conceptually (not to mention practical difficulties) to accomplish the goal set forth by our critics.

Air pollution differs, however, in that the lower atmosphere acts as a sink in which pollutants accumulate and interact. In theory, it might be possible to develop an estimate of the changes in value of the stock of clean air over a given region. We have made a modest attempt to move in that direction by using ambient air quality data to construct a revised time series for the cost of air pollution. We continued to use nitrogen oxides, sulphur dioxide, and particulates as the basis for our estimates. For the years 1977 to 1988, data exist in the *Statistical Abstract* on ambient air quality with respect to the three relevant pollutants. Giving each type of pollution equal weight, we constructed an index which shows a 22% improvement for those years. This compares to a 14% improvement from 1977 to 1984 in emissions. In other words, ambient quality improved more rapidly than emissions curtailment. In the absence of data for years prior to 1977, we have assumed that air quality improved or declined in the same direction as changes in emission levels, but at a faster rate. Thus we assumed that air quality declined by 1% per year from 1950 to 1960, declined by 2.4% per year from 1961 to 1970, and improved by 3% per year from 1971 to 1976. We estimated 1989-90 as an extrapolation from 1988, and assumed no deterioration or improvement.

Columns R and S

In the matter of the cost to society due to loss of wetlands and farmland, Eisner has criticized the ISEW for failing to include "the value of land gain" to offset the losses that the ISEW records. If in fact that were the case, this would be a serious problem in the ISEW. However, those gains are already included in personal consumption figures and need not be added again. If a swamp is drained in order to be used for farming or if a farm is paved in order to build a subdivision or a shopping center, the returns from the "higher" (more profitable) use are reflected in the national accounts as the value added. In the case of wetlands, the loss of the former use is not recorded at all because the benefits (flood control, water-fowl habitat, etc.) are not traded in the market. In the case of farmland, part of the loss is recorded in national accounts as lower agricultural output (though this may be offset by higher agricultural output from other land). The ISEW does not subtract that loss, since that is a type of loss incurred anytime resources are shifted from one use to another. Instead, in the column dealing with farmlands, we have sought to measure a subtler loss: the loss of productivity of land that will eventually be evident when the level of soil depletion can no longer be masked by petrochemical inputs. In other words, the loss we are trying to capture has to do with sustainability of agricultural production, not with losses in the current year. We understand that this way of thinking does not fit in well with the prevailing orthodoxy among economists about the relation between present and future costs. We hope, nevertheless, that this will serve to make our own position clearer.

Column T

Eisner criticizes our assumption that market prices inadequately reflect scarcity of nonrenewable resources. He and Gottfried suggest that the use of a zero discount rate to equalize present and future prices leads to absurd results. Yet, they offer no explanation of how one should deal with the depletion of natural capital in national accounts. The use of current prices for calculating "depreciation" of these stocks ignores the crux of the problem of developing a measure of *sustainable* welfare. Current prices merely reflect the time preference or discount rate of the present population. Observable market transactions by themselves do not take into account the interests of future generations. This poses an ethical dilemma: from whose perspective, present vs. future, are the resources to be valued? If those perspectives are given equal consideration, should we seek to determine some estimate of the social rate of discount that differs from the discount (interest) rate as generated by the market? These questions may have no practical answers. Thus the issue for us is how to devise a method that includes future interests without resorting to the use of a zero discount rate that would value finite resources without good substitutes at astronomical prices.

A second issue, related to valuing changes in the stock of nonrenewable resources, is how to account for changes in the stock of natural capital assets. Is it appropriate simply to subtract the amount of stock depleted each year? Or should an accounting method be adopted, as Eisner suggests, that also adds the value of new discoveries (i.e., new information about the size of the stock of capital)? Or should changes in the value of the resource over time also be included in the valuation? (In the last case, if a resource is partly depleted but its market value increases dramatically, the accounting procedure would show an increase in the capital stock despite the depletion of some physical stock.) Our inclination is to choose the first alternative, simply subtracting an amount representing the amount of depletion. Although new discoveries might have an impact on current market prices, they are not of great significance for long term welfare. Moreover, when retrospective work is done, as in the ISEW, the date of new discoveries of resources should not influence the estimates.

With regard to the problem of depreciating natural capital, economist Herman Daly has suggested in a personal conversation that our previous method could be modified slightly by calculating the amount of rent from resource production that should be reinvested in a process to create a perpetual stream of output of a renewable substitute for the nonrenewable resource being depleted. Calculating on the basis of an actual physical product equivalent to an existing product reduces the problem of speculating about the changes in price of a nonrenewable resource and the discount rate at which those prices should be evaluated. Thus one way to deal with the problem of estimating the long-run value of the oil that is extracted would be to consider the marginal cost of producing close substitutes such as "gasohol" from sugar cane or other organic material. This procedure obviates the need to use a zero discount rate because it assumes that depletable resources can be used in the present to create the capital necessary to provide a permanent stream of substitutes.

As a consequence, we have followed a procedure whereby we estimated the amount of money that would have had to be spent in each year to replace the amount of resources extracted (produced) in that year. We have focused on energy resources because they account for 75 to 80% of the value of raw materials produced in the United States and because we have used a physical measure of energy to aggregate various sources (coal, oil, natural gas, and nuclear power) into a single number, which is not possible for other minerals. Moreover, cheap energy can compensate for the costs of extracting minerals from low-grade ores, but high-grade zinc or copper ores can do little to provide more energy.

Starting with the total amount of nonrenewable energy produced each year (measured in quadrillions of BTUs), we divided that number by 5.8 million (the approximate number of BTUs per barrel of oil) to estimate the barrel equivalent of energy produced.[4] We then multiplied that number by the constant dollar replacement cost per barrel, which, by assumption, increased at 3% per year from 1950 to 1990. In 1988, we assumed that the cost of replacement was $75 per barrel in nominal dollars or approximately $26.50 in 1972 constant dollars.

The estimate of $75 per barrel as the nominal replacement cost in 1988 might seem rather high at first glance, particularly since the world price of oil that year was around $12. However, that lower figure has little to do with the cost of providing replacement fuel from a renewable source. (If the replacement is not from a renewable source, then this methodology does not overcome the problem of how to compare the claims of present and future consumers of a nonrenewable resource. In that case, the appropriate price to use in the accounting is completely indeterminate.) Yet even renewable energy from biomass could be produced for less than $75 per barrel in 1988. Why have we used such a high figure?

According to one 1988 study ethanol would have been cost-competitive with oil selling at $40 per barrel if biomass conversion were not receiving a subsidy and if corn were selling at $2.00 per bushel.[5] If the price of corn were $4.00 per bushel, the break-even price of ethanol would rise to $50 per barrel. This is not the full story, however. The authors of the study note that ethanol now accounts for about one-half of one percent of the energy content of gasoline in the United States and that doubling or tripling production

> would begin to place strong upward pressure on corn and other grain prices, thereby increasing the production cost of ethanol and reducing its competitiveness with alternative energy sources.[6]

In other words, devoting millions of acres to growing crops for alcohol would drive up the price of land, of food, and of the crops grown for fuel as well. Using tens or hundreds of millions acres of cropland to increase the production of ethanol by a factor of one hundred (to one-half of the energy content of gasoline used in the U.S.) would presumably drive agricultural prices up much further than current agricultural price supports. The price of corn might reach $15 or $20 per bushel, which would drive the cost of producing ethanol up to over $100 per barrel.

These estimates do not even consider the cost of increased erosion if the organic residue of corn and other crops were removed from the land. According to a 1984 report, removal of crop residues could increase erosion by up to nine times.[7] The energy cost of conservation measures to counteract those effects could be high enough to eliminate any net energy derived from ethanol production.

Even without consideration of the energy costs of conservation measures, the energy produced from ethanol may be less than the energy required to produce it. According to one study, the net energy derived from sugar cane that is transformed into alcohol ranges from 0.8 to 1.7, according to whether the processing plant uses petroleum or bagasse (the sugar cane stalk) as its source of energy.[8] The 0.8 figure signifies that 8 units of energy are produced for every 10 units consumed. In other words, the net energy is negative. Even the 1.7 figure is low, and it does not include the cost of transporting the ethanol to its end use. Since the energy cost of ethanol production is so high, the high monetary cost is not surprising.

Consequently, $75 would appear a conservative estimate in 1988 of the cost per barrel of replacing the energy produced in the U. S.[9]

The estimated 3% annual growth of the real replacement cost of energy is based on several factors. First, the growth of the amount of energy produced would require more farmland to be devoted to the purpose of providing biomass as a feedstock for ethanol production. Also, as world population grows, the demand for alternative uses of the land (for growing food) has grown as well. Second, since a large part of the cost of the production of ethanol (planting, harvesting, processing) is the cost of energy, higher energy costs form a positive feedback or self-reinforcing loop. Third, the energy cost of extracting all of the resources needed for the production of the capital equipment used in the ethanol production process are rising as well.

The choice of the 3% estimated growth rate is partly arbitrary. However, a comparison with the rate of growth of the cost per foot of oil drilling will show that it is not unreasonable. Drilling costs per well rose by 5.7% per year from 1970 to 1975, 7.4% from 1975 to 1980 and by 12.4% in 1981 and 6.5% in 1982.[10] After that, the world price of oil fell, exploration was cut back, and drilling was presumably limited to wells with lower cost. Nevertheless, during the period of rising oil prices, the rising drilling cost is indicative of the basic principle that when the limits of a resource are being reached, the cost of extracting the next unit is more costly than the previous unit. This principle presumably applies also to renewable fuels, though not as dramatically as to oil and gas. Thus we used a growth rate of cost per barrel approximately half the one revealed for fossil fuels extraction in the 1970s.

Column U
Eisner has also criticized the use of $.50 per barrel equivalent as an appropriate measure of the cumulative damage inflicted on the environment by energy use. We agree that this number is arbitrary, and we make no claim to know that the relation between energy use and environmental deterioration is in fact linear. Having acknowledged our limitations, we are not, however, willing to ignore major issues for lack of an accepted methodology for treating them. We have reckoned that current energy consumption patterns will impose costs in the hundreds of billions or trillions of dollars in the next century, and that those costs ought to be subtracted from current income. In part this includes the oil equivalent of atomic power production. The disposal of wastes at the Hanford weapons development center already costs several billion dollars per year, and those wastes comprise only a portion of the total that have been generated in the United States. The costs of maintaining and protecting these facilities will continue indefinitely. There are still not reliable estimates of the costs of decommissioning

atomic power reactors and disposing of their high-level wastes. Thus, the cumulative costs imposed on future generations by atomic power generation may amount to several tens of billions of dollars per year.

As large as the costs of radioactive waste management may be, they pale by comparison with the potential costs of climate change. The costs to the future imposed by industrial and agricultural activities that add carbon dioxide, nitrous oxide and methane to the atmosphere (thereby contributing to the "greenhouse effect" and global climate change) have only recently begun to be assessed. Although there is scientific controversy over the expected magnitude of the greenhouse effect, due to the limited capacity of computer models to simulate all of the key interactions in global climate, the most likely effect of a doubling of carbon dioxide (and other heat trapping compounds) would be an increase of 1.5 to 4.5 degrees Centigrade, with the greatest warming occurring at high latitudes. Although some elements of the models may overstate the effect of greenhouse gases other elements that could accelerate global warming are understated. As an example of acceleration, warmer average temperatures increase the release of carbon dioxide and methane due to higher levels of biological decomposition, which in turn contributes to further warming.[11] If the temperature in the northern polar region rises sufficiently to thaw land containing large peat deposits, the decay of that peat could add considerable amounts of carbon dioxide to the atmosphere. Thus, human releases of greenhouse gases could set in motion irreversible processes that would alter climate even more than current models predict. In addition, since the models presume a gradual increase in temperature over a period of decades, a climate shift resulting from changes in ocean currents could cause unforeseen problems to arise rapidly.[12]

Because the weather patterns of the earth are determined largely by temperature differences between the poles and the equator, warmer poles will mean that ocean currents and continental weather systems will become less vigorous.

The extent of global warming has generally not been as great since around 1950 as computer models have predicted would be caused by the increased level of carbon dioxide in the atmosphere. One plausible explanation of this anomaly is that the increased levels of humanly generated sulfates in the atmosphere have counteracted warming trends in the Northern Hemisphere. However, since sulfates remain in the atmosphere for months, whereas greenhouse gases remain for years, the warming trend is likely to be dominate in the long run.[13]

The full extent of the physical damage likely to ensue from the cumulative effects of climate change is difficult to predict. The flooding of cities and erosion of beaches as a result of higher sea levels represent only the first level of the threat. Even the disruption of established patterns of agriculture as a result of drought and increased variations and unpredictability of weather will not be the most serious consequence of these changes. The greatest threat is ecological. The almost instantaneous change (on a geological scale) of the global climate could have harmful effects on all but the most resilient species of plants and animals in those regions of the planet most drastically affected by climate change. A 3 degree Centigrade increase in temperature in the United States, for example, would force vegetation belts around 200 miles northward, causing the extinction of thousands of species that cannot disperse at the required speed.[14]

A recent economic study by Willliam R. Cline, who relies on the view of the majority of scientists on the Intergovernmental Panel on Climate Change (IPCC), indicates that a 2.5 degree Centigrade warming by 2025 would generate around $60 billion (1990 dollars) in annual tangible losses and perhaps another $60 billion annually in intangible losses, particularly species loss.[15] Cline points out that the IPCC "best guess" probably underestimates the amount of warming by ignoring the short-term "masking" of potential warming by sulfates from urban pollution. There are various other positive feedback mechanisms that may have been underestimated by the IPCC, such as the release of methane from peat deposits and increased trapping of heat by clouds in the upper atmosphere as warming causes a redistribution of clouds from the lower to the upper atmosphere.

In bending over backwards to take account of criticism of the global warming hypothesis, Cline may have bent too far. Thus, his $120 billion per year damage figure in 2025 is probably conservative. In addition to accepting temperature change estimates that he acknowledges are probably underestimates, he also assigns too much weight to conservative damage estimates. For example, when he examines the effects of warming on agriculture, he focuses on the carbon fertilization effects of increased carbon dioxide, even after noting that the laboratory results which demonstrate this effect are biased by the presence of adequate water and fertilizer. In addition, these studies ignore the fact that weeds will have access to increased carbon dioxide as well and that increased biomass production may lead to a higher ratio of carbohydrate to protein, hardly a nutritional gain.

Although we recognized that greenhouse gases vary in the extent to which they trap heat and that spent fuels from atomic power plants vary in their toxicity and persistence, we have continued to assume, for simplicity, that the amount of long-term environmental damage or the added cost of protecting the environment is directly proportional to the consumption of nonrenewable energy (fossil fuels and fissionable materials). We have therefore calculated long-term environmental damage in the same manner as before: calculating the damage as $.50 per cumulative barrel equivalent of nonrenewable energy consumed. If Cline's estimate of $120 billion in annual damage is approximately right, that would mean the accumulated condition of damage in 2025 (from which annual damage would "flow") would be around $1.2 trillion. That serves as an indirect confirmation of the reasonableness of our estimate of $285 billion (1972 dollars) as the "stock" of damage in 1990.

Column V

As a result of the observation by Carson and Young that our inclusion of government capital in net capital growth was inconsistent with our exclusion of the services of that capital elsewhere, we modified column V so as to include only the stock of private capital in our computations. (In the revised calculations, we have estimated the stock of private capital for the years 1945 to 1949 based on the ratio of private to total capital stocks in the early 1950s.)

With respect to the revision suggested by Gottfried, however, that we should not mix flows of services from capital and changes in stocks of capital, we have not modified this column. His recommendation of greater consistency in the use of stocks and flows may not be appropriate when we are trying to combine current enjoyment (measured by service flows) and future sustainability (measured by changes in stock). In this column, changes in stock reflect changes in sustainable levels of capital available. Thus, we have not altered it.

Eisner has taken us to task for the ISEW's failure to include human capital in estimates of changes in the stock of capital. According to his analysis, human capital is "the most critical factor of production" and constitutes "the largest single share of the total capital of the nation." We have no quarrel with this evaluation of the importance of human capital. We do, however, dispute that any causal relation has ever been demonstrated between expenditures on education and the stock of human capital. In almost every study we have seen, the relation is assumed rather than tested. When Eisner describes the large number of "functionally illiterate school dropouts" and "declining scores on scholastic aptitude examinations," he ignores the fact that these phenomena have coincided with continuous growth in inflation-adjusted expenditures per pupil.

In an early version of the ISEW, we included an estimate of human capital based on educational expenditures for members of the labor force. We found that real per pupil expenditures quadrupled between 1945 and 1985, and our estimate of human capital showed an almost eleven-fold increase during that period. However, since the quality of education does not appear to have improved during that period (and may have declined), the use of school expenditures to measure human capital seems completely inappropriate. If indeed human capital is "the most critical factor of production," it would appear to derive largely from on-the-job training and experience, in spite of schooling rather than because of it. Until someone devises an ingenious method of measuring the value of the knowledge embodied by workers and managers, a plausible measure of the stock of human capital will remain beyond our reach.

Column W

Eisner has raised an important objection to our methodology in treating net international investment. The problem is that we have relied on official figures which are based on historic purchase price of assets instead of current market value. He argues that since the U.S. invested overseas in the past and foreigners have invested in the U.S. recently, the figures we have used considerably underestimate the value of American assets abroad and overestimate foreign investments in the U.S. He further points out that making adjustments along the lines he proposes would have the effect of raising the rate of growth of the ISEW in recent years.

Carson and Young suggest 1) that we should assume that some of the net foreign investment in the U.S. adds to productivity of our economy and 2) that we should distinguish capital flows from changes in exchange rates and price. With respect to the first question, we recognize that at a certain stage of economic development, net inflows of capital may be a healthy sign, assuming they are used for investment rather than consumption. However, in a mature economy such as the United States, we assume that net inflows of capital represent a fundamental weakness, especially when they are used to finance unproductive government spending. Furthermore, if the flow of capital into the U.S. is financing productive investment, this will show up in the column "Net Capital Growth." With respect to the second question, it is not clear why the decline of the dollar should be factored out of the calculation of sustainable welfare, since the decline in buying power represents a real loss of capacity to enhance well-being. Thus, the figures we used *may* have overstated the changes in sustainable welfare for the reasons they suggest, but without further information, we cannot assume that to be the case.

Fortunately, recent calculations by the Bureau of Economic Analysis have made possible more appropriate estimates of the changes in net international position from 1982 to 1990.[16] The values for 1950 to 1981 that we have used continue to be based on historic costs rather than market value, but for those years the difference between historic costs and market value would not have altered the net international position substantially. For the period from 1982 to 1990, however, the BEA's new estimates, which are based on market value, provide a more reliable estimate of net investment, more so than historic cost estimates.

New Columns

Personal pollution control expenditures. Carson and Young propose that we account for personal expenditures for pollution control devices, and we gladly accept their advice since they also offer estimates that can used in a time series. Using the figures they provide in table B.4.2 of their paper, we have subtracted the expenditures that are attributed to personal consumption of pollution control equipment and their operation. We then calculated backwards for previous years, assuming that prior to 1972, personal expenditures on pollution abatement and control had increased by 20% per year. In the ISEW, we subtracted these expenditures because they represent defensive expenditures; they do not improve welfare, but merely attempt to restore it to some baseline level. Since business and government expenditures are not included in personal consumption expenditures (column B), we have not subtracted their pollution abatement expenditures.

Ozone depletion. Eisner points out correctly that our assumption that all long term environmental damage is related to energy use is not supported. We had already included examples of long term damage that is not tied to energy use in columns dealing with loss of wetlands and farmland. Nevertheless, we were especially concerned that we had omitted a damage estimate from the cumulative release of chlorofluorocarbons into the upper atmosphere. Consequently, we did further research and discovered a data series on quantities of CFCs released.

The column we have introduced is derived by multiplying the cumulative world production of CFC-11 and CFC-12 by $5 per kilogram.[17] (Since about one-third of CFC production has taken place in the U.S., the $5 per kilogram estimate actually amounts to $15 per kilogram of U.S. production.) The lifetimes of CFC-11 and CFC-12 are 75 and 110 years, respectively. (Other CFCs and halogenated compounds also contribute to ozone depletion, but the only time series data we found were for CFC-11 and CFC-12, so we have restricted our estimates to those compounds.)

In the eight years between November 1978 and October 1986, the amount of ozone in the stratosphere above the mid-northern hemisphere declined by somewhere between 4.4% and 7.4%.[18] One likely effect of the increased ultraviolet radiation reaching the earth's surface as a result will be a higher incidence of skin cancer, particularly among fair-skinned people. The risk of contracting malignant melanoma is already rising: from a lifetime risk factor of 1 in 600 in 1950 to 1 in 135 in 1987.[19] In fact, the direct consequences to humans in terms of skin cancer represent only the least significant of the effects of allowing increased ultraviolet radiation to reach the earth's surface. In theory, humans could protect themselves from the harmful effects of increased radiation (though even this behavior change would constitute a cost imposed on the future). However, plants and animals cannot protect themselves from changes brought about by reduced ozone in the upper atmosphere. Thus the ecological effects of greater ultraviolet radiation are likely to be much greater than the health effects, though no one knows precisely what they will be.

Our assumption that the damage from ozone depletion due to cumulative CFC production and release in the U.S. is equal to $15 per kilogram amounts to the same as assuming that each individual in the U.S. would demand about $960 (1972 dollars) in 1985 to compensate for the risks involved in producing and having produced CFCs. Or it may be thought of as the amount that would need to be set aside to compensate future generations for having made their planet less habitable.

Two Additional Issues

Leisure Reconsidered

In our original analysis, we suggested that one reason to omit leisure it that it has varied little during the period of our study. Subsequently we came across information that indicated that leisure time had been declining. According to the Louis Harris poll, the amount of leisure time decreased substantially from 26.2 hours per week in 1973 to 16.6 hours per week in 1987, an almost 40 percent decline.[20] If this revealed a true reduction in leisure and a corresponding rise in the number of hours worked per week, this would imply a much greater reduction in measured welfare during that period than we have indicated in the ISEW as it stands now. However, there is good reason to believe that Harris's figures are misleading. According to Richard Hamilton, the Harris pollsters asked in 1973 how many hours per week an interviewee worked, whereas in 1980, they asked how many hours per week a respondent worked *or studied or did housework*.[21] The increased hours of work reported in the latter year could easily have been accounted for by the difference in the questions asked, and leisure would have declined correspondingly. Based on evidence provided by the National Opinion Research Center General Social Survey and the Bureau of the Census Current Population Survey, Hamilton argues that the hours of work per week have remained approximately constant throughout the 1970s and 1980s. We believe that if anyone does include leisure in a measure of economic welfare that the amount of leisure should be recorded as being constant in recent years.

Mishan correctly points out that even if leisure has not varied during the period of analysis, that is no basis for excluding it. By leaving out a variable that remains relatively constant we have tended to overstate the rate of growth in sustainable economic welfare from 1950 to the present. (If we added as the value of leisure a large constant amount--perhaps $4,000 per year per person--to the per capita ISEW as it appears in table A.1, the effect would be to reduce the percentage changes in per capita ISEW over time. For example, an increase from $7,000 to $7,500 or a corresponding decrease is a much smaller change than the shift from $3,000 to $3,500.

Nevertheless, we chose not to include leisure as an element in our index. Interestingly, although Mishan provides one good reason to include leisure, other points he raises inadvertently serve as new objections to including leisure in the ISEW.

One problem with the measurement of leisure that Mishan's comments raise has to do with the number of hours per day that are to be classified as leisure. Mishan suggests that there is no reason to exclude the time spent sleeping as leisure, so that the number of hours of leisure per day for someone working 8 hours would be 16. The total amount of leisure per year would then be approximately 6766 hours per fully employed member of the labor force (and more for part-time employees). (This is equal to the total hours in a year minus approximately 2000 hours of work, assuming two weeks of vacation time.) If we assume an average real wage rate of $5 per hour and that the value of the marginal hour of leisure is equal to the wage rate, then the value of leisure to the average worker per year is $33,830, and the total for the work force is in the neighborhood of $3.7 trillion. This would be approximately double the value of GNP in 1989 in 1972 dollars. In fact, according to Mishan, the actual value of leisure should be higher than this because the value of infra-marginal hours would be higher than the marginal hour. (In other words, if someone had already worked 20 hours in a day, it would require a higher payment to induce a 21st hour of work than it would to induce a 9th hour from someone who has worked only 8.) Thus the value of leisure might range from $4 to $5 trillion per year. As far as we are concerned, this kind of calculation, which Mishan seems to propose quite seriously, amounts to a *reductio ad absurdum* of the difficulties posed by including leisure in an index of economic welfare. It would so totally swamp all other figures in such an index as to make every other aspect of welfare trivial by comparison. Yet there is no particular reason within economic theory for not following Mishan's proposal quite literally. It is only a sense of proportion and the bounds of plausibility that tell us that there is something terribly out of balance in this calculation.

Mishan also raises for us a second doubt about the use of foregone income as the basis of estimating the value of leisure in his discussion in another context of the difference between compensating variation (CV) and equivalent variation (EV). The valuation of leisure should not be based on EV (How high must a wage be to induce someone to work an extra hour?) but rather on CV (How much would it be necessary to pay someone to compensate for a loss of an hour of leisure IF total income were not at issue?) To put the matter bluntly, we feel uneasy about assigning more worth to an hour of idleness of a rich person than a similar hour in the life of a poor person. Does a steak likewise taste better in the mouth of the person who can afford it than it would in the mouth of someone who cannot?

In the abstract we agree with Mishan and others that leisure time is related to current enjoyment or welfare. However, there are simply too many unresolved issues and ambiguities in the exact meaning of leisure. Combining the problems we find in Mishan's analysis with those raised in Part A, we continue to be convinced that including leisure in the ISEW is not appropriate.

Stocks, Flows, and the Treatment of Capital

Upon reflection, it seems to us that the measure of current welfare should be based on the level of services flowing from an existing stock of capital and that the measure of sustainability or capacity to generate services in the future should be based on changes in capital stocks. The ISEW combines both of those features in a single index on the theory that true welfare is current enjoyment that does not take away enjoyment from future generations. Consequently, despite the call for consistency from Gottfried, we regard the use of two different methods for two different purposes as justifiable. Sustainability involves maintaining a given stock of capital to allow an equal level of income or service from it in the future. Increases in the stock enhance the potential for future production of services, while decreases in the stock diminish future potentialities. The columns in the ISEW dealing with loss of wetlands, loss of farmland, resource depletion, long-range environmental damage, ozone depletion, net capital growth, and net international position all deal with sustainability and thus ought to be calculated on the basis of changes in the stock of capital.[22] In other cases, where current enjoyment is concerned, valuation ought to be on the basis of services from that capital.

Implications of the ISEW

The ISEW will serve its purpose if it focuses attention on the need to think in terms of sustainable welfare. Within the field of economics that would represent a significant shift. The work of Nordhaus and Tobin provided a model for thinking about economic welfare, but they did not go far enough. They did not recognize the seriousness of the need to develop a methodology to account for depletion of natural capital, including long-term environmental damage. In the almost twenty years since their study appeared, human activity has approached biological limits and threatens to disrupt global ecological systems. Leaving the question of preserving natural capital in the background is no longer justifiable. It must become as central to economic thinking as full employment and controlling inflation. Yet this cannot occur unless there is an accounting system that includes sustainability as one of its central features.[23]

During the Reagan and Bush administrations, there have been frequent claims that government regulations block economic growth. A number of conservatives have criticized plans to cut the emission of carbon dioxide and other greenhouse gases by arguing that limiting industrial or agricultural activities to control those emissions will reduce the well-being of society. These claims implicitly assume that GNP is an accurate measure of economic well-being. Productivity is defined purely in terms of the output of measured goods and services. Yet if the meaning of "the economy" were broadened to encompass the costs of pollution, as in the case of the ISEW, the reduction of pollution would be seen as contributing directly to economic growth. In other words, if citizens could buy cleaner air in the market, those payments would contribute to a realistically measured economy, and there would be no conflict between economics and environmental concerns.

The habits of mind that have developed in conjunction with the GNP have inhibited conservation policies that could be justified even in terms of traditional national accounts. Thus proposals to raise energy taxes have been attacked as inflationary or damaging to the economy, based on the assumption that those taxes would raise production costs and reduce the growth rate of GNP. Yet higher taxes on energy consumption would make possible higher growth of real GNP over the long run, particularly if the energy tax offset income taxes. The energy tax would induce innovations to improve efficiency, while the reduced income tax would increase buying power and employment. In addition, in a world market, equipment that is not energy-efficient has become increasingly uncompetitive because the price of energy is higher in the rest of the world than in the United States. American cars, farm equipment, and industrial machinery that are designed to run on fuel priced at $1 per gallon are at a disadvantage in countries where fuel prices are as high as $4 per gallon.

Although the case for higher energy taxes can thus be made in terms of conventional accounts, alternative accounts that include depletion costs and environmental damage costs would reveal the need for those taxes much more strongly. If economic accounts automatically considered the side-effects of energy use on the environment, they would have revealed the value of higher energy taxes long ago. Only an antiquated view of "the economy" prevents us from seeing the obvious positive contribution that higher energy taxes would make to our lives.

Cultural Conflict Over the Evaluation of Progress

Since the relatively simple idea of broadening the national accounts has been around since their inception, the failure to include income distribution, natural resources, household work, and other factors is not accidental. The implications of the ISEW or other similar measures can be appreciated only in the context of the cultural conflict over how to define progress. That conflict is hundreds of years old and might be described as the difference between a mechanistic and an organic view of the world.

The mechanistic view focuses on simple, measurable cause-and-effect relationships. This presupposes that one set of events can be isolated from all other events in the world for the sake of analysis. In that way each causal relationship can be considered separately. The world is thus seen as a machine composed of exchangeable units that can be rearranged and controlled from the outside by human intervention. The measure of success is the ability to predict and control.

The organic view, by contrast, stresses the inseparability of events. The isolation of events for purposes of studying them is a useful fiction, but it tells only part of the story. Parts interact to form wholes that cannot be defined as the sum of the parts. Prediction and control are possible in limited contexts, but efforts to control events have unforeseeable repercussions.

Economics is tied closely to the mechanistic model. In order to be able to predict and control, economics defines its boundaries to include only measurable behavior and events. Precision (based on measurement of an event) is more important than accuracy (based on analysis of the meaning of an event). This bias is obvious in the case of the national income accounts. Economists want to protect the precision of their measurements because they are expected to provide advice that will enable political leaders to control the future and protect citizens from uncertainty and distress. Thus, economists ignore messy components that do not lend themselves to simple measurement and direct control.

The ISEW represents a small movement away from a purely mechanistic model to a more organic one. It breaks down the rigid boundaries that separate the measured and the unmeasured. Indeed the ambiguity of the meaning of well-being--the fact that there is no boundary that determines what should be included in a welfare measure--is one of the key objections to the ISEW and similar projects, as the quotation from Ruggles pointed out in the introduction. To those steeped in the ideology of mechanism, this absence of boundaries is disturbing (and it may even provoke condescending remarks toward those outside the economics fraternity who do not play by its rules.)

Judgments about economic progress thus heavily depend on the extent to which one allows "soft" imputations to mix with the "hard" data of market prices. Thus, "hardliners" tend to favor growth of measurable output and to gloss over the side-effects, whereas those who take seriously the soft data regard that sort of growth as inherently ambiguous, particularly when the conditions necessary for growth are imposed on a population by economic elites. Since the hardliners also believe that events can be controlled, they are likely to blame their soft critics if policies fail. For example, the cessation of growth of atomic power, despite considerable federal subsidies, is still often blamed on environmental critics rather than inherent economic problems with the technology.

The debate over how we should evaluate the welfare of a society is far more than a technical dispute over what elements to include. It amounts to a choice of the type of future we will pursue. In a nation that is prone to be swayed by numbers, the strife over which numbers (if any) to use is a conflict over power: who will have it and how they will be allowed to use it. Those who would use technology to increase output without regard to the social consequences prefer a measure such as the GNP that disregards the damage that may occur. Those who are concerned about qualitative dimensions of life must find some alternative that can undermine the emphasis on GNP as the symbol of our culture.

The International Implications

The change of focus we are proposing is relevant in every country, not only the United States. Nevertheless, we do not suppose that an accounting framework modeled precisely on the ISEW could be replicated around the world. Diefenbacher's work in Germany demonstrates the difficulty of trying to reproduce the ISEW in its exact form in other countries. Perhaps it is not important for welfare measures to transcend national boundaries. Their more important function would be to help determine whether a nation was becoming better off over time, not whether it is better or worse off than other nations.

Developing indicators similar to the ISEW in other countries is not a mere academic exercise. For example, if the work performed in households, primarily by women, were included in a composite measure of welfare, this could lead to changes in national policies that would treat the subsistence work of households on a par with the type of work that is valued in the market. Or if the ongoing value of forests, wetlands, and other features of the natural world that provide flood control, water quality, and wildlife preservation services at no cost were included in calculations of welfare, the political will to protect those lands would be strengthened.

Alternative economic indicators similar to the ISEW could be used by groups that are seeking to fend off the giant development projects sometimes proposed by the World Bank or by national governments. Policies promoting sustainability may slow the rate of deforestation in the tropics, and those policies require statistical justification of the sort that alternative indicators could provide.

Bridging Economics and Ecology

New indicators will have little constructive value, however, unless the operative meaning of sustainability is ecological rather than narrowly economic. In recent years, the term "sustainable" has lost the connection with its biological origins. A sustainable ecological system is one that maximizes complexity and minimizes throughputs of energy. This corresponds to Herman Daly's idea of a steady-state economy. Instead, the dominant mode of economic thought has coopted the term to mean "capable of continued growth," which historically has meant sustained growth of energy consumption from nonrenewable sources. The idea of the sustainability of life has given way in practice to the idea that society must sustain an increase in production.

From the larger perspective, ecological and economic sustainability should coincide because the basis of economic life is ultimately the earth and the resources it provides. If the life-sustaining capacity of the earth is depleted, economic life will also come to an end. Yet, if the information provided through the economic system (primarily through relative prices) misrepresents the true scarcity of ecological resources, the two systems will diverge. Since economic thinking has focused attention almost exclusively on human activity, to the neglect of nature's contribution, divergence has become the norm.

Thus, the development of new indicators should be understood as an effort to bring ecological and economic knowledge into a closer relationship. Precise estimates of currently unmeasured values are not as important as including some figure of the right order of magnitude. Only by beginning the task of deriving monetary estimates of these often hidden values will it be possible for the elements of the natural world and of society that sustain the economy to receive due recognition. An accounting system that takes into account only a limited range of actions inevitably distorts the decisions made in a society. If individuals, businesses, and governments are to take actions that will genuinely enhance welfare, each nation needs a way to analyze and measure what constitutes well-being. We hope that our work on the ISEW has contributed to an understanding of the significance and the difficulties associated with that endeavor.

The Revised Tables

In the revised tables that follow, we have included only those we have revised in accordance with the foregoing discussion. The table dealing with cost of urbanization has been omitted because the corresponding column has been removed from the ISEW. Tables dealing with commuting, agricultural land, and long-term environmental damage (Tables A.6, A,9, and A.10 in the original) are not included because the only change has been to update them to 1990. In Table C.1 columns dealing with housework, consumer durables services, commuting, water and noise pollution, and loss of wetlands and farmland have been updated by means of extrapolation from the previous year rather than with new data. Table C.1 omits two columns that were in the original ISEW table (advertising expenditures and the cost of urbanization) and adds two new columns: one for personal expenditures on pollution abatement and control and the second for damage due to ozone depletion. Thus, there has been some rearrangement of columns K through U in the revised summary table.

Table C.13 summarizes the rate of annual growth of per capita ISEW after accounting for all of the changes we have made. This table provides a general sense of whether our society is getting better off, worse off, or staying the same by indicating the direction and rate of change of sustainable welfare.

The results reveal slight growth of per capita ISEW in the 1950s, considerable growth in the 1960s (at 60% of the growth rate of per capita GNP), slow growth again in the 1970s, followed by a decline in the 1980s. According to Table C.1, per capita ISEW in 1990 was slightly below the level in 1966, and the level in 1984 was below the level of 1956.

Whereas per capita ISEW grew by only 16.5% from 1951 to 1990, per capita personal consumption expenditures (calculation not shown) increased by 170%. The main factors contributing to this difference were a widening gap in income distribution, the slow increase in the value of housework services, depletion of natural resources, long-term systemic environmental damage (in contrast to improvements in localized environmental management), and the growing need to rely on foreign capital to finance consumption.

Figure C.1

Alternative Measures of Economic Welfare

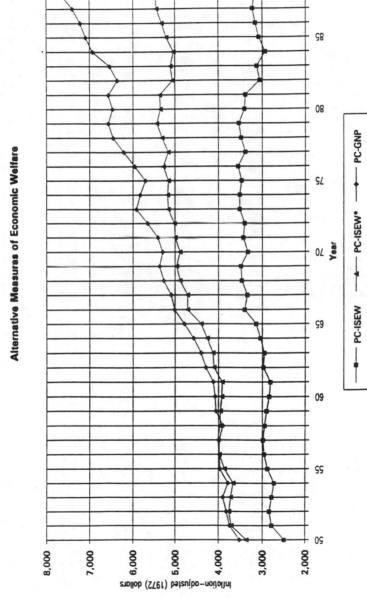

Note: ISEW is Index of Sustainable Economic Welfare (Table C.1, Col. Y); ISEW* is ISEW without Cols. S and T. This graph presents annual changes in per capita ISEW and GNP. It is a revised form of the graph presented on page 79 in Part A. Revisions are discussed in the text of chapter 11.

Table C.1. Index of Sustainable Economic Welfare 1950-1990

Year A	Personal consump- tion B	Distribu- tional inequality C	Weighted personal consumption (B/C) D	Services of house- hold labor E(+)	Services of consumer durables F(+)	Services of streets and highways G(+)
1950	337.3	111.1	303.6	311.4	30.2	6.2
1951	341.6	100.0	341.6	315.4	32.9	6.3
1952	350.1	102.0	343.1	319.5	34.9	6.5
1953	363.4	106.4	341.6	323.6	37.3	6.7
1954	370.0	111.1	333.0	327.8	39.3	7.0
1955	394.1	104.2	378.3	332.0	42.2	7.4
1956	405.4	100.0	405.4	336.3	44.2	7.7
1 957	413.8	98.0	422.1	340.6	45.7	8.1
1958	418.0	100.0	418.0	345.0	46.3	8.5
1959	440.4	102.0	431.6	349.5	47.6	9.0
1960	452.0	104.2	433.9	354.0	48.8	9.5
1961	461.4	106.4	433.7	358.5	49.4	9.9
1962	482.0	100.0	482.0	363.2	51.0	10.4
1963	500.5	100.0	500.5	367.9	53.0	11.0
1964	528.0	98.0	538.6	372.6	56.2	11.6
1965	557.5	96.2	579.8	377.4	60.4	12.1
1966	585.7	89.3	656.0	382.3	65.2	12.7
1967	602.7	90.9	663.0	387.2	69.6	13.3
1968	634.4	89.3	710.5	392.2	75.2	13.9
1969	657.9	89.3	736.8	397.2	80.3	14.4
1970	672.1	92.6	725.9	402.4	83.9	14.8
1971	696.8	90.9	766.5	407.5	88.5	15.3
1972	737.1	92.6	796.1	412.8	94.7	15.7
1973	767.9	90.9	844.7	418.1	101.9	16.0
1974	762.8	90.9	839.1	423.5	106.2	16.2
1975	779.4	92.6	841.8	429.0	109.7	16.3
1976	823.1	92.6	888.9	434.5	115.0	16.5
1977	864.3	96.2	898.9	440.1	121.7	16.6
1978	903.2	96.2	939.3	445.8	128.9	16.7
1979	927.6	96.2	964.7	451.5	135.0	16.7
1980	931.8	98.0	950.4	457.3	137.9	16.8
1981	950.5	100.0	950.5	463.2	141.1	16.8
1982	963.3	106.4	905.5	469.2	143.4	16.9
1983	1009.2	106.4	948.6	475.3	148.7	16.9
1984	1058.6	106.4	995.0	481.4	156.6	17.1
1985	1108.2	108.7	1019.5	487.6	167.2	17.3
1986	1151.3	108.7	1059.2	493.9	179.4	17.4
1987	1184.0	108.7	1089.3	500.3	190.3	17.5
1988	1226.7	108.7	1128.5	506.7	204.3	17.7
1989	1250.3	108.7	1150.3	513.2	216.2	17.8
1990	1265.6	108.7	1164.4	519.8	224.9	18.0

Table C. 1 continued

Year A	Public expenditures on health and education H	Expenditures on consumer durables I	Defensive private expenditures health and education J	Costs of commuting K(-)	Personal expenditures pollution control L(-)	Costs of auto accidents M(-)	Costs of water pollution N(-)
1950	4.9	42.6	13.9	9.0	0.0	11.6	9.0
1951	4.9	39.1	14.5	8.5	0.0	13.2	9.2
1952	5.1	38.0	14.9	8.4	0.0	13.3	9.4
1953	5.3	42.1	15.5	9.3	0.0	13.9	9.7
1954	5.5	42.5	16.1	9.6	0.0	13.3	9.9
1955	5.8	51.1	16.9	10.9	0.0	13.9	10.2
1956	6.2	48.8	17.9	10.4	0.0	14.4	10.4
1957	6.5	48.6	18.9	10.5	0.0	14.3	10.7
1958	6.9	45.3	19.5	9.9	0.1	14.0	10.9
1959	7.3	50.7	20.2	10.7	0.1	14.3	11.2
1960	7.8	51.4	21.1	11.3	0.1	14.4	11.5
1961	8.6	49.3	22.9	10.9	0.1	14.4	11.8
1962	9.4	54.7	24.8	11.7	0.1	15.4	12.1
1963	10.4	59.7	26.6	12.4	0.2	16.2	12.4
1964	11.4	64.8	28.5	12.8	0.2	17.4	12.7
1965	12.5	72.6	30.2	14.3	0.3	18.8	13.1
1966	15.4	78.4	31.9	14.9	0.3	19.4	13.4
1967	17.9	79.5	32.6	15.2	0.4	19.5	13.8
1968	19.4	88.3	33.7	16.7	0.5	20.8	14.1
1969	20.8	91.8	34.2	17.7	0.7	23.0	14.5
1970	22.6	89.1	34.5	17.4	0.8	25.3	14.9
1971	23.9	98.2	35.9	19.5	1.0	26.3	15.3
1972	25.5	111.1	38.1	21.6	1.3	28.7	15.3
1973	27.3	121.3	39.9	23.1	1.4	28.6	15.3
1974	29.7	112.3	39.4	22.4	1.6	25.8	15.3
1975	30.4	112.7	39.3	22.4	1.7	28.1	15.3
1976	32.2	126.6	40.7	25.0	1.9	30.1	15.3
1977	32.7	138.0	42.0	27.2	2.1	32.1	15.3
1978	34.0	146.8	43.2	28.2	2.4	33.7	15.3
1979	35.3	147.2	44.4	29.2	2.6	32.5	15.3
1980	37.1	137.5	45.8	28.6	2.9	29.0	15.3
1981	38.4	140.9	47.7	29.0	3.2	27.0	15.3
1982	37.9	140.5	48.4	27.7	3.6	26.1	15.3
1983	38.2	157.5	49.9	30.2	4.3	26.3	15.3
1984	38.6	177.9	51.9	32.8	4.7	27.8	15.3
1985	39.9	195.5	53.0	35.3	5.1	29.6	15.3
1986	40.1	211.7	54.1	33.5	5.5	30.5	15.3
1987	41.4	215.5	56.8	32.0	4.6	31.3	15.3
1988	42.4	230.3	60.0	34.3	5.0	31.5	15.3
1989	43.9	235.7	62.6	34.8	5.0	31.7	15.3
1990	45.1	234.6	63.2	34.6	5.0	31.9	15.3

Table C.1 continued

Year A	Costs of air pollution O	Costs of noise pollution P	Loss of wetlands Q(-)	Loss of farm land R(-)	Depletion of nonrenewable resources S(-)	Long term environmental damage T(-)	Cost of ozone depletion U(-)
1950	21.6	2.0	10.0	7.2	46.8	84.0	1.1
1951	21.8	2.1	10.4	7.8	53.0	86.9	1.3
1952	22.0	2.2	10.7	8.5	53.4	89.9	1.6
1953	22.2	2.2	11.1	9.1	55.6	92.9	1.9
1954	22.5	2.3	11.4	9.7	54.8	95.8	2.2
1955	22.7	2.4	11.8	10.4	62.5	99.0	2.7
1956	22.9	2.5	12.2	11.0	68.6	102.4	3.2
1957	23.2	2.5	12.5	11.7	71.4	105.7	3.7
1958	23.4	2.6	12.9	12.4	68.2	109.1	4.2
1959	23.6	2.7	13.2	13.0	73.8	112.5	4.8
1960	23.9	2.8	13.6	13.7	77.7	116.2	5.6
1961	24.1	2.9	14.0	14.4	81.0	120.2	6.4
1962	24.7	2.9	14.3	15.1	86.5	124.0	7.5
1963	25.3	3.0	14.7	15.8	94.1	128.0	8.7
1964	25.9	3.1	15.0	16.5	100.9	132.2	10.1
1965	26.6	3.2	15.4	17.2	107.3	136.6	11.6
1966	27.2	3.3	15.8	17.9	117.2	141.2	13.4
1967	27.9	3.4	16.1	18.7	127.0	146.0	15.4
1968	28.6	3.5	16.5	19.4	135.3	151.0	17.7
1968	29.3	3.7	16.8	20.1	144.6	156.3	20.2
1970	30.0	3.8	17.2	20.9	157.0	161.8	22.7
1971	29.1	3.9	17.6	21.6	159.2	167.4	26.1
1972	28.2	4.0	17.9	22.4	167.1	173.3	29.5
1973	27.4	4.0	18.3	23.2	171.2	179.5	33.4
1974	26.6	4.1	18.5	24.0	171.9	185.4	37.4
1975	25.8	4.1	18.6	24.7	174.2	191.2	40.9
1976	25.0	4.2	18.8	25.5	180.2	197.4	44.7
1977	24.3	4.2	19.0	26.3	189.0	203.7	48.2
1978	23.6	4.2	19.2	27.1	195.8	210.2	51.6
1979	23.2	4.3	19.4	27.8	211.2	216.7	54.8
1980	22.5	4.3	19.5	28.6	221.2	223.0	58.0
1981	21.5	4.4	19.7	29.4	227.3	229.1	61.2
1982	19.5	4.4	19.9	30.2	230.5	234.9	64.2
1983	19.2	4.5	20.1	31.0	225.8	240.6	67.4
1984	19.6	4.5	20.3	31.7	252.2	246.6	70.9
1985	18.8	4.6	20.4	32.5	257.1	252.7	74.4
1986	18.7	4.6	20.6	33.3	262.3	258.8	76.6
1987	18.7	4.6	20.8	34.1	274.8	265.1	78.8
1988	18.9	4.7	21.0	34.9	290.1	271.8	81.0
1989	18.9	4.7	21.2	35.7	296.9	278.5	83.2
1990	18.9	4.8	21.3	36.5	312.6	285.3	85.3

Table C.1 continued

Year A	Net capital growth V(+)	Change in net interna- tional position W(+)	Index of Sustainable Economic Welfare ISEW X(sum)	Per capita ISEW Y	Gross National Product Z	Per capita GNP AA
1950	-17.2	0.0	380.2	2496.9	534.8	3512.2
1951	-1.0	0.2	432.5	2792.6	579.4	3741.0
1952	11.1	0.2	448.1	2844.4	600.8	3813.3
1953	17.6	0.2	446.8	2789.1	623.6	3893.0
1954	23.1	0.2	445.6	2733.4	616.1	3779.2
1955	27.3	0.2	478.8	2885.3	657.5	3962.5
1956	22.4	2.4	499.9	2959.8	671.6	3976.2
1957	21.3	2.3	513.1	2983.4	683.8	3976.0
1958	21.5	2.3	516.0	2950.7	680.9	3893.5
1959	20.9	2.2	517.0	2907.5	721.7	4058.4
1960	21.2	2.2	514.1	2845.6	737.2	4080.3
1961	25.4	4.8	518.1	2820.7	756.6	4118.9
1962	28.1	4.8	555.1	2975.8	800.3	4290.3
1963	28.5	4.7	559.0	2953.7	832.5	4399.1
1964	28.7	4.7	583.5	3040.6	876.4	4567.2
1965	30.4	4.6	610.1	3140.1	929.3	4782.7
1966	31.0	-0.9	667.3	3394.7	984.8	5010.2
1967	28.0	-0.8	662.8	3335.6	1011.4	5089.8
1968	29.6	-0.7	693.8	3456.9	1058.1	5271.9
1969	29.0	-0.7	705.0	3478.5	1087.6	5366.2
1970	28.6	-0.7	682.1	3326.6	1085.6	5294.3
1971	27.3	3.2	711.3	3425.2	1122.4	5405.0
1972	23.2	3.1	712.5	3394.3	1185.9	5649.9
1973	19.1	3.0	743.5	3508.6	1254.3	5919.1
1974	17.1	2.8	750.0	3506.9	1246.3	5827.8
1975	17.9	2.5	748.4	3465.4	1231.6	5702.6
1976	14.0	7.1	773.0	3545.4	1298.2	5954.1
1977	12.8	-7.8	743.8	3377.2	1369.7	6219.2
1978	9.0	2.3	774.7	3480.5	1438.6	6463.1
1979	7.8	11.3	793.8	3527.1	1479.4	6573.5
1980	3.8	6.4	773.5	3396.3	1475.0	6476.7
1981	5.1	17.9	777.4	3379.3	1512.2	6573.6
1982	4.8	-2.0	710.5	3058.1	1480.0	6369.8
1983	12.5	-16.0	732.3	3122.5	1534.7	6543.5
1984	13.1	-50.3	695.3	2933.9	1642.5	6930.4
1985	19.0	-20.0	736.3	3077.3	1697.5	7094.3
1986	19.8	-21.1	763.1	3158.5	1744.1	7219.0
1987	24.4	-23.3	785.4	3220.1	1803.8	7395.4
1988	24.9	-43.0	782.8	3178.0	1884.3	7649.7
1989	28.5	-44.6	801.2	3220.4	1931.6	7764.4
1990	29.4	-34.0	818.2	3253.1	1950.8	7755.9

Table C.2a (revised)
Alternative Income Distribution Indexes

Year a	Harmonic mean index b	Top quintile index c	Low quintile index d	Weighted ratios index e	Gini co-efficient index f
50	109.0	102.6	111.1	112.2	104.4
51	100.0	100.0	100.0	100.0	100.0
52	102.0	100.7	102.0	102.2	101.4
53	100.8	98.3	106.4	106.3	98.9
54	106.2	100.5	111.1	111.7	102.2
55	101.2	99.3	104.2	104.1	100.0
56	98.1	98.6	100.0	99.8	98.6
57	95.3	97.1	98.0	97.5	96.7
58	97.1	97.6	100.0	99.6	97.5
59	99.6	98.8	102.0	102.0	99.4
60	101.3	99.3	104.2	104.4	100.3
61	105.3	101.4	106.4	107.2	103.0
62	99.6	99.3	100.0	100.1	99.7
63	99.2	99.0	100.0	100.0	99.7
64	98.5	99.0	98.0	98.0	99.4
65	96.5	98.3	96.2	95.9	98.1
66	92.0	97.4	89.3	88.7	96.1
67	92.5	97.1	90.9	90.3	95.9
68	92.0	97.4	89.3	88.6	95.9
69	92.4	97.6	89.3	88.6	96.1
70	95.0	98.3	92.6	92.1	97.5
71	94.9	98.8	90.9	90.6	98.1
72	96.6	99.5	92.6	92.6	99.2
73	95.1	98.8	90.9	90.7	98.1
74	94.7	98.6	90.9	90.6	98.1
75	95.9	98.8	92.6	92.5	98.6
76	95.9	98.8	92.6	92.5	98.9
77	99.0	99.8	96.2	96.4	100.3
78	99.0	99.8	96.2	96.3	100.3
79	99.5	100.2	96.2	96.6	100.6
80	100.1	100.0	98.0	98.5	100.6
81	102.4	100.7	100.0	100.7	101.9
82	107.9	102.6	106.4	107.7	105.0
83	108.1	102.6	106.4	107.8	105.2
84	108.9	103.1	106.4	107.9	105.5
85	110.8	104.6	108.7	108.2	107.2
86	112.8	105.0	108.7	110.6	108.0
87	113.0	105.3	108.7	110.8	108.3
88	113.9	105.8	108.7	110.9	108.8
89	115.9	107.2	108.7	111.2	110.5
90	114.5	106.5	108.7	111.1	109.1

Lowest year of each index divided by highest year: (low numbers signify a more dispersed index)

| | 0.7938 | 0.9058 | .8038 | .7897 | .3678 |

Table C.2b
Effects of Alternative Income Distribution
Indexes of Per Capita ISEW

Year	Harmonic mean index PC-ISEW	Top quintile index PC-ISEW	Low quintile index PC-ISEW	Weighted ratios index PC-ISEW	Gini co-efficient index PC-ISEW
50	2536.0	2661.4	2496.9	2478.4	2624.9
51	2792.6	2792.6	2792.6	2792.6	2792.6
52	2844.8	2872.9	2844.4	2841.0	2858.6
53	2906.3	2964.0	2789.1	2791.3	2950.5
54	2828.4	2949.5	2733.4	2721.8	2911.4
55	2951.3	2997.6	2885.3	2885.9	2980.3
56	3005.8	2995.0	2959.8	2964.2	2993.4
57	3052.9	3006.7	2983.4	2997.5	3017.5
58	3023.0	3009.6	2950.7	2960.7	3011.5
59	2966.5	2987.2	2907.5	2909.4	2970.8
60	2914.2	2963.9	2845.6	2840.0	2938.8
61	2844.7	2935.7	2820.7	2802.4	2897.5
62	2987.5	2994.6	2975.8	2973.8	2983.0
63	2973.8	2979.4	2953.7	2953.0	2961.0
64	3028.8	3012.3	3040.6	3040.6	3000.8
65	3129.6	3074.5	3140.1	3148.7	3081.8
66	3295.3	3118.0	3394.7	3418.3	3156.6
67	3279.1	3122.4	3335.6	3358.3	3163.0
68	3352.7	3163.4	3456.9	3482.9	3213.8
69	3357.5	3168.9	3478.5	3506.1	3219.2
70	3238.3	3120.5	3326.6	3344.2	3147.7
71	3269.7	3130.4	3425.2	3436.7	3155.6
72	3237.2	3130.4	3394.3	3393.3	3142.7
73	3334.1	3190.4	3508.6	3518.0	3217.5
74	3350.4	3202.4	3506.9	3519.2	3220.3
75	3329.1	3220.6	3465.4	3470.5	3227.1
76	3402.9	3289.4	3545.5	3550.8	3285.5
77	3260.7	3229.7	3377.2	3366.6	3209.4
78	3358.3	3328.0	3480.5	3473.9	3307.0
79	3384.2	3352.3	3527.1	3509.3	3339.6
80	3310.6	3314.5	3396.3	3376.8	3292.0
81	3284.0	3349.7	3379.3	3350.4	3301.1
82	3001.8	3200.1	3058.1	3009.1	3111.0
83	3058.1	3269.8	3122.5	3069.5	3166.7
84	2837.7	3066.6	2933.9	2873.6	2968.7
85	2994.6	3245.5	3077.3	3096.4	3138.3
86	2999.1	3310.8	3158.5	3081.2	3187.2
87	3048.4	3364.7	3220.1	3135.8	3237.9
88	2970.6	3304.8	3178.0	3085.7	3173.0
89	2933.4	3284.4	3220.4	3115.7	3146.2
90	3016.6	3348.9	3253.1	3152.8	3236.3

Table C.3
Value. of the Services of Highways and Streets

Year a	Net stock of federal, state and local highways b	Imputed services of highways 7.5%b c
50	82.8	6.2
51	84.3	6.3
52	86.5	6.5
53	89.5	6.7
54	93.4	7.0
55	98.2	7.4
56	102.5	7.7
57	107.7	8.1
58	113.8	8.5
59	119.9	9.0
60	126.0	9.5
61	132.6	9.9
62	139.1	10.4
63	147.0	11.0
64	154.4	11.6
65	161.8	12.1
66	169.8	12.7
67	177.3	13.3
68	185.1	13.9
69	191.7	14.4
70	197.8	14.8
71	203.9	15.3
72	208.8	15.7
73	213.2	16.0
74	216.2	16.2
75	218.0	16.3
76	220.2	16.5
77	221.2	16.6
78	222.5	16.7
79	223.1	16.7
80	223.5	16.8
81	224.1	16.8
82	225.1	16.9
83	226.0	16.9
84	227.7	17.1
85	230.3	17.3
86	231.7	17.4
87	233.9	17.5
88	235.8	17.7
89	237.7	17.8
90	240.1	18.0

Table C.4
Public Expenditures on Health and Education
Counted as Personal Consumption

Year a	Public expenditures on higher education b	Public expenditures on higher education for consumption (b/2) c	Public expenditures on health d	Public expenditures on improving health (d/2) e	Public expenditures on health and education for consumption (c+e) f
50	2.2	1.1	7.6	3.8	4.9
51	2.0	1.0	7.9	3.9	4.9
52	2.2	1.1	8.1	4.0	5.1
53	2.2	1.1	8.4	4.2	5.3
54	2.4	1.2	8.7	4.3	5.5
55	2.6	1.3	9.0	4.5	5.8
56	2.9	1.4	9.5	4.7	6.2
57	3.2	1.6	9.9	4.9	6.5
58	3.6	1.8	10.1	5.1	6.9
59	4.1	2.1	10.4	5.2	7.3
60	4.8	2.4	10.7	5.4	7.8
61	5.4	2.7	11.8	5.9	8.6
62	6.0	3.0	12.9	6.4	9.4
63	7.0	3.5	13.9	7.0	10.4
64	7.8	3.9	14.9	7.5	11.4
65	9.2	4.6	15.9	7.9	12.5
66	10.8	5.4	20.0	10.0	15.4
67	12.5	6.3	23.2	11.6	17.9
68	12.6	6.3	26.2	13.1	19.4
69	13.2	6.6	28.5	14.2	20.8
70	14.8	7.4	30.5	15.3	22.6
71	15.4	7.7	32.4	16.2	23.9
72	16.1	8.0	35.0	17.5	25.5
73	17.2	8.6	37.3	18.7	27.3
74	17.8	8.9	41.5	20.7	29.7
75	18.9	9.5	41.9	21.0	30.4
76	19.3	9.7	45.1	22.6	32.2
77	19.6	9.8	45.9	22.9	32.7
78	19.9	10.0	48.1	24.0	34.0
79	20.6	10.3	50.0	25.0	35.3
80	21.7	10.9	52.4	26.2	37.1
81	22.2	11.1	54.5	27.3	38.4
82	21.3	10.6	54.5	27.3	37.9
83	21.6	10.8	54.7	27.4	38.2
84	21.5	10.8	55.7	27.8	38.6
85	22.0	11.0	57.8	28.9	39.9
86	22.1	11.1	58.0	29.0	40.1
87	22.7	11.3	60.1	30.0	41.4
88	23.6	11.8	61.3	30.6	42.4
89	24.5	12.2	63.4	31.7	43.9
90	25.4	12.7	64.8	32.4	45.1

Table C.5
Defensive Private Expenditures
on Health and Education

Year	Private expenditures on education	Private expenditures on higher education	Defensive expenditures on private education b−(c/2)	Private expenditures on health	Defensive expenditures on private health (e/2)	Defensive expenditures on private health and education (d+f)
a	b	c	d	e	f	g
50	3.6	1.6	2.9	22.1	11.1	13.9
51	3.8	1.6	3.0	22.9	11.5	14.5
52	4.0	1.6	3.2	23.6	11.8	14.9
53	4.1	1.7	3.3	24.5	12.2	15.5
54	4.3	1.7	3.4	25.3	12.7	16.1
55	4.6	1.8	3.7	26.4	13.2	16.9
56	4.8	1.9	3.9	28.0	14.0	17.9
57	5.2	2.1	4.1	29.4	14.7	18.9
58	5.4	2.2	4.3	30.5	15.2	19.5
59	5.6	2.3	4.5	31.5	15.7	20.2
60	6.0	2.4	4.8	32.6	16.3	21.1
61	6.2	2.5	5.0	35.9	17.9	22.9
62	6.6	2.6	5.3	39.0	19.5	24.8
63	7.0	2.7	5.6	42.0	21.0	26.6
64	7.4	2.9	5.9	45.1	22.6	28.5
65	7.9	3.3	6.3	47.8	23.9	30.2
66	8.7	3.5	6.9	50.1	25.0	31.9
67	9.0	3.6	7.2	50.7	25.4	32.6
68	9.8	3.8	7.9	51.5	25.8	33.7
69	10.3	4.0	8.4	51.7	25.8	34.2
70	10.7	4.1	8.6	51.9	25.9	34.5
71	10.9	4.3	8.8	54.1	27.1	35.9
72	11.4	4.4	9.2	57.7	28.9	38.1
73	11.5	4.5	9.3	61.2	30.6	39.9
74	11.1	4.4	9.0	61.0	30.5	39.4
75	11.5	4.4	9.3	60.0	30.0	39.3
76	11.8	4.4	9.6	62.2	31.1	40.7
77	11.7	4.4	9.5	64.9	32.5	42.0
78	12.2	4.5	9.9	66.5	33.2	43.2
79	12.4	4.6	10.1	68.6	34.3	44.4
80	12.6	4.7	10.2	71.2	35.6	45.8
81	12.8	4.9	10.4	74.6	37.3	47.7
82	12.9	4.8	10.5	75.9	38.0	48.4
83	13.5	5.0	11.1	77.7	38.9	49.9
84	14.1	5.1	11.6	80.5	40.3	51.9
85	15.1	5.3	12.5	81.1	40.5	53.0
86	15.8	5.4	13.1	82.1	41.0	54.1
87	16.6	5.5	13.9	85.8	42.9	56.8
88	17.9	5.7	15.1	89.8	44.9	...
89	19.1	5.8	16.2	92.8	46.4	62.6
90	19.6	5.9	16.7	93.0	46.5	63.2

Table C.6
Cost of Commuting

Year a	User operated transportation b	Purchased local transportation c	Cost of commuting (.21b+.3c) d
50	34.2	6.1	9.0
51	32.4	5.6	8.5
52	32.3	5.4	8.4
53	37.1	5.1	9.3
54	39.2	4.7	9.6
55	45.7	4.4	10.9
56	43.3	4.3	10.4
57	43.8	4.2	10.5
58	41.8	3.9	9.9
59	45.6	3.9	10.7
60	48.4	3.9	11.3
61	46.6	3.6	10.9
62	50.5	3.6	11.7
63	53.9	3.5	12.4
64	56.2	3.4	12.8
65	63.2	3.3	14.3
66	66.5	3.3	14.9
67	67.5	3.2	15.2
68	74.7	3.3	16.7
69	79.2	3.5	17.7
70	78.3	3.4	17.4
71	87.8	3.4	19.5
72	97.8	3.4	21.6
73	105.3	3.4	23.1
74	101.5	3.5	22.4
75	101.8	3.5	22.4
76	113.8	3.6	25.0
77	124.4	3.6	27.2
78	129.0	3.7	28.2
79	133.4	3.8	29.2
80	131.2	3.5	28.6
81	133.6	3.2	29.0
82	127.8	3.0	27.7
83	139.4	3.0	30.2
84	152.1	3.0	32.8
85	163.6	3.0	35.3
86	155.3	2.9	33.5
87	148.0	3.1	32.0
88	159.2	3.0	34.3
89	161.7	2.9	34.8
90	160.5	2.9	34.6

Table C.7
Cost of Air Pollution

Year	NO$_x$	SO$_2$	Particulate matter	Ambient air pollution index	Air pollution cost
		(Index number 1977 = 100)			
50				89.0	21.6
51		assumed		89.9	21.8
52		ambient air		90.8	22.0
53		pollution		91.7	22.2
54		increase		92.7	22.5
55		of 1.0%		93.6	22.7
56		per year		94.5	22.9
57		from 1950		95.5	23.2
58		to 1960		96.5	23.4
59				97.4	23.6
60				98.4	23.9
61				99.4	24.1
62		assumed		101.9	24.7
63		increase		104.4	25.3
64		of 2.4%		106.9	25.9
65		per year		109.6	26.6
66		from 1961		112.2	27.2
67		to 1970		115.0	27.9
68				117.8	28.6
69				120.7	29.3
70		assumed		123.7	30.0
71		decrease		120.0	29.1
72		of 3.0%		116.4	28.2
73		per year		112.9	27.4
74		from 1971		109.5	26.6
75		to 1977		106.2	25.8
76				103.0	25.0
77	100.0	100.0	100.0	100.0	24.3
78	100.0	93.0	99.0	97.3	23.6
79	100.0	86.0	101.0	95.7	23.2
80	97.3	78.1	102.7	92.7	22.5
81	95.0	74.6	96.6	88.7	21.5
82	92.2	68.8	80.2	80.4	19.5
83	91.5	66.0	79.6	79.0	19.2
84	92.6	67.3	81.9	80.6	19.6
85	91.5	63.0	78.1	77.5	18.8
86	92.6	60.9	77.8	77.1	18.7
87	92.2	59.5	79.6	77.1	18.7
88	92.6	60.2	80.8	77.9	18.9
89		(no data; assumed = 1988)		77.9	18.9
90		(no data; assumed = 1988)		77.9	18.9

Table C.8
Loss of Agricultural Land
(Erosion, Compaction, Urbanization)

Year a	Erosion productivity loss b	Compaction productivity loss c	Agricultural land lost by urbanization d	Total loss of agricultural land (b+c+d) e
50	5.6	0.7	1.0	7.2
51	6.1	0.7	1.0	7.8
52	6.7	0.7	1.1	8.5
53	7.3	0.7	1.1	9.1
54	7.9	0.8	1.1	9.7
55	8.5	0.8	1.2	10.4
56	9.0	0.8	1.2	11.0
57	9.7	0.8	1.2	11.7
58	10.3	0.9	1.2	12.4
59	10.9	0.9	1.3	13.0
60	11.5	0.9	1.3	13.7
61	12.1	0.9	1.3	14.4
62	12.8	1.0	1.4	15.1
63	13.4	1.0	1.4	15.8
64	14.0	1.0	1.4	16.5
65	14.7	1.1	1.5	17.2
66	15.4	1.1	1.5	17.9
67	16.0	1.1	1.5	18.7
68	16.7	1.2	1.5	19.4
69	17.4	1.2	1.6	20.1
70	18.1	1.2	1.6	20.9
71	18.7	1.3	1.6	21.6
72	19.4	1.3	1.7	22.4
73	20.1	1.3	1.7	23.2
74	20.8	1.4	1.7	24.0
75	21.5	1.4	1.8	24.7
76	22.2	1.5	1.8	25.5
77	22.9	1.5	1.8	26.3
78	23.6	1.6	1.8	27.1
79	24.3	1.6	1.9	27.8
80	25.0	1.7	1.9	28.6
81	25.7	1.7	1.9	29.4
82	26.4	1.8	2.0	30.2
83	27.1	1.8	2.0	31.0
84	27.8	1.9	2.0	31.7
85	28.5	1.9	2.1	32.5
86	29.2	2.0	2.1	33.3
87	29.9	2.1	2.1	34.1
88	30.6	2.1	2.1	34.9
89	31.3	2.2	2.2	35.7
90	32.0	2.2	2.2	36.5

Table C.9
Depreciation of Nonrenewable Resources
(Using replacement cost of energy as proxy)

Year a	Nonrenewable energy production (quadrillions of BTUs) b	Barrel equivalents (b/5.8) (billions of barrels) c	Replacement cost/barrel @ 3%/yr. increase (based on 1988=26.5) d	Total replacement cost (c x d) e
50	32.6	5.6	8.3	46.8
51	35.8	6.2	8.6	53.0
52	35.0	6.0	8.9	53.4
53	35.4	6.1	9.1	55.6
54	33.8	5.8	9.4	54.8
55	37.4	6.4	9.7	62.5
56	39.8	6.9	10.0	68.6
57	40.1	6.9	10.3	71.4
58	37.2	6.4	10.6	68.2
59	39.1	6.7	11.0	73.8
60	39.9	6.9	11.3	77.7
61	40.3	7.0	11.6	81.0
62	41.8	7.2	12.0	86.5
63	44.1	7.6	12.4	94.1
64	45.8	7.9	12.8	100.9
65	47.3	8.2	13.2	107.3
66	50.1	8.6	13.6	117.2
67	52.7	9.1	14.0	127.0
68	54.5	9.4	14.4	135.3
69	56.4	9.7	14.9	144.6
70	59.4	10.2	15.3	157.0
71	58.5	10.1	15.8	159.2
72	59.5	10.3	16.3	167.1
73	59.2	10.2	16.8	171.2
74	57.6	9.9	17.3	171.9
75	56.6	9.8	17.8	174.2
76	56.8	9.8	18.4	180.2
77	57.8	10.0	19.0	189.0
78	58.1	10.0	19.6	195.8
79	60.8	10.5	20.2	211.2
80	61.8	10.6	20.8	221.2
81	61.5	10.6	21.4	227.3
82	60.5	10.4	22.1	230.5
83	57.5	9.9	22.8	225.8
84	62.3	10.7	23.5	252.2
85	61.6	10.6	24.2	257.1
86	61.0	10.5	24.9	262.3
87	62.0	10.7	25.7	274.8
88	63.5	10.9	26.5	290.1
89	63.1	10.9	27.3	296.9
90	64.5	11.1	28.1	312.6

Table C.10
Energy Consumption as a Measure of Long Term
Environmental Damage

Year a	Total energy consumption (quadrillions of BTUs) b	Barrel equivalent of energy consumption (b/5.8) billions of (barrels) c	Cumulative $.50 tax per barrel (billions of $) d	Year e	Total energy consumption (quadrillions of BTUs) f	Barrel equivalent of energy consumption (b/5.8) billions of barrels) g	Cumulative $.50 tax per barrel (billions of $) h
1900	7.3	1.3	0.6	1945	30.1	5.2	70.7
1901	8.0	1.4	1.3	1946	29.0	5.0	73.2
1902	8.4	1.5	2.0	1947	31.4	5.4	75.9
1903	9.9	1.7	2.9	1948	32.5	5.6	78.7
1904	9.8	1.7	3.7	1949	30.0	5.2	81.3
1905	11.0	1.9	4.7	1950	31.7	5.5	84.0
1906	11.5	2.0	5.7	1951	34.1	5.9	86.9
1907	13.4	2.3	6.8	1952	33.8	5.8	89.9
1908	11.8	2.0	7.9	1953	34.9	6.0	92.9
1909	13.0	2.2	9.0	1954	33.9	5.8	95.8
1910	14.3	2.5	10.2	1955	37.4	6.4	99.0
1911	14.0	2.4	11.4	1956	38.9	6.7	102.4
1912	15.1	2.6	12.7	1957	38.9	6.7	105.7
1913	16.1	2.8	14.1	1958	38.8	6.7	109.1
1914	14.9	2.6	15.4	1959	40.5	7.0	112.5
1915	15.4	2.7	16.7	1960	42.1	7.3	116.2
1916	17.1	2.9	18.2	1961	46.2	8.0	120.2
1917	18.8	3.2	19.8	1962	44.7	7.7	124.0
1918	19.7	3.4	21.5	1963	46.5	8.0	128.0
1919	16.8	2.9	22.9	1964	48.6	8.4	132.2
1920	19.0	3.3	24.6	1965	50.6	8.7	136.6
1921	15.8	2.7	25.9	1966	53.6	9.2	141.2
1922	16.5	2.9	27.4	1967	55.3	9.5	146.0
1923	21.0	3.6	29.2	1968	58.7	10.1	151.0
1924	19.8	3.4	30.9	1969	61.5	10.6	156.3
1925	20.2	3.5	32.6	1970	63.7	11.0	161.8
1926	21.7	3.7	34.5	1971	65.0	11.2	167.4
1927	21.0	3.6	36.3	1972	68.4	11.8	173.3
1928	21.5	3.7	38.2	1973	71.3	12.3	179.5
1929	22.9	4.0	40.1	1974	69.1	11.9	185.4
1930	21.5	3.7	42.0	1975	67.2	11.6	191.2
1931	18.1	3.1	43.6	1976	71.2	12.3	197.4
1932	15.7	2.7	44.9	1977	73.7	12.7	203.7
1933	16.2	2.8	46.3	1978	74.9	12.9	210.2
1934	17.2	3.0	47.8	1979	75.7	13.1	216.7
1935	18.3	3.2	49.4	1980	72.8	12.6	223.0
1936	20.6	3.6	51.1	1981	70.8	12.2	229.1
1937	21.9	3.8	53.0	1982	67.1	11.6	234.9
1938	19.0	3.3	54.7	1983	66.5	11.5	240.6
1939	20.8	3.6	56.4	1984	70.1	12.1	246.6
1940	23.0	4.0	58.4	1985	70.4	12.1	252.7
1941	25.7	4.4	60.6	1986	70.6	12.2	258.8
1942	26.7	4.6	62.9	1987	73.4	12.7	265.1
1943	29.1	5.0	65.5	1988	77.3	13.3	271.8
1944	30.4	5.2	68.1	1989	78.2	13.5	278.5
				1990	78.3	13.5	285.3

Table C.11
Cumulative Damage from Ozone Production

| Year | Cumulative production CFC-11 | Cumulative production CFC-12 | Sum | Damage 1 kg. = $5 annual damage |
| | (000s metric tons) | | (b+c) | (.005xd) |
a	b	c	d	e
50	18.6	198.3	216.9	1.1
51	27.6	234.5	262.1	1.3
52	41.2	271.7	312.9	1.6
53	58.5	318.2	376.7	1.9
54	79.4	367.1	446.5	2.2
55	105.6	425.0	530.6	2.7
56	138.1	493.6	631.7	3.2
57	172.0	567.8	739.8	3.7
58	201.6	641.2	842.8	4.2
59	237.1	728.8	965.9	4.8
60	286.9	828.3	1115.2	5.6
61	347.3	936.8	1284.1	6.4
62	425.4	1064.9	1490.3	7.5
63	518.7	1211.3	1730.0	8.7
64	629.8	1381.4	2011.2	10.1
65	752.6	1571.4	2324.0	11.6
66	893.7	1787.6	2681.3	13.4
67	1053.4	2030.4	3083.8	15.4
68	1236.5	2297.9	3534.4	17.7
69	1453.8	2595.1	4048.9	20.2
70	1619.9	2916.2	4536.1	22.7
71	1955.1	3257.8	5212.9	26.1
72	2262.0	3637.7	5899.7	29.5
73	2611.1	4061.0	6672.1	33.4
74	2980.8	4503.8	7484.6	37.4
75	3294.8	4884.8	8179.6	40.9
76	3634.7	5295.5	8930.2	44.7
77	3955.1	5678.3	9633.4	48.2
78	4264.0	6050.4	10314.4	51.6
79	4553.5	6407.6	10961.1	54.8
80	4843.1	6757.8	11600.9	58.0
81	5130.0	7109.1	12239.1	61.2
82	5401.5	7437.1	12838.6	64.2
83	5693.2	7792.5	13485.7	67.4
84	6005.6	8174.6	14180.2	70.9
85	6332.4	8550.9	14883.3	74.4
86			15320.6	76.6
87			15757.9	78.8
88			16195.2	81.0
89			16632.4	83.2
90			17069.7	85.3

Table C.12
Net Capital Growth

Year a	Labor force (000's) b	% change in labor force c	Rolling average % change in labor force d	Net stock fixed capital e	Rolling average net stock fixed capital f	Change in rolling average of capital stock $f-f_{(t-1)}$ g	Capital requirement for labor $dxf_{(t-1)}$ h	Net capital growth (g-h) i
45	53060			735.8				
46	56720	6.90%		743.1				
47	59350	4.64%		750.3				
48	60621	2.14%		757.5				
49	61286	1.10%	3.69%	764.8	750.3			
50	62208	1.50%	3.26%	772.0	757.5	7.2	24.4	-17.2
51	62017	-0.31%	1.81%	806.8	770.3	12.7	13.7	-1.0
52	62138	0.20%	0.93%	841.6	788.5	18.3	7.1	11.1
53	63015	1.41%	0.78%	876.4	812.3	23.8	6.2	17.6
54	63643	1.00%	0.76%	911.2	841.6	29.3	6.2	23.1
55	65023	2.17%	0.89%	946.0	876.4	34.8	7.5	27.3
56	66552	2.35%	1.42%	981.2	911.3	34.9	12.5	22.4
57	66929	0.57%	1.50%	1016.4	946.2	35.0	13.7	21.3
58	67639	1.06%	1.43%	1051.6	981.3	35.0	13.5	21.5
59	68369	1.08%	1.45%	1086.8	1016.4	35.1	14.2	20.9
60	69628	1.84%	1.38%	1122.0	1051.6	35.2	14.0	21.2
61	70459	1.19%	1.15%	1168.8	1089.1	37.5	12.1	25.4
62	70614	0.22%	1.08%	1215.6	1129.0	39.8	11.8	28.1
63	71833	1.73%	1.21%	1262.4	1171.1	42.2	13.7	28.5
64	72091	1.75%	1.35%	1309.2	1215.6	44.5	15.8	28.7
65	74455	1.87%	1.35%	1356.0	1262.4	46.8	16.4	30.4
66	75770	1.77%	1.47%	1416.2	1311.9	49.5	18.5	31.0
67	77347	2.08%	1.84%	1476.4	1364.0	52.2	24.1	28.0
68	78737	1.80%	1.85%	1536.6	1418.9	54.8	25.3	29.6
69	80734	2.54%	2.01%	1596.8	1476.4	57.5	28.5	29.0
70	82771	2.52%	2.14%	1657.0	1536.6	60.2	31.6	28.6
71	84382	1.95%	2.18%	1720.0	1597.4	60.8	33.4	27.3
72	87034	3.14%	2.39%	1783.0	1658.7	61.3	38.2	23.2
73	89429	2.75%	2.58%	1846.0	1720.6	61.9	42.8	19.1
74	91949	2.82%	2.64%	1909.0	1783.0	62.4	45.4	17.1
75	93775	1.99%	2.53%	1972.0	1846.0	63.0	45.1	17.9
76	96158	2.54%	2.65%	2034.3	1908.9	62.8	48.9	14.0
77	99009	2.96%	2.61%	2096.5	1971.6	62.7	49.9	12.8
78	102251	3.27%	2.72%	2158.8	2034.1	62.5	53.6	9.0
79	104962	2.65%	2.68%	2221.0	2096.5	62.4	54.6	7.8
80	106940	1.88%	2.66%	2270.0	2156.1	59.6	55.8	3.8
81	108670	1.62%	2.48%	2327.1	2214.7	58.6	53.4	5.1
82	110204	1.41%	2.17%	2360.3	2267.4	52.8	48.0	4.8
83	110550	0.31%	1.58%	2400.0	2315.7	48.3	35.7	12.5
84	113544	2.71%	1.59%	2470.3	2365.6	49.9	36.8	13.1
85	115461	1.69%	1.55%	2548.2	2421.2	55.6	36.6	19.0
86	117834	2.06%	1.64%	2623.8	2480.6	59.3	39.6	19.8
87	119865	1.72%	1.70%	2692.8	2547.0	66.5	42.1	24.4
88	121669	1.51%	1.94%	2771.0	2621.2	74.2	49.3	24.9
89	123869	1.81%	1.76%	2843.0	2695.8	74.5	46.0	28.5
90	124787	0.74%	1.57%	2906.2	2767.3	71.6	42.2	29.4

Table C.13
Rates of Growth of Per Capita Measures from 1950/51 to 1990

Compound Growth of

	PC-GNP	PC-ISEW	PC-ISEW*		PC-GNP	PC-ISEW	PC-ISEW*
50-60	1.51%	1.32%	1.56%	51-60	0.97%	0.21%	0.65%
51-60	0.97%	0.21%	0.65%	60-70	2.64%	1.57%	2.22%
50-65	2.08%	1.54%	1.82%	70-80	2.04%	0.21%	0.91%
51-65	1.77%	0.84%	1.24%	80-90	1.82%	-0.43%	0.52%
50-77	2.14%	1.12%	1.61%				
51-77	1.97%	0.73%	1.29%				
50-90	2.00%	0.66%	1.30%				
51-90	1.89%	0.39%	0.08%				

Notes: • PC-ISEW* means per capita ISEW not including columns S (resource depletion) and T (long-term environmental damage) in table C.1.

• We have given 1950 and 1951 as alternative base years for calculations of annual changes because the change in per capita ISEW between those years was greater than at any other time during the period from 1950 to 1990. (See table C.1, column Y.) Because of this anomaly, we consider 1951 to be the appropriate year from which to make comparisons.

Notes and References

Introduction Notes

1. Manfred Max-Neef. 1985. "Reflections on a Paradigm Shift in Economics," in *The New Economic Agenda*, ed. Mary Inglis and Sandra Kramer (Inverness, Scotland: Findhorn Press), p. 151. Max-Neef also points out the failure of GNP to include the value of subsistence activities, particularly household work.

2. Robert Repetto, William Magrath, Michael Wells, Christine Beer, and Fabrizio Rossini. 1989. *Wasting Assets: Natural Resources in the National Income Accounts* (Washington, D.C.: World Resources Institute).

3. See especially the essays by Salah El Serafy, Henry Peskin, Roefie Hueting, and others in Part 2 of *Ecological Economics: The Science and Management of Sustainability*, Robert Costanza, ed. (New York: Columbia University Press, 1991).

4. Herman Daly. 1991. *Steady-State Economics*, second edition (Covelo, CA: Island Press), p. 103. Daly compares a steady-state economy to a mature eco-system that maximizes complexity for each unit of energy. Young ecosystems and young economies, by contrast, are ones that maximize the flow of energy in order to grow rapidly. The transition from a growth economy to a steady-state economy, according to Daly, is equivalent to ecological succession.

5. Herman Daly, *Steady State Economics*, op. cit., p. 23, citing George Woodwell. 1974. "Short-Circuiting the Cheap Power Fantasy," *Natural History* (October).

6. Ivan Illich. 1981. *Shadow Work* (Salem, New Hampshire: Marion Boyars). Illich argues that the modern economy (in contrast to the classical economy) is bifurcated between the types of work in the public realm and in the private realm. The possibility of work for wages depends on uncompensated "shadow work," which includes housework, most schooling, and commuting.

7. Robert Eisner. 1989. *The Total Incomes System of Accounts* (Chicago: University of Chicago Press).

8. Thomas Power. 1988. *The Economic Pursuit of Quality* (Armonk, NY: M.E. Sharpe).

9. See, for example, Ezra Mishan. 1967. *The Costs of Economic Growth* (New York: Praeger).

Chapter 1 Notes

1. Richard Ruggles. 1983. "The United States National Income Accounts, 1947-1977: Their Conceptual Basis and Evolution," in *The U.S. National Income and Product Accounts*, ed. Murray F. Foss (Chicago: University of Chicago Press), p. 17.

2. Marilyn Waring. 1988. *If Women Counted: A New Feminist Economics* (San Francisco: Harper and Row).

3. Simon Kuznets. 1954. *National Income and Industrial Structure* (London: Economic Change), pp. 177-78, cited in Waring, *If Women Counted,* pp. 53-54.

4. J. Viner. 1953. *International Trade and Economic Development* (Oxford: Clarendon Press), pp. 99-100, cited in Waring, p. 58.

5. Otto Eckstein. "The NIPA Accounts: A User's View," in Foss, *The National Income and Product Accounts*, p. 316.

6. Richard Ruggles. "The United States National Income Accounts, 1947-1977: Their Conceptual Basis and Evolution," in Foss, *The National Income and Product Accounts*, p. 32.

7. Ibid.

8. Ibid., p. 35.

9.   Ibid., pp. 41-43.

10. William Nordhaus and James Tobin. 1972. "Is Growth Obsolete?" in *Economic Growth*, (New York: National Bureau of Economic Research).

11. Ibid., p. 4.

12. Ibid., p. 5.

13. Ibid., p. 7.

14. Ibid., p. 8.

15. Ibid., pp. 31-32.

16. Ibid., p. 13. They incorrectly report the growth of MEW on this page as 1.1 percent. In fact the growth rate of per capita MEW from 1929 to 1965 was only 1.0% per year. The correct calculation can be found in Table A.18 on page 56 of their study.

17. We have chosen to compare per capita MEW with per capita GNP rather than per capita NNP as Nordhaus and Tobin have done. We do this for the sake of consistency with other studies (especially the one by Zolotas, discussed below). The differences in annual growth rates are not large, though the growth of per capita NNP is slightly slower than for per capita GNP.

18. Interestingly, though Nordhaus and Tobin calculate the growth rate of per capita NNP and per capita sustainable MEW for the period 1929-1947 and 1947-1965 (see Table A.18 on page 56 of their text), they never refer to the remarkable difference between those two periods in their discussion. To do so would have required them to explain why the growth rate for per capita sustainable MEW had flattened out, even as per capita NNP kept rising.

19. Ibid., p. 39.

20. William Nordhaus. 1977. "Metering Economic Growth," in *Prospects for Growth: Changing Expectations for the Future*, ed. Kenneth D. Wilson (New York: Praeger Publishers), p. 197.

21. Xenophon Zolotas. 1981. *Economic Growth and Declining Social Welfare* (New York: New York University Press).

22. Edward F. Denison. 1962. *The Sources of Economic Growth in the United States and the Alternatives before Us* (New York: Committee for Economic Development), pp. 68 ff. Theodore W. Schultz. 1961. "Education and Economic Growth," in Nelson B. Henry, ed. *Social Forces Influencing American Education* (Chicago: University of Chicago Press).

23. Lester C. Thurow. 1972. "Education and Economic Equality." *The Public Interest* 28 (Summer): 61-81, reprinted in Donald M. Levine and Mary Jo Bane, eds. 1975. *The "Inequality" Controversy: Schooling and Distributive Justice* (New York: Basic Books, Inc.), pp. 170-184.

24. Lester Thurow, in *The "Inequality" Controversy,* p. 172.

25. Ibid., p. 182 (emphasis in original).

26. Jacob Mincer. 1974. *Schooling, Experience, and Earnings* (New York: National Bureau of Economic Research), p. 44. In the eighth year after completion of schooling, the level of education accounts for about one-third of variation in incomes, though this proportion falls rapidly in succeeding years.

27. Nordhaus and Tobin, p. 6.

28. Net capital growth, which is added to MEW, is equal to the change in the net capital stock minus the growth requirement, which is composed of changes in the labor force and productivity. If productivity decreases, the growth requirement would grow more slowly, and MEW would grow more rapidly.

29. Ibid., p. 14.

30. Edward F. Denison, *The Sources of Economic Growth,* p. 13.

31. Harold J. Barnett and Chandler Morse. 1963. *Scarcity and Growth* (Baltimore: Johns Hopkins University Press), Part III.

32. John Gever, Robert Kaufmann, David Skole, and Charles Vorosmarty. 1986. *Beyond Oil: The Threat to Food and Fuel in the Coming Decades* (Cambridge, Mass.: Ballinger Publishing Company), p. 70. Cited from C. J. Cleveland, R. Costanza, C.A.S. Hall, and R. Kaufmann. 1984. "Energy and the U.S. Economy: A Biophysical Perspective," *Science* 225: 890-897. *Beyond Oil* uses

the term "energy profit ratio" to refer to the amount of output energy available relative to the amount of input energy used in a system. We have chosen the term "energy output/input ratio" instead to avoid the possible confusion that the term profit might refer to financial profit rather than surplus energy.

33. According to Gever, et al., *Beyond Oil*, p. 70, the energy output/input ratio of electricity production is 4 for nuclear power (less if the cost of reactor decommissioning is included) and 2.5 for Western strip-mined coal if the cost of using scrubbers is included.

34. Gever, et al., *Beyond Oil*, p. 20.

35. Ibid., p. 20.

36. As the authors of *Beyond Oil* note (on page 72), there are already practical reasons for doubting that fusion will provide a technical fix that is commercially viable. They cite Lawrence Lidsky of MIT, a leading fusion researcher, who argues that the deuterium-tritium process, which is being intensively pursued, will always be too costly to serve as a major power source. Lidsky believes that the per unit cost of electricity from fusion would be higher than from today's fission reactors because fusion requires more sophisticated safety and control technology to prevent dispersal of radioactivity.

37. Cleveland, et al., "Energy and the U.S. Economy," cited in Gever, et al., *Beyond Oil*, p. 101.

38. Gever, et al., *Beyond Oil*, p. 102-103, citing D. Pimentel, et al. 1973. "Food Production and the Energy Crisis," *Science* 182: 443.

39. See, for example, Robert Solow. 1974. "Intergenerational Equity and Exhaustible Resources," *Review of Economic Studies*, Symposium on the Economics of Exhaustible Resources, Vol. 41, (supplement 1974): 29-45.

40. E. J. Mishan. 1984. "GNP--Measurement or Mirage," *National Westminster Bank Quarterly Review* 5: 13.

41. A. C. Pigou. *The Economics of Welfare.* 1924. (London: Macmillan and Company). Quoted in Sandra S. Batie. 1986. "Why Soil Erosion: A Social Science Perspective," in Stephen B. Lovejoy and Ted L. Napier, eds. *Conserving Soil: Insights from*

Socioeconomic Research (Ankeny, Iowa: Soil Conservation Society of America), p. 10.

42. We suspect that the inclusion of an imputation for leisure in the ISEW would have similarly widened the gap between its growth rate and that of GNP, thus strengthening our conclusion that an alternative measure of sustainable economic welfare is needed. However, we did not attempt this calculation because we could not find a conceptually sound and empirically well grounded basis for imputing the value of leisure.

43. Lisa Leghorn and Katherine Parker. 1981. *Women's Worth: Sexual Economics and the World of Women* (Boston and London: Routledge and Kegan Paul), cited in Marilyn Waring, *If Women Counted*, p. 161.

44. Nordhaus and Tobin, "Is Growth Obsolete," p. 44.

45. Zolotas, *Economic Growth*, p. 95. The survey he cites comes from J.P. Robinson and P.E. Converse. 1967. *66 Basic Tables of Time Budget Research Data for the United States* (Ann Arbor: University of Michigan, Survey Research Center).

46. Zolotas, *Economic Growth*, p. 97.

47. Ibid., p. 94.

48. Richard A. Berk and Sarah Fenstermaker Berk. 1979. *Labor and Leisure at Home: Content and Organization of the Household Day* (Beverly Hills: Sage Publications).

49. Sarah Fenstermaker Berk. 1985. *The Gender Factory* (New York: Plenum Press), p. 69. "The accomplishment of household labor involves thinking about or planning for the task, as well as the actual work demanded by the task itself . . . [O]ur early research . . . revealed a clear distinction between "help" with and "responsibility" for household labor."
   See also Berk and Berk, *Labor and Leisure at Home*, p. 232: "[H]ousehold work and child care remain the primary responsibility of the wife (even if employed full-time), with husbands providing a "reserve" source of labor in times of particular need."

50. Ruth Schwartz Cowan. 1983. *More Work for Mother* (New York: Basic Books). For the 1910s, Cowan cites (on page 159) an unpublished doctoral dissertation by Leeds from 1917. For the 1920s and 1930s, she refers (on page 178) to U.S. Department of Agriculture surveys that found a range of hours spent in housework from a high of 61 to a low of 48. For the 1960s, she cites John P. Robinson. 1977. *How Americans Use Time: A Social-Psychological Analysis of Everyday Behavior* (New York: Praeger Publishers), pp. 63-64.

51. Berk, *The Gender Factory,* p.64.

52. Ibid., p. 8.

53. Robert Eisner. 1985. "The Total Incomes System of Accounts," *Survey of Current Business* (January): 30.

54. Richard Easterlin. 1974. "Does Economic Growth Improve the Human Lot? Some Empirical Evidence," in *Nations and Households in Economic Growth* (New York: Academic Press).

55. We are indebted to comments by C. O. Matthews on Nordhaus and Tobin's study for this idea. See *Economic Growth* (note 10 above), pp. 88-89.

Chapter 2 Notes

1. Robert Eisner. 1985. "The Total Income System of Accounts," *Survey of Current Business* (January): 30.

2. United States Bureau of the Census. 1980. *1980 Census of Population: General Social and Economic Characteristics,* Vol. C 3.223/7:980, p. 70.

3. See Leonard P. Gianessi and Henry M. Peskin. 1981. "Analysis of National Water Pollution Control Policies: 2. Agricultural Sediment Control," in *Water Resources Research* 17(4): 803-821. See especially pages 813-817.

4. Gianessi and Peskin. "Analysis of National Water Pollution Control Policies," Table 1, page 804.

5. A. Myrick Freeman. 1982. *Air and Water Pollution Control: A Benefit-Cost Assessment* (New York: John Wiley and Sons), Chapter 9.

6. Conservation Foundation. 1985. *State of the Environment: An Assessment at Mid-Decade* (Washington, D.C.: The Conservation Foundation), p. 109.

7. Freeman, *Air and Water Pollution Control*.

8. Ibid., p. 107.

9. *Congressional Quarterly Almanac*. 1972. (Washington, D.C.: Congressional Quarterly Service), p. 980.

10. T.R. Gupta and J.H. Foster in "Economic Criteria for Freshwater Wetland Policy in Massachusetts," *The American Journal of Agricultural Economics*, 57(1): 40-45; cited in John H. Foster. 1979. "Measuring the Social Value of Wetlands," in *Wetland Functions and Values: The State of Our Understanding*, edited by Philip Greeson, John Clark, and Judith Clark, (Minneapolis: American Water Works Association), p. 88.

11. See Lugo and Brinson, "Calculations of the Value of Saltwater Wetlands," in *Wetland Functions and Value*, op. cit., p. 124.

12. Ralph W. Tiner. 1984. *Wetlands of the U.S.: Current Status and Recent Trends* (Washington, D.C.: National Wetlands Inventory, U.S. Fish and Wildlife Service, U.S. Department of Interior), p. 29.

13. Robert G. Healy, in a discussion note to Michael Brewer and Robert Boxley. 1982. "The Potential Supply of Cropland," in *The Cropland Crisis: Myth or Reality?*, Pierre R. Crosson, ed. (Baltimore: Johns Hopkins), p. 115.

14. *Statistical Abstract*, 1982, Table 1154, p. 658, from U.S. Department of Agriculture, *Major Uses of Land in the United States: 1978*.

15. From Soil Conservation Service. 1985. *Background for 1985 Farm Legislation*, Agricultural Information Bulletin Number 486 (Washington, D.C.: U.S. Department of Agriculture, January); cited in Council on Environmental Quality. 1984. *Environmental Quality*, 15th Annual Report, (Washington, D.C.: CEQ).

16. R. Neil Sampson. 1981. *Farmland or Wasteland*, (Emmaus, PA: Rodale).

17. Salah El Serafy. 1988. "The Proper Calculation of Income from Depletable Natural Resources," in *Environmental and Resource Accounting and their Relevance to the Measurement of Sustainable Income*, edited by Ernst Lutz and Salah El Serafy (Washington: World Bank).

18. El Serafy presumes to take the conceptual problem of rising extraction costs into account by proposing that "reserves . . . be adjusted downward by a factor that would reflect [the] rising future cost of extraction." This adjustment would reflect the closure of mines and wells when market prices are below extraction (and processing) costs. Even though this adjustment may be correct for short run fluctuations in market prices, over time the rise of resource prices will mean that increasing extraction costs can be passed on to consumers. Thus extraction costs cannot define the size of n. Moreover, since neither the exact size of deposits nor the appropriate amount of adjustment for future increases in extraction costs are known, this method would not offer a practical way of dealing with the difficulty of changing costs.

19. Talbot Page. 1977. *Conservation and Economic Efficiency* (Baltimore: Johns Hopkins University Press), Chapter 8.

20. For 1900 to 1949, see *Historical Statistics of the U.S.: Colonial Times to 1970*, Series M76-92. For 1950 onward, see Energy Information Administration. 1988. *Annual Energy Review,* Table 3.

21. See "Where's the Beach?" *Time*, August 10, 1987, for anecdotal evidence.

Chapter 3 Notes

1. In particular, Kendrick (1976 and 1979), Jorgenson and Fraumeni (1987) and Ruggles and Ruggles (1982).

2. Eisner and Pieper, (1989).

Chapter 3 References

Robert Eisner. 1985. "The Total Incomes System of Accounts." *Survey of Current Business* (January): 24-48.

Robert Eisner. 1988. "Extended Accounts for National Income and Product." *Journal of Economic Literature* (December): 1-78.

Robert Eisner. 1989. *The Total Incomes System of Accounts*. (Chicago: University of Chicago Press).

Robert Eisner and Paul J. Pieper. 1989. "The World's Greatest Debtor Nation?" to be published in *The Review of Economics and Finance*.

Dale W. Jorgenson and Barbara M. Fraumeni. 1987. "The Accumulation of Human and Non-Human Capital, 1948-1984." Unpub. ms., Harvard, University.

John W. Kendrick. 1976. *The Formation and Stocks of Total Capital*. (NY: Columbia University Press for NBER).

John W. Kendrick. 1979. "Expanding Imputed Values in the National Income and Product Accounts." *Review of Income and Wealth* 25(4): 349-363.

William D. Nordhaus and James Tobin. 1972. "Is Growth Obsolete?" in *Economic Growth*. Fiftieth Anniversary Colloquium V. (New York: NBER).

Richard Ruggles and Nancy D. Ruggles. 1982. "Integrated Economic Accounts for the United States, 1947-1980." *Survey of Current Business*.62(5): 1-53.

Xenophon Zolatas. 1981. *Economic Growth and Declining Social Welfare*. (Athens: Bank of Greece).

Chapter 4 Notes

1. See the preface of United Nations. 1977. *The Feasibility of Welfare-Oriented Measures to Supplement the National Accounts and Balances: A Technical Report*, Studies in Methods, Series F., No. 22 (New York: United Nations): iii.

2. The Study Group's index of inequality is

$$X = \left(\frac{S_5}{S_1} + \frac{S_5}{S_2} + \frac{S_5}{S_3} + \frac{S_5}{S_4} + \frac{S_5}{S_5}\right)/\,5,$$

where S_i is the share of total income received by the ith quintile. Because the ratio of the share of total income received by one quintile to that received by another quintile is equal to the ratio of average income of one quintile to that of another quintile, the index of inequality may be written in terms of the average incomes of the quintiles.

3. To make this calculation, it is necessary to substitute $\bar{I}$ for $\tilde{I}$ in the Study Group's table A.1. The percentage change in $\bar{I}$ may be calculated directly from column f in table A.2 because the change in $\bar{I}$ is proportional to the change in the share of total income received by the fifth quintile. From 1980 to 1986, I in column h increases 13 percent; $\bar{I}$ calculated from column f increases 5 percent.

4. For a survey, see Arnold J. Katz. 1983. "Valuing the Services of Consumer Durables," *Review of Income and Wealth* 29: 405-428.

5. The Study Group's method of calculating the estimate of the value of services on consumer durables is to take 10 percent of the net stock of consumer durables in constant (1972) dollars. The 10 percent is derived by reference to housing; it is described as "the ratio of housing services to net housing stock given in the National Income and Product Accounts (NIPA)." With only this limited information, we were unable to replicate the 10 percent beginning in the 1970's. "Housing services" presumably represent the personal consumption expenditures for housing, which includes the services provided by both farm and non-farm owner- and tenant-occupied dwellings. It seems likely that this is the component the Study Group used because it is in the Study Group's table 7, which underlies component M. (In that table, for some reason, the Study Group calculated a 1972-dollar measure using the current-dollar estimates in NIPA table 2.4 rather than using the ones provided in the NIPA table 2.5; for most years, the two estimates are quite close. However, the Study Group's estimates beginning in 1982 are suspect because they show an uncharacteristic decline in 1982 and little growth in 1983.) One might argue that the subcomponent for hotels, motels, and other

transient and group housing should be omitted, but it is too small to account for the problem of replicating the 10 percent. "Net housing stock" presumably represents the total stock of residential capital. One might argue that the subcomponents owned by government or consisting of equipment rather than structures should be omitted, but they are too small to account for the problem. The tabulation below shows estimates for selected years for housing services (billions of 1972 dollars), from NIPA table 2.5, and for the net housing stock (billions of 1972 dollars), from table A8 of *Fixed Reproducible Tangible Wealth in the United States, 1925-79* (and updates in the *Survey of Current Business*), the ratio calculated from these estimates, and the Study Group's ratio.

	Housing services	Net stock	Ratio: Housing services to net stock	
			Calculated	Study Group
1960	64.0	592.8	10.8	10.7
1965	81.6	711.4	11.5	11.7
1971	106.4	850.0	12.5	11.2
1974	124.2	949.8	13.1	10.0
1977	142.5	1,015.5	14.0	9.7
1980	159.8	1,091.1	14.6	9.5
1983	171.3	1,139.9	15.0	11.3

6. In the years designated as the base year (in this case, 1972), current- and constant-dollar estimates for the flows--services, expenditures, and depreciation--are equal. For stocks, which are as of the end of the year rather than the average for the year, the current- and constant-dollar estimates differ slightly.

7. These figures include expenditures on durables; that is, we did not subtract the expenditures on durables and add an estimate of the value of the services of these durables, as would be consistent with the ISEW.

8. A 1968 publication, often called the *Blue Book*, can be taken as representing the present SNA: United Nations, *A System of National Accounts*, Studies in Methods, Series F, No. 2, Rev. 3 (New York: United Nations). A subsequent publication rounded

out the guidelines on balance sheets: United Nations. 1977. *Provisional International Guidelines on the National and Sectoral Balance-Sheet and Reconciliation Accounts of the System of National Accounts,* Statistical Papers, Series M, No. 60 (New York: United Nations). A useful overview of the present SNA is in the annual UN compilation of economic accounts statistics: United Nations. 1989. *National Accounts Statistics: Main Aggregates and Detailed Tables 1986,* Parts I and II, ST/ESA/STAT/ SER.X/11 (New York: United Nations).

9.   Satellite accounts are especially useful in developing new concepts and systems. They allow data problems to be worked out and conceptual refinements to be introduced from experience without disrupting the accounts with which users are familiar.

10. In addition, the Study Group, in the section "GNP and Related Measures," speculates that perhaps GNP should be calculated purely in terms of market activity--that is, without any imputations. Later, a quotation from Richard Ruggles mentions the desirability of separating market transactions from imputations. Although these references seem to us to raise issues outside the Study Group's main argument, it is perhaps worth noting that the revised SNA makes provision for complementary classifications--for example, of output and household final consumption--that identify transactions in kind and other imputations. The complementary classification, like the satellite accounts, are designed to provide flexibility for analysis.

11. *The Feasibility of Welfare-Oriented Measures,* p. 6.

12. See "Improving the Quality of Economic Statistics," which summarizes the recommendations, in the February 1990 *Survey of Current Business.*

13. U.S. Congress, Senate, *National Income, 1929-32,* S. Doc. 124, 73rd Cong., 2d sess., 1934, as summarized in Carol S. Carson. 1975. "The History of the United States National Income and Product Accounts: The Development of an Analytical Tool." *Review of Income and Wealth* 21: 153-181.

14. Edward F. Denison. 1947. "Report on Tripartite Discussions of National Income Measurement," in Conference on Research in Income and Wealth, Vol. 10: *Studies in Income and Wealth* (New York: National Bureau of Economic Research).

15.   F. Thomas Juster, Paul N. Courant, and Greg K. Dow. 1981. "A Theoretical Framework for the Measurement of Well-being," *Review of Income and Wealth* 27 (March): 2-3.

16.   *The Development Data Book.* 1988. 2nd ed. (Washington, DC: World Bank).

17.   Richard Ruggles, "The United States National Income Accounts, 1947-1977: Their Conceptual Basis and Evolution," in Murray F. Foss, ed. 1983. *The U.S. National Income and Product Accounts: Selected Topics*, Vol. 47: *Studies in Income and Wealth* (Chicago: University of Chicago Press), p. 18. The evolution from emphasis on a single aggregate to an accounting structure featuring several analytically useful aggregates is one of the main themes traced in Carol S. Carson. 1975. "The History of the United States National Income and Product Accounts: The Development of an Analytical Tool," *Review of Income and Wealth* 21 (June): 153-181.

18.   Much of the work that was completed was collected in U.S. Department of Commerce, Bureau of Economic Analysis. 1982. "Measuring Nonmarket Economic Activity: BEA Working Papers. Working Paper 2 (Washington, DC: Bureau of Economic Analysis).

Chapter 5 Notes

1.   Talbot Page. 1977. *Conservation and Economic Efficiency: Resources for the Future.* (Baltimore: Johns Hopkins University Press).

2.   Ernest Hemingway. 1987. *Green Hills of Africa.* (N.Y.: Collier).

3.   G. R. Conway. 1985. "Agroecosystem Analysis." *Agricultural Administration* 20: 31-55; Michael Dover and Lee M. Talbot. 1987. *To Feed the Earth: Agro-Ecology for Sustainable Development.* (Washington, DC; World Resources Institute).

4.   This is inspired by Holling who views ecosystem stability as depending more upon what is connected to what and how and less upon the numbers of different types of organisms present. (See C.S. Holling. 1978. "The Nature and Behavior of Ecological Systems." in Holling, ed. *Adaptive Environmental Assessment*

and Management. International Institute for Applied Systems Analysis. NY: John Wiley & Sons.)

5. If one assumes that the economy has become less sustainable, the compensating variation measure (CV) of the value of sustainability would be the willingness of the population to accept compensation for the loss. However, should society gain a degree of sustainability not attained before, then the CV measure of the value of that sustainability would be the amount of money people would be willing to pay in order to obtain it. (See E. J. Mishan. 1976. *Cost-Benefit Analysis.* New and Expanded Edition. New York: Praeger.)

6. Talbot. *Conservation and Economic Efficiency.*

Chapter 6 Notes

1. T. M. Power. 1988. "The Folk Economics of Local Economic Development." Unpublished paper presented at the 1988 Western Regional Science Association Meetings, Napa Valley, California.

2. Gregory Jackson et al. 1981. *Regional Diversity: Growth in the United States 1960-1990.* (Boston: Auburn House), pp. 114 and 118; George E. Johnson. 1983. "Intermetropolitan Wage Differentials in the United States," Chapter 8 in *The Measurement of Labor Cost.* Jack E. Triplett, ed., (Chicago: U. of Chicago Press).

3. Ann R. Markusen. 1987. *Regions: The Economics and Politics of Territory.* (Rowman and Littlefield), p. 136.

4. William Nordhaus and James Tobin. 1972. "Is Growth Obsolete?" in *Economic Growth,* National Bureau of Economic Research, Vol. 5 of *Economic Research: Retrospect and Prospect.*

5. Don Bellante. 1979. "The North-South Differential and the Migration of Heterogeneous Labor." *American Economic Review* 69(1): 166-175; Shelby Gerking and William N. Weirick. 1983. "Compensating Differences and Interregional Wage Differentials." *Review of Economics and Statistics* 65(3); Leonard G. Sahling and Sharon P. Smith. 1983. Regional Wage Differen-

tials: Has the South Risen Again." *Review of Economics and Statistics* 65(1): 131-135.

6. Johnson, "Intermetropolitan Wage Differentials," op. cit.; Richard J. Cebula. 1983. *Geographic Living-Cost Differentials.* D.C. Heath.

7. Ronald J. Krumm. 1983. "Regional Labor Markets and the Household Migration Decision." *Journal of Regional Science* 23(3): 361-376.

8. Johnson, "Intermetropolitan Wage Differentials," op cit.; Sahling and Smith, "Regional Wage Differentials," op cit.; and Stephen C. Farber and Robert J. Newman. 1987. "Accounting for South/ non-South Real Wage Differentials and for Changes in those Differentials over Time. *Review of Economics and Statistics,* pp. 215-223.

9. T. M. Power. 1988. *The Economic Pursuit of Quality.* (New York: M. E. Sharpe), Chapter 6.

10. Ibid., pp. 139-145.

11. T. M. Power. 1980. *The Economic Value of the Quality of Life.* (Boulder: Westview Press); Power, *The Economic Pursuit of Quality,* op. cit., pp. 141-147.

12. David Clark et al. 1988. "City Size, Quality of Life, and the Urbanization Deflator of the GNP." *Southern Economic Journal* 54(3): 701-14; Gerking and Weirick, "Compensating Differences;" and Malcolm Getz and Yuh-Ching Huang. 1978. "Consumer Revealed Preference for Environmental Goods." *Review of Economics and Statistics* 60 (August): 449-58; Johnson, "Intermetropolitan Wage Differentials," op. cit.

13. Jennifer Roback. 1982. "Wages, Rents, and Quality of Life." *Journal of Political Economy* 90(6): 1257-1278; John P. Hoehn, et al. 1987. "A Hedonic Model of Interregional Wages, Rents and Amenity Values." *Journal of Regional Science* 27(4): 605-620; Patricia E. Beeson and Randall W. Eberts. 1987. "Identifying Amenity and Productivity Cities Using Wage and Rent Differentials." *Economic Review.* Cleveland Federal Reserve Bank, Quarter 3, 1987, pp. 16-25.

14.   Philip E. Graves. 1983. "Migration with a Composite Amenity: The Role of Rents." *Journal of Regional Science* 23(4): 541-546.

15.   Roback, "Wages, Rents, and Quality of Life," op. cit., pp. 1259 and 1275.

16.   Getz and Huang, "Consumer Revealed Preference," op. cit.

17.   Reuben Gronau. 1980. "Home Production: A Forgotten Industry." *Review of Economics and Statistics* (72): 412.

18.   William H. Gauger and Kathryn E. Walker. 1980. "The Dollar Value of Household Work." New York State College of Human Ecology, Cornell University, Information Bulletin 60, p. 11.

19.   Ibid., p. 6.

20.   Daniel S. Hamermesh and Albert Rees. 1984. *The Economics of Work and Pay.* 3rd ed., (Harper and Row), pp. 12-13.

21.   Ibid., p. 31.

22.   Power, *The Economic Pursuit of Quality*, op. cit., Chapter 9.

Chapter 6 References

Mark Dickie and Shelby Gerking. 1987. "Interregional Wage Differentials: An Equilibrium Perspective." *Journal of Regional Science* 27(4): 571-585.

Randall W. Eberts and Joe A. Stone. 1986. "Metropolitan Wage Differentials: Can Cleveland Compete?" *Economic Review*, Cleveland Federal Reserve Bank, Quarter 2, 1986, pp. 2-8.

Theodore Morgan. 1975. *Economic Development: Concept and Strategy.* (Harper and Row).

Chapter 7 Notes

1.   It is as well to bear in mind also that income differences are quite strongly age-related. Lifetime earnings are the more significant

data, and will be much smaller than annual differences. In a limiting case, the lifetime earnings of all families in a community could be equal while in any one year the differences could be very great.

2.   Analysis of the error can be found in Chapter 18 of my *Economic Efficiency and Social Welfare* (London, 1981).

3.   The economist who is not so much interested in changes in net consumption but rather in changes over time of the productive power of the economy will not need to bother about variations in leisure or hours worked. He can safely restrict himself to changes in the value of output per man hour, this being an index of technical progress in a comprehensive sense.

4.   Reasons for this belief are given in S. Linder's *Harried Leisure Class* (New York, 1971), also in Chapter 28 of my *Economic Growth Debate* (London, 1977).

5.   Thus the value of leisure is treated as being on all fours with the value of a range of personal services--including hair-cutting, teaching, waitering, acting, gardening, and chauffeuring--whose quality and productivity do not change much with the passage of time. The payments for such personal services do, however, follow the rise over time in money wages. Their prices therefore rise faster than the prices of finished products from industries showing continual increases in productivity. In a limiting case where money wages rise no faster than productivity, the prices of manufactured goods remain constant whereas the prices of personal services will continue to rise in the same proportion as money wages.

   Included as they are in the over-all price index, the higher prices of personal services exert a deflationary effect in converting the money value of aggregate consumption into a 'real' value.

   (For a personal service whose quality or productivity *did* improve over time, all, or some part, of its rise in price may be attributed to an increase in its real value.)

6.   By a "significant" activity I mean one taking up a significant proportion of the average working week, say more than 2 per cent. Incidentally, the so-called "managerial" component of housework which, it is sometimes alleged, should be valued at sums comparable with the earnings of managers in industry is rather far-fetched. It can hardly be as important with respect either to

time or quality, being in the main little more than giving instructions to the home-help and later inspecting the work done.

7.   The causal effect is, of course, the reverse of this: for example, a rise in the price of corn resulting from an increase in population will, *cet. par.*, cause a rise in the price of land and therefore also a rise in the rent of land, as in the primitive Ricardian model. Thus, if the working population doubled and, in the limiting case, there was no way of expanding the output of corn, there would be a decline in the per capita consumption of corn, one that could be estimated by reference to the price-rise.

The landlords themselves do indeed make real gains inasmuch as rents rise relative to the price of corn. Yet if all the gain in rents were confiscated and costlessly redistributed among the working population, the resulting per capita 'real' income would clearly remain unchanged--lower, that is, than it was before the population doubled.

Extending this simplified model to urban rents, or elaborating it to comprehend additional capital resources, does not alter the basic conclusion.

8.   Thus, for all goods on the market, the CV for an individual is the largest sum he would pay for the opportunity of buying his chosen batch of goods at their given prices when the alternative is the removal of this opportunity which leaves him with his income to hold on to. The CV in this limiting case is exactly equal to his income.

9.   Most recently in my *Cost Benefit Analysis*, 4th ed. (London, 1988).

10. The Equivalent Variation is defined as the sum paid to or received from the individual in lieu of the change which would make him as well off as if he had the change. Thus if the change is for the better, he receives a sum of money; if for the worse, he pays a sum of money.

11. To be sure, the cunning economist may elect to call the latter state (when the damage is already done) state 1, so that the resulting CV_{12} does indeed correspond with the maximum the victims are willing to pay in order to return to their earlier situation, state 2. But this contrived CV_{12} is unacceptable in these circumstances for two reasons.

First, it is manifestly inequitable inasmuch as those who will suffer from the profitable actions of others are held to be responsible for paying the perpetrators to refrain from the damaging activity, rather than the reverse.

Second, determining resource allocation by reference to this contrived CV_{12} (equal to Hicks' EV) may violate the allocation criterion. In the above example it would countenance the siting of the plant in the area since the residents' offer of $100 million falls short of the $180 million that is just acceptable to the corporation. Yet such an outcome could not be vindicated by the Pareto criterion which--being defined as a potential Pareto improvement--is met only when the gainers from the change are able to (over)compensate losers. And in our example, clearly, the most the gainers (the corporation) can pay, $180 million, for a change from the original situation, is not enough to compensate the losers (the residents). In short, if we are attentive to the norms of resource allocation, we should never countenance the proposed siting in the first place; the original state 2 would not be actualized.

12.   In my *Twenty-One Popular Economic Fallacies* (London, 1969), I argue that if it is information and entertainment that are at issue, more comprehensive and less biased information, and also better entertainment, can be made available to the public at a total cost no greater than it currently pays for its commercial advertisements.

13.   Postwar economic growth has given rise to some fearsome advances in small weapons technology, to increased mobility and communication, and to the spread of vast urban development which lends itself admirably to criminal operation and concealment.

Accompanying these things has been a change in lifestyles that has produced an erosion of neighborhoods and the neighborhood mentality. Moreover, with the ascendancy of science a more secular society comes into being and, inevitably, a collapse of traditional norms of propriety hastened by the promiscuity of programs filtered into the homes of millions by expanding television media competing for mass audiences.

For arguments about the connecting links between economic growth and crime see Chapter 6 of my *Pornography, Psychedelics, and Technology* (London, 1980).

14. The rise of material prosperity and the rapid pace of technological change looks to be culminating in a frenzy of opportunism and hedonistic pursuit which, along with a growing immersion in computerized recreations, leaves us with less time and apparently less need of others.

Chapter 8 Notes

1. S. Kuznets. 1966. *Modern Economic Growth: Rate, Structure and Spread.* (New Haven and London: Yale University Press).

2. S. Levy and L. Guttman. 1975. "On the Multivariate Structure of Wellbeing." *Social Indicators Research* 2(3): 361-388.

3. J. Tinbergen. 1985. "Measurability of Utility (or Welfare)." *De Economist* (133): 411-414; J. Tinbergen. 1987. "Measuring Welfare of Productive Consumers." *De Economist* (135): 231-236.

4. R. Summers, et al. 1984. "Changes in World Income Distribution." *Journal of Policy Modeling* 6(2): 237-270.

5. J. Tinbergen. 1987. *Revitalizing the United Nations System.* Booklet 13, Waging Peace Series, Nuclear Age Peace Foundation. Santa Barbara, CA.

Chapter 9 Notes

1. Barbara Tuchman. 1981. *Practicing History.* (Alfred A. Knopf), p. 289.

2. William Manchester. 1988. *The Last Lion,* Vol. II: *Alone.* (Little, Brown).

3. Kenneth E. Boulding. 1984. "The Fallacy of Trends," *National Forum of Phi Kappa Phi Journal* LXIV(3).

4. William James Durant and Ariel Durant. 1968. *The Lessons of History.* (Simon and Schuster)

5. Albert A. Bartlett. 1989. "Fusion and the Future," *Physics and Society* 18(3).

6. Henry Kissinger. As quoted in "Future Development Dimensions," (Los Angeles: DMJM).

7. Ralph Buultjen. 1978. *The Decline of Democracy*. (Mary Knoll, NY: Orbis Books).

8. Arnold Toynbee. 1974. "An Age of Economic Siege is Approaching, *" Denver Post*, May 5, 1974.

9. Buultjens, *The Decline of Democracy*.

10. Kenneth Winetrout. 1975. *Arnold Toynbee*. (Twayne), p. 53.

11. Paul Blumberg. 1980. *Inequality in an Age of Decline*. (Oxford University Press), p. xi.

12. Peter Schwartz. "Future Development Dimensions." (Los Angeles: DMJM).

Chapter 10 Notes

I want to thank Thomas Baumgartner of Belfort, and Friedhelm Küppers of Hanover, for many discussions and their help collecting data.

1. A comprehensive overview of the German discussion in this field is the paper of F. Rubik. 1985. "Das Bruttosozialprodukt als Indikator für Lebensqualität? Kritik und Alternativen," in Projektgruppe Ökologische Wirtschaft (ed.): *Arbeiten im Einklang mit der Natur*. Freiburg i.Brsg.: Dreisam-Verlag, pp. 145-176.

2. U. Wehner. 1976. *Ökologische soziale Kosten und volkswirtschaftliche Gesamtrechnumg*. Köln: Diss.

3. U. P. Reich and C. Stahmer (eds.) 1983. *Gesamtwirtschaftliche Wohlfahrtsmessung und Umweltqualität*. Frankfurt/M.: Campus-Verlag.

4. A. Theobald. 1985. *Das Ökosozialprodukt - Lebensqualität als Volkseinkommen*. Osnabrück: Verlag A. Fromm.

5. F. Beckenbach and M. Schreyer (eds.). 1988. *Gesellschaftliche Folgekosten - was kostet unser Wirtschaftssytem?* Frankfurt/M.: Campus.

6. R. Müller-Wenk. 1978. *Die ökologische Buchhaltung - ein Informations - und Steuerungsinstrument für umweltkonforme Unternehmenspolitik.* Frankfurt/M.: Campus-Verlag.

7. L. Wicke. 1986. *Die ökologischen Milliarden.* München: Kösel-Verlag.

8. Ch. Leipert. 1989. *Die heimlichen Kosten des Fortschritts - wie Umweltzerstörung das Wirtschaftswachstum fördert.* Frankfurt/M.: Verlag S. Fischer.

9. See Th. Baumgartner. 1985. "Wer was wie mißt," in *Arbeiten im Einklang*, op. cit., pp. 177-206.

10. Figures derived from Statistisches Bundesamt (ed.): *Lange Reihen;* Vol. 1973, 150ff. and Vol. 1988, 208ff.

11. Statistisches Bundesamt (ed.): *Jahrbücher*, Vols. 1955 - 1989.

12. See Fn 13.

13. Figures derived from Statistisches Bundesamt (ed.): *Lange Reihen;* Vol. 1973, 156ff and Vol. 1988, 220ff.

14. See W. Glatzer. 1984. "Einkommensverteilung und Einkommenszufriedenheit," in W. Glatzer and W. Zapf (eds.): *Lebensqualität in der Bundesrepublik.* Frankfurt: Campus-Verlag, pp. 45-72.

15. K. -D. Bedau. 1988. "Einkommensverteilung," in H. -J. Krupp and J. Schupp (eds.): *Lebenslagen im Wandel - Daten 1987.* Frankfurt: Campus-Verlag, pp. 61-87.

16. See Part A, Table A.2, column g.

17. See K. -D. Bedau, op. cit., p. 68.

18. Figures for the period of 1950 to 1959 and again augmented to include Saarland and West-Berlin; figures derived from

Statistisches Bundesamt (ed.): *Lange Reihen*, Vol. 1973, p. 160f. and Vol. 1988, p. 258ff.

19. Statistisches Bundesamt (ed.): *Lange Reihen*, Vol. 1973, p. 30ff and Vol. 1988, p. 36ff.

20. Sachverständigenrat zur Begutachtung der gesamtwirtschaftlichen Entwicklung (ed.): *Jahresgutachten 1988/89*, Anhang, table 26.

21. See H. Fürst. 1956. *Einkommen, Nachfrage, Produktion und Konsum des privaten Haushaltes in der Volkswirtschaft.* Stuttgart: Köln, p. 87; H. Schmucker. 1961. "Über die Hälfte des Volkseinkommens geht durch die Hände der Frau," in *Bayern in Zahlen*, Vol. 1961, No. 1, p. 21; E. Langfeld. 1983. "Ursachen der Schattenwirtschaft und ihre Konsequenzen für die Wirtschafts-, Finanz- und Gesellschaftspolitik," Institut für Weltwirtschaft an der Universität Kiel, *Forschungsauftrag des Bundesministeriums für Wirtschaft;* R. Schettkat. 1985. "The Size of Household Production: Methodological Problems and Estimates for the Federal Republic of Germany in the Period 1964 to 1980," *Review of Income and Wealth*, Vol. 1985, No. 3, p. 315; M. Hilzenbecher. 1986. "Die schattenwirtschaftliche Wertschöpfung der Hausarbeit," *Jahrbücher für Nationalökonomie und Statistik*, Vol. 1986, No. 2, p. 107ff; as an overview, see "Haushalts-produktion in gesamtwirtschaftlicher Betrachtung," *Wirtschaft und Statistik*, Vol. 1988, No. 5, p. 309ff.

22. This is the estimation of E. Langfeld (1983).

23. M. Hilzenbecher (1986) computes the size of household production in the year 1982 as between 54% and 58% of GNP.

24. L. Goldschmidt-Ciermont. 1982. *Unpaid Work in the House-hold.* Geneva; V. Tanzi (1982). *The Underground Economy in the United States and Abroad.* Lexington/Toronto: Lexington Books; K. Gretschmann 1983. *Wirtschaft im Schatten von Markt und Staat.* Frankfurt: Fischer-Verlag; K. Gretschmann, R. G. Heinze and B. Mettelsiefen (eds.). (1984. *Schattenwirtschaft.* Göttingen: Vandenhoek und Ruprecht.

25. See R. Schettkat (1984), p. 159.

26. Statistisches Bundesamt (ed.). *Jahrbuch*, Vol. 1988, 458.

27. F. W. Peren. 1986. *Einkommen, Konsum und Ersparnis der privaten Haushalte in der Bundesrepublik Deutschland seit 1970 - Analyse unter Verwendung makroökonomischer Konsumfunktionen.* Frankfurt/Bern: Peter Lang, p. 207.

28. Statistisches Bundesamt (ed.). *Jahrbücher,* table "Entwicklung der Ausgaben der Öffentlichen Haushalte."

29. Ibid., table "Ausgaben der Öffentlichen Haushalte für ausgewählte Aufgabenbereiche."

30. Ibid., table "Wohnbevölkerung nach Art des Krankenversicherungsschutzes."

31. Ibid., table "Krankenversicherungsunternehmen" and table "Einnahmen und Ausgaben der sozialen Krankenversicherungsträger."

32. Zentralausschuß der Werbewirtschaft. 1989. *Werbung, 1988.* Köln: Selbstverlag.

33. X. Zolotas. 1981. *Economic Growth and Declining Social Welfare.* New York: New York University Press.

34. Ch. Leipert. 1989. op. cit., p. 267.

35. See Statistisches Bundesamt (ed.). *Jahrbücher,* tables "Übersiedler," "Aussiedler," and "Vertriebene."

36. Ch. Leipert. (1989). op. cit., p. 284 and p. 289.

37. Ibid., pp. 276-289.

38. Ibid., p. 256; Antwort der Bundesregierung auf die Große Anfrage des Abgeordneten Drabiniok und der Fraktion Die Grünen zum Thema Gesellschaftliche Kosten des Autoverkehrs; *Bundestagsdrucksache* 10/2348, p. 21.

39. L. Wicke. 1986. op. cit., chapters I-VI.

40. Ibid., p. 85.

41. Ibid., p. 56; Index derived from Umweltbundesamt (ed.). 1987. *Daten zur Umwelt 1987.* Berlin: Selbstverlag.

42. L. Wicke. op. cit., p. 120.

43. Ibid., p. 107; Ch. Leipert, op. cit., 162ff., 180ff.

44. Figures derived from Statistisches Bundesamt (ed.). *Jahrbücher,* table "Produktion bergbaulicher Erzeugnisse."

45. Figures for the period of 1950 to 1987 derived from Sachverständi-genrat zur Begutachtung der gesamtwirtschaftlichen Entwicklung (ed.). *Jahresgutachten.*

46. Figures are derived from Statistisches Bundesamt (ed.). *Jahrbücher,* tables "Erwerbspersonen," and Vermögensrechnun-gen der Volkswirtschaftlichen Gesamtrechnung.

47. Ibid., table "Kapitalbilanz."

48. It does not include 1987 because at the time these computations were made there was no 1987 ISEW for the United States available.

49. See H. Diefenbacher. 1988. "Armaments and Poverty in the Industrial Nations," *Concilium,* No. 215, pp. 61-68.

50. Named as "Satellitensysteme zur Volkswirtschaftlichen Gesam-trechnung."

Chapter 11 Notes

1. John Rawls. 1971. *A Theory of Justice* (Cambridge: Harvard University Press).

2. See Bureau of the Census, *Measuring the Effect of Benefits and Taxes on Income and Poverty,* Current Population Reports, Consumer Income, Series P-60, No. 176-RD (for 1989 and 1990), No. 170-RD (for 1987-88) and No. 164-RD (for 1986).

3. The lowest quintile of families (as opposed to households) received 4.6 percent of pre-tax income in 1990. We have used family income in the development of the distributional index. However, the only after-tax data are for households, which are not precisely comparable to families.

4. For the total production of nonrenewable energy produced in the U.S. each year, we subtracted renewable sources from the total in Energy Information Administration. 1992. *Annual Energy Review* (Washington, D.C.: U.S. Department of Energy), Table 2.

5. Economic Research Service. 1988. *Ethanol: Economic and Policy Tradeoffs*, Agricultural Economic Report No. 585 (Washington, D.C.: U.S. Department of Agriculture).

6. Ibid.

7. Council for Agricultural Science and Technology. 1984. *Energy Use and Production in Agriculture*, Report No. 99 (Ames, Iowa: CAST).

8. C. S. Hopkinson, Jr. and J. W. Day, Jr. 1980. "Net Energy Analysis of Alcohol Production from Sugarcane," *Science*, vol. 207 (January 18).

9. As another basis of comparison, we might also consider that the United States has already been spending the equivalent of over $400 per barrel of oil from the Persian Gulf, if the cost of military expenditures to guarantee supplies are factored into the cost. Of course, this cost shows up in taxes, not consumer prices, so it is not relevant to our analysis. However, it suggests that subsidizing energy self-sufficiency would be cost-effective as a national policy. Amory B. and L. Hunter Lovins. 1987. "Energy: The Avoidable Oil Crisis." *The Atlantic* (December): 26-27.

10. Energy Information Administration. 1992. *Annual Energy Review 1991*, (Washington, D.C.: U.S. Department of Energy), Table 45.

11. Dean E. Abrahamson. "Global Warming: The Issue, Impacts, Responses," in Dean E. Abrahamson, ed. 1989. *The Challenge of Global Warming* (Washington, D.C.: Island Press), p. 12.

12. Wallace S. Broecker. "Greenhouse Surprises," in Abrahamson, *Challenge of Global Warming*, chapter 13.

13. William R. Cline. 1992. *Global Warming: The Economic Stakes* (Washington, D.C.: Institute for International Economics). A more comprehensive book by Cline, entitled *The Economics of Global Warming*, was not available at the time of this writing.

14. Robert L. Peters. "Effects of Global Warming on Biological Diversity," in Abrahamson, *Challenge of Global Warming*, chapter 6.

15. Cline, *Global Warming: The Economic Stakes.*

16. *Survey of Current Business*, June 1991. Or see *Economic Report of the President*, 1992, table B-99, p. 411.

17. Data on cumulative production (from major producers in reporting countries) comes from hearings before Subcommittee on Health and Environment, Committee on Energy and Commerce, U.S. House of Representatives, *Ozone Layer Depletion*, Serial 100-7, March 9, 1987, pp. 435-436. The estimates that we have used for 1986 through 1990 are extrapolations based on regression analysis. Although the regression on the logarithm of production provides a better fit ($R^2 = .97$) than the linear model ($R^2 = .91$), we used the latter, more conservative, growth estimate. Using the logarithm would have produced a 1990 damage estimate of $133.4 billion instead of $85.3 billion. In that case per capita, ISEW would have been around $3,060, indicating a decline rather than improvement in the last years of the 1980s.

18. Donald Heath of NASA's Goddard Space Flight Center, testimony in the *Ozone Layer Depletion* hearings, p. 32.

19. Darrel Rigel, testimony in *Ozone Layer Depletion*, pp. 70-80.

20. *Sacramento Bee*, June 24, 1990, p. H1. Also see Louis Harris. 1987. *Inside America* (New York: Vintage).

21. Richard F. Hamilton. "Work and Leisure: On the Reporting of Poll Results," *Public Opinion Quarterly* 55: 347-356.

22. The calculation of the value of loss of wetlands and farmland in columns S and T might seem to violate this principle. Yet unlike nonrenewable resources the value of which is used up in one year, the value of renewable resources is the stream of benefits produced in perpetuity. A reduction in the stock of the latter type of resource is in fact a reduction in the stream of benefits. To avoid the problems posed by discounting the value of that stream of benefits (see discussion earlier on discounting), we estimated cumulative losses of services from these resources.

23. Recent work by Nordhaus has, however, focused on the question of sustainability. In October 1992 he delivered a paper entitled "Is Growth Sustainable? Reflections on the Concept of Sustainable Growth" at the International Economic Association. In that paper, he calculates "Hicksian Income" (the maximum consumption each year that leaves the stock of capital intact) for the years 1950 to 1986, in which there is some overlap with the categories in his original MEW, some with Eisner's TISA, and some with the ISEW. Long-term environmental damage plays a much smaller role in his analysis than in the ISEW because he estimates that the present value of future damage from global warming in 1990 was approximately $5 per ton of carbon equivalent or a total of only $14 billion in costs in 1986.

Nordhaus compares his calculation of Hicksian Income with the ISEW (in its original form in part A of this book). Hicksian Income grew by 4.41 percent per year from 1950 to 1965 and by 2.35 percent from 1965 to 1986. By contrast, the ISEW grew at annual rates of 3.81 and 1.02 percent during the same two periods. Thus, the growth slowdown was 2.79 percent for ISEW and 2.06 percent for Hicksian Income. (The growth slowdown on a per capita basis was 2.18 for ISEW and 1.45 for Hicksian Income.) Although Nordhaus emphasizes the difference between the dramatic slowdown of ISEW and the lesser reduction in the growth rate of Hicksian Income, the latter slowed down three times as much as the decline in the GNP growth rate (it went from 3.75 per cent per year to 3.05, for a reduction of only .70 percent.) Thus, his own figures suggest that GNP is not a good indicator of permanent income or sustainable well-being.

INDEX